FIGHTING LIKE THE FLOWERS

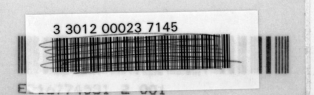

Fighting Like the Flowers

An Autobiography

by
Lawrence D. Hills

'As merry as the ancient sun,
And fighting like the flowers.'

G. K. Chesterton

GREEN BOOKS

First published in 1989 by
Green Books
Ford House, Hartland
Bideford, Devon EX39 6EE

Typeset by
Fine Line Publishing Services
Witney, Oxon

Printed on recycled paper

Printed by Hartnolls
Victoria Square, Bodmin
Cornwall

British Library Cataloguing in Publication Data
Hills, Lawrence D. (Lawrence Donegan), *1911* —
Fighting like the flowers.
1. Gardens. Organic cultivation — Biographies
I. Title
635'.0484'0924

ISBN 1-870098-29-3
ISBN 1-870098-30-7 pbk

Contents

List of Illustrations

The following are brief descriptions by the author of the photographs in the centre of the book. For full captions please see under the photographs.

Foreword

ON A WARM summer's day, some time in the late 1960s though I forget which year, I saw Lawrence Hills for the first time. My eye had been caught by a figure in the distance, tall and thin, wearing a panama hat with the tropical linen suit he says later in this book he bought from an Oxfam shop, surrounded by a small crowd of his own, talking nineteen to the dozen, clearly a person of importance. A voice beside me said; 'That's Lawrence Hills.'

I knew the name, of course. The occasion of this first fleeting glimpse was a Soil Association Open Day, at the experimental farms the Association maintained at Haughley in Suffolk. I worked in the editorial department of the Association and I had read many of Lawrence's articles. I knew of the Henry Doubleday Research Association, as a kind of sister organization to our own, promoting organic gardening as we promoted organic farming. In the years since then I have read much more of Lawrence's writing and have enjoyed the even greater pleasure of a personal friendship with Lawrence and his wife, Cherry, that has developed against the background of the phenomenal growth of the environmental movement, the years when we both wrote for *The Ecologist* — the Soil association editorial department handled the magazine's production in the early years — attended a conference together in far-off San Francisco, and, more important perhaps, that has seen the increasing acceptance of 'the organic idea'.

These days organic methods of cultivation are fashionable. Even Government ministers speak favourably of them when they wish to sound 'green'. A bandwagon is rolling, with passengers leaping aboard at every opportunity to join a motley crew whose members may well find one another's company less congenial as the journey progresses. It is worth recalling, therefore, that Lawrence Hills did not board a bandwagon — he is one of those who set it in motion and he is still one of its drivers.

He joined the Soil Association in 1948, not long after it was formed, and for several decades his was one of a very few voices speaking against a great weight of accepted orthodoxy.

He had to put up with being dismissed as a crank, a romantic dreamer whose grip on scientific and economic reality was at best tenuous. I suspect he may have rather enjoyed the label, but he did not choose it and at times heterodoxy can seem synonymous with loneliness. E. F. Shumacher saw the bandwagon coming and warned of its dangers. At first, he said, an idea is dismissed as outrageous. Then, but for a very short time, people admit there may be something in it. After that the idea is absorbed, people think they have always known it, and its origins are forgotten.

For several years in the 1970s Lawrence was a member of the Soil Association Council but his main work has always centred on his own Association, dedicated to Henry Doubleday, the Essex Quaker Lawrence rescued from obscurity. When I first came to know of the work of the Henry Doubleday Research Association and read its booklets what I did not know was the extent to which that Association was Lawrence's own creation. The H.D.R.A. was Lawrence D. Hills and Lawrence D. Hills was the H.D.R.A. Today the H.D.R.A. is by far the largest society of organic growers in Britain, and perhaps in the world. Doubtless fortune has smiled on an idea whose time has come, but without all those years of work, hardship and ingenuity fortune would not have smiled. Lawrence's dedication was an act of faith and its reward is richly deserved.

His central idea is very simple. If a large number of amateur organic gardeners, working different soils in different climates, can test plants, devices and techniques, useful amounts of practical information can be gathered from them very cheaply for dissemination to others. That is what the H.D.R.A. does. It sounds obvious, but so far as I know it is unique.

My first impression, on that sunlit Suffolk day, was correct. The man in the Oxfam suit was a person of some significance. Yet, as I learned by reading this book, Lawrence is more interesting and his personal achievement greater than such bald facts reveal. No one who has read one of his gardening books or articles can doubt that his knowledge of horticulture is profound. Here he describes how it was acquired, working in nurseries where he was taught by gardeners who learned their craft before the days of chemical 'crutches' and who survived only if they made a profit against fierce competition. It was hard work, but Lawrence was not strong. Handicapped by an illness that was not fully understood until he was middle aged, and that frequently laid him low even then, until Cherry devised a diet that sustained him and that he was able to digest, Lawrence could never feel secure in any job. He took up writing at least partly because it meant his bouts of illness would no longer jeopardize the jobs and capital investment of others.

He describes his wartime experiences in the R.A.F., and the long, hand-written letter from Albert Howard that answered questions from an ordinary airman half a world away and, coincidentally, recruited that airman into an organic movement that was just coming into existence. The other man to change the direction of Lawrence's life was, of course, Henry Double-day, who introduced what he called 'Russian' comfrey but who was also an inventor, naturalist and visionary who 'observed the works of God in humbleness'. Lawrence tells us as much as is known about Henry. Perhaps he himself is some kind of reincarnation of that good man.

His is a rich life, he is a skilled and witty writer, and this is a a rich book, full of detail and often very funny. I have read it with delight for itself because it is a 'good read' but also for the window it opens on the life and personality of the person I am honoured to call my friend and whom I have no hesitation in describing as the most senior figure in the British organic move-ment today.

Michael Allaby

Wadebridge, Cornwall
July 1989

Introduction

THROUGH the quarter-century in the middle of my life when I was publisher's reader in farming and gardening to Faber and Faber, in the years when they were publishing the thin and thoughtful books that built the organic movement, I was probably thanked more in prefaces than any other writer in literary history. I learnt to help others to write better books than I could write myself, but it is as hard for authors to help themselves as for dentists to draw their own teeth.

Canadian peach orchard owners have the custom of thinning each other's crops for they know that no one will be sufficiently drastic with his own peachlings. Again and again I advised my friend the late Richard de la Mare of Faber and Faber that 'there was nothing wrong with a manuscript that a fuller wastepaper basket would not cure'. Now my words come home to roost and I have cut my life short enough to print in an age when a book designer would take one look at *Silent Spring* and say 'Far too long', and dismiss the Bible with 'No pictures. It will never sell'.

I have carried out faithfully two pieces of my own advice to authors. The first is 'Always write about what you know' and ever since my first book *Miniature Alpine Gardening* in 1944 I have done this, and I must apologise to those who expect more of what I know that will be of value to them in their own gardens. This book is my opportunity to say what I think in words I like, and I trust that they will make my past come alive and grow for others like the many plants of which I have written. I plead that I have practical experience of being 'me' that goes back to 1911.

The other advice I always gave is 'Never waste Chapter One in your introduction because so few people read these. They skim through the Contents and List of Illustrations and glance at the 'blurb' on the inside front flap of the dust-jacket. Introductions should be brief and mainly acknowledgements of illustrations.' So I will start by thanking Messrs HTV Ltd, producers of the H.D.R.A. 'Muck and Magic' Television Series for the photograph of our 'Give up Smoking Bonfires' exhibit at my fortieth Chelsea Flower Show; Godfrey Parris for the photographs of his father 'Mr George' and his uncle 'Mr Fred'; and my cousin John Saunders for the photographs of my father and his father at the gates of his home Hadleyhurst, and for the wet plate picture of my mother aged fourteen. She hated being photographed and this is the only portrait we have of her that will reproduce. The daguerrotype of Henry Doubleday, taken at the 1851 Exhibition, was given by Thomas Doubleday, his nephew and our Member No. 1.

My brother Geoffrey drew the maps of the Trial Ground and gave me much valuable chemical advice from his position in the ICI, which may well be as full of organic gardeners as a sausage factory is of vegetarians. I would like to thank 'Haro' and the editor of *The Observer* for the drawing of the nimble over-ninety who first appeared above the letter that launched my wife's *Basic Food Guide to a Green Old Age* and to forestall a fleet of letters telling me that the sprightly gardener is holding a manure fork, not one for digging. I remember the row over Earl Haig's horse when hundreds of indignant cavalrymen wrote the the Press. It was not it seems a charger, but a milk-round horse, borrowed as a model from Express Dairies by the sculptor.

The little picture of Henry Doubleday's comfrey needs no acknowledgement for it is over a hundred years old. It is from Messrs Sutton & Sons Farm Seeds Catalogue for 1878 when they sold his original F.1 hybrid, which looks like a blend of Bocking No. 7 and Bocking No. 14.

The picture that means most to me is a coloured one that is not there, so I express my deepest and most heartfelt thanks not to the photographer, but to the staff at Bocking through the years when we built The Henry Doubleday Research Association together. From left to right they stand as I see them still in 1979: Patrick Hughes, Paul Brammall, myself, Cherry, Pauline Pears, Jackie Gear, Teresa Hughes, Sandra Kent, Alan Gear, Eileen Johnson, Lucille Bouthay, Anne Long, Rose Whybrow, and Violet Asling. Thank you again for all the dedication and hard work you gave to the small beginnings that have grown so large and famous. They were good old days when we were all younger than we are now, among the friendly neighbours of Convent Lane, who put up with the traffic and helped us grow into history.

Introduction

I shall use that picture as the frontispiece of the next book of my autobiography which will carry further the story of the H.D.R.A. and myself, for it has been and still is my life.

Lawrence D. Hills

Ryton Court Bungalow
Ryton-on-Dunsmore
July 1989

The cartoon by Haro of a sprightly organic gardener over ninety, illustrating Lawrence D. Hills' letter in The Observer *that he wrote to publicize Cherry's* Basic Food Guide to a Green Old Age.

1

Quiet Homes and Small Beginnings

'From quiet homes and small beginning, out to the undiscovered ends.'

Hillaire Belloc

THIS BOOK is the story of my journey from an ailing childhood spent in a wheelchair to becoming founder, builder, Director and President of the Henry Doubleday Research Association, the largest body of organic gardeners in Britain, perhaps in the world. When I began the Association, in 1954, there were relatively few followers of the pioneers of the organic movement. According to Dr G. H. Hessayon, Britain's best known inorganic gardener, speaking at a press conference, in 1979 one gardener in three was unwilling to use chemical fertilizers or sprays. The proportion is probably still higher today.

As an organic gardener myself, I shall begin my story by defining organic gardening as briefly as I can. It is the art of growing healthy vegetables, fruit, flowers and lawns without using chemical fertilizers, pesticides, fungicides or herbicides. Organic gardeners endeavour to control pests and diseases by cunning, using biological controls, resistant varieties and tricks of timing and cultivation whenever they can. They employ sprays of mainly vegetable origin because these break down in the soil rather than leaving residues to accumulate, and do not evolve resistant varieties of pests or diseases by unnatural selection or build up to danger along Nature's chains of eaters and eaten. Ideally they spare such garden friends as ladybirds, and destroy only our foes. Shortages of calcium, magnesium, phosphorus, potassium, and trace elements, if they occur, are corrected and maintained with

1

ground minerals made available slowly by root secretions and micro-organisms. The living soil is fed by aiding nature's recycling processes with compost, manure, green manures and organic fertilizers rather than with rapidly soluble chemicals that can overfeed crops, reducing their disease resistance and, like nitrates, polluting drainage water and endangering both environmental balance and human health.

I was born on July 2nd 1911 at 4 Valetta Terrace, Dartmouth, Devon, one of six houses in a row, crammed so closely against a hillside that washing had to be hoisted on a kind of mast with pulleys because the backyards were tiny and front gardens were non-existent — front doors opened straight on the street. Our house was different because while in the others bath water was heated in coppers and carried upstairs in brown-painted cans, ours went up in state, pumped by a trawler's hand bilge pump ingeniously adapted by my father.

He was a Civilian Science Master at the Royal Naval College, at first on the *Brittania* and later in the shore establishment. He went there after leaving the Royal Masonic School, then working as a laboratory assistant to Sir Alfred Ewing on early experiments on 'wireless telegraphy' in the 1890s when Marconi was not the only worker in this field. My father often recalled the weekend he stayed on working with iron pyrites from coal, which could have given him the crystal detector before Marconi found the coherer, which was small, simple and the first step on the road to radio.

My parents married when both were 21, on the strength of the new job. With a salary that worked out at £2.50 a week this even employed a daily servant, a Mrs. Pockett.

During the Dartmouth years my father studied hard — long before correspondence colleges were thought of — to take his matriculation intermediate and B.Sc. engineering degree. He sat his finals as an external student at London University in the year I was born, passing them at the second attempt, just as my brother Geoffrey, two years my senior, did many years later.

My mother was one of a family of 14, for my grandmother married twice, carrying over four daughters from her first marriage to 'Woodhill', the big house at Ealing bought by John Sanders, her second husband and a prosperous farmer, to accommodate his ever-increasing family. My grandfather on my father's side also married twice. This left my brother Geoffrey, my younger sister Iris and me rather over-uncled and over-aunted, even by Victorian standards.

2

The two families met because of the photographer's business at Windsor where Robert Hills, my grandfather, was one of the pioneers of photography, and the firm of Hills and Saunders held the contract for photographing the Eton boys. The Saunders money, and the Hills ingenuity that used four wet-plate cameras to take four glass negatives simultaneously, then fitted them together into the first large group photographs ever taken, made this a prosperous business.

The family opposed the match because my parents were first cousins, but they married as soon as they were of age and the arrival of Geoffrey, all golden curls, dimples and with a solemn interest in all things mechanical and mathematical that has never left him, soon won their hearts. We three children have kept to Mendel's law as faithfully as though we were tall and dwarf peas. Geoffrey has inherited a double dose of my father's engineering and mathematical mind, Iris my mother's and my grandmother's artistic ability, and in the opinion of my mother I am a blend of both parents, more a Saunders than a Hills, with no mathematical or mechanical attributes whatever.

As miniatures, painted on ivory by my grandmother show, my mother was darkly beautiful when she was young. She played the piano well and had a clear soprano voice, while my father sang Gilbert and Sullivan in a jocular baritone. They fitted into the civilian side of the social life of Dartmouth when Dreadnought class battleships, each with twelve 12-inch guns, were as new as Tridents today. Among their friends was G. A. Henty, who made a fortune from writing books for boys, and there were several trips on his ninety-foot schooner *Egret* which began my father's interest in maritime painting.

We left Dartmouth when I was 21 months old and my sister a two-month-old baby. Soon after I was weaned I developed attacks of diarrhoea, which left me a small, skinny, white-faced child whom my mother was told she would 'never rear'. There was little that could be done for 'sickly' children. Even my grandmother reared only 11 of her 14.

When I was three I composed a poem which I recited to my mother. At least it had the virtue of brevity:

When it rains the ground is wet,
And all the puddles are as full as they can get.

My mother has since told me she determined then that I

should be writer, on the evidence of this concise statement of observed facts in short and simple words.

There was always a deep bond between my mother and myself, forged through the years she spent fighting for my health (since I am a coeliac, undiagnosed until I was 52), arguing with doctors and doing her best to keep me alive despite medical ignorance which can still handicap the estimated quarter million people with my very debilitating chronic condition. My recurring childhood memory is of my mother, with her thick black hair hanging right down her back. I also recall Geoff piping up during the craze for bobbed and shingled hair, 'Mummy, I'm the only boy in our class whose mother can sit on her hair.' How often she would come in the night wearing a white flannel nightgown with frills at the throat and wrists and bare feet peeping below, to comfort me and cope with what we called my 'attacks'.

When my father, with his new and hard won B.Sc., won the combined posts of science master at Bishop Vesey's Grammar School and Vice Principal of the Sutton Coldfield Technical Institute, which were next door to each other and shared laboratory and workshop facilities, we moved to Sutton Coldfield, near Birmingham. The Principal of the Institute was Harold Pochin, a biologist who was also a captain in the Territorials.

There we lived in a house that was called 27 Upper Holland Road until we re-christened it 'Woodhill' after Mother's childhood home. A large semi-detached property of three storeys, it had an enormous attic which ran from front to back where my father fitted up a workshop and photographic studio. The rent was 40 a year, and we could afford it out of my father's increased salary. The house was lit by gas, some jets with mantles and others only fish tail burners which gave off quite a bit of heat. I still recall their cosy roaring on cold days.

When war came in 1914, Harold Pochin was called up at once and my father took charge of the Technical Institute, organizing extra metal-working classes where students made shell parts. He had dropped a heavy weight on his foot at the Cambridge laboratories which left him with a permanently weak ankle, making him unfit for military service in both world wars.

Soon we moved from Sutton Coldfield to Worcester where my father organized the training of unskilled labour and the machinery for making cartridges, demanded in millions for machine guns in the air and on the ground. He developed the phosphorus bullet that brought down Zeppelins so effectively it ended these airship raids on London. None of his inventive ideas made money, for they were used in the service of his country when others were dying in the mud of Paschendale and the Somme.

At Worcester we lived at 'Belmont', another three-storey semi-detached house with the high rental of 50 a year. A large walnut tree dominated the back garden where we three were allowed beds with which to do what we liked. We made 'trenches' and dugouts mainly, but mine included a small pond, cemented by my father, in which I reared batches of frog and toad tadpoles. As medical opinion held that I should be rested as much as possible, Mother always wheeled me in a bath chair, with Geoffrey on one side and Iris on the other, and on my lap lay model boats to sail in the Worcester and Birmingham Canal. It was a red letter day for us if we saw 'The Barge Lady', a bargee's wife who wore a man's cap and smoked a clay pipe as she steered her slowly gliding craft while far ahead her husband drove the hardworking horse.

I regularly kept the other two enthralled making up stories and ideas for games, but I was often laid low by my 'attacks'. One of the worst ended my first and only period of formal education. My brother went first to Tredenic, a preparatory school, and then to Worcester Grammar School, while Iris went to Miss Tysoe's kindergarten, and then shared a governess with Veronica Sharrock, the vicar's daughter. I, too, started to go to Miss Tysoe's where I can remember a plump and vigorous boy named Geoffrey Ford, in a red jersey and dark blue shorts, who was always being told to make less noise. But after two weeks I had to give up because of my 'attacks'.

It was no good trying to educate me, much less spend any real money on teaching me. I should never be able to pass matriculation because in orthodox medical opinion I could not live long enough. My mother refused to believe this and fed my eager mind on heavy books from the library. I had learned to read early, Nansen's *Farthest North*, Scott's *Last Expedition*, Shackleton's *Heart of the Antarctic*, Bates's *Naturalist on the Amazon*, Kipling, E. Nesbit, Ernest Thompson Seton, anything to widen my horizons as I lay white and small in bed. I used to dream of building a yacht and sailing round the world, writing out long lists of things I would need, including 'nails' and 'more nails', and drawing lines in old atlases to show where I should some day voyage, little thinking that I would one day fly to the distant places I had dreamed of sailing to in tall ships with stars to steer them by.

When the Armistice came in 1918, the cartridge factory shut down fast, and after an interval my father, my Uncles Charlie and Kenneth, his brothers, and Mr Caink, a friend from the factory, started an enterprise making gold paint from smashed up cartridge cases and scrap brass. This failed when the fall of the mark brought the Germans into competition with us, and by the end of 1919 our family fortunes were at a low ebb, though we children carried on happily with our lives.

We were never bored, we always had plenty to do, and we rarely had other children to tea. I cannot recollect that we ever ate cakes; Mother made everything, with the help of the faithful Mrs. Ashcroft, and the fact that we ate fruit rather than cakes and puddings may well have saved my life, though no one at that date realized this. I think now that my father must have lost money we could not afford on the Radiant Products Company. The turning point came when Major Pochin was demobilized in 1919 and became headmaster of Dartford Grammar School in Kent, with instructions from the governors to strengthen the science side which was badly run down. So he sent for Father who arrived in 1921, taking lodgings with the Youens family, a Dutch widow with two daughters, Olive and Margery, who became additional Aunties to us. We stayed behind at 'Belmont', where Mother took in schoolmistresses as lodgers, to help cover the costs of running two homes.

During this period my grandmother died, leaving about 800 for Mother during her lifetime and then to us, her three children. My Uncle Gordon who, like Uncle Peter, had been articled to a firm of estate agents and was by now a partner in John D. Wood of Berkeley Square, was trustee, for my grandmother did not want to risk letting 'Willy' as she called my father, to his great disgust, spend the money financing some other invention. Out of this money Mother paid to have me examined by a Harley Street specialist, Dr Sanders. I cannot remember much of the long rail journey in the winter of 1922. I think Auntie Daisy, my mother's elder sister, came to 'Belmont' to look after Iris and Geoffrey, but Mother and I stayed with the Youens's and we took a taxi from Charing Cross to Harley Street.

Dr Sanders dismissed the idea of my having T.B. of some kind, but recommended an outdoor life. He said my condition went by sevens: I had nearly died when I was seven, I should be greatly improved by 14, and well by 21. It was not known then that coeliacs absorb vitamin D very badly and this prevents their bodies absorbing calcium. As the skin can synthetize this vitamin from sunlight my outdoor life as a gardener indeed has saved me from the crippling effects of a calcium shortage which I have seen in other coeliacs less fortunate than I.

In April 1923 we moved from Worcester to Dartford, where the legacy bought us No. 1 Tower Road for 500. Our new home was a four-bedroom semi-detached with a large coal cellar, room for a workshop for my father, a small front garden and a long back one, with a giant William pear tree at the bottom. At first it was lit by gas, but later we had electricity installed. This gave my father scope to devise a convector heater for drying clothes using very thin wires that never got red hot, using less current than conventional fires. This was the basis of his last and most successful private invention.

Geoffrey went to the grammar school and Iris started at the Dartford County School for Girls, while I continued to read widely and omnivorously. I started keeping fish in two half tubs holding four and 12 gallons respectively. My father fixed up a windmill, a vertical shaft that played a small fountain in the large tub or pumped in a stream of bubbles to provide oxygen for my collection of stone loach and minnows — not sticklebacks but *Phoxinus phoxinus*, the true minnow, which can grow up to seven inches long.

Stone loach (*Misgornus fossilis*) are about six inches long, with six barbels round their mouths. They live on the bottom in clear running streams or rivers by cleaning algae off stones, and eating small insects from under them. They are interesting because they are the only British equivalent to the lung-fish of the tropics. They can breathe by swallowing air as newts do, using their swim bladders as temporary lungs.

I had a female loach, 'Brownie', with a damaged eye, so I could put a hand gently in the water on her blind side and stroke her side when she would push against me like a cat rubbing round my legs. I made her the subject of the very first experiment I ever designed. I boiled some water on the gas cooker (electric cookers came much later) to expel the oxygen, let it cool overnight, then poured it into a pie dish and placed it in our large outdoor lavatory where we kept the garden tools. After catching my loach with a small net I kept for inspections, I deposited her in my dish. Then I sat down with my father's stopwatch to await results.

At first Brownie stayed on the bottom, using up the residual oxygen, till I began to think nothing would happen. But suddenly she rose with a leisurely swish of her tail, took a good gulp of air and returned to nuzzling the stones I had put in the dish to make her feel at home. Gradually the intervals shortened until she was coming up very 40 seconds. Then I carried out the second part of the experiment with some Canadian pondweed I had ready in a jam jar of water. I put in some branches of this very powerful photosynthesizer, and noted that after about ten minutes the intervals began to lengthen. Gradually, six per cent of the sunlight streaming through the lavatory door provided the energy to split some of the water drawn into the pondweed to oxygen and hydrogen, and some of the carbon dioxide breathed out by my lady loach into oxygen and carbon, fitted the carbon on the hydrogen to make carbohydrates (starches and sugars) and released enough oxygen to keep Brownie peacefully on the bottom. I put her back in the large tub (the small one was for newts) and went indoors to tell Mother all about it.

I wrote up results in the red exercise books with useful information about firkins, rods, poles and perches on the back. Later they all vanished as war time 'salvage'. At that time I was able to go for walks on my own, freed from the bathchair, so my father made me a telescope with a two-and-a-half-inch lens he had ground. It had a short focal length, a wide field of vision, and a microscope eyepiece. It served me well for bird-watching on Dartford Heath, home of the Dartford Warbler.

My first 'published' writing was an account of how to rear tadpoles, which I wrote because the science mistress at the county school was having trouble with hers in the windowsill aquarium, and my sister insisted that her brother had reared hundreds of tadpoles with no trouble at all. I think it was in 1926 that I produced this and it may still be in use for it had been jellygraphed with hectographic ink — that messy ancestor of photostating. The science mistress had not realized that tadpoles are not vegetarians, so hanging a small piece of meat in the tank provides the vitamin B12 and other nutrients, naturally supplied by eating pond snails, which they need to keep them happily wriggling their way to froghood.

It was not possible to make a career of any kind of biology without matriculation and mathematics. My parents tried a governess, and Mr Pell, the art master from the grammar school, tried to teach me drawing, but in every case the result was an 'attack'. Every time I had a diarrhoea attack I was put on a diet of milk and cream cracker biscuits. The milk was all right, for I was not milk intolerant as some coeliacs are, but the biscuits were giving me the gluten that was the cause of the trouble. An ordinary meat, vegetable, and fruit meal would have given my villi a chance to recover. 'Villi' are the human equivalent of a plant's feeding roots, working on the insides of our intestines, and gluten makes them lie down and give up absorbing nutrients. I think mine became more tolerant for a time as I grew older, but an extra heavy intake of anything containing wheat, oats, rye, or barley, would lay me low again.

It was in this period, between 1924 and 1928, that my father wrote his three textbooks. They stayed in print year after year for they were used in certain overseas colleges until they were swept away before the flood of '11 plus' and 'A' and 'O' levels. *Mechanics and Applied Mathematics* Part I, published in 1925, Part II in 1926 and *Elements of Mechanics*, 1928, were published by the English Universities Press, a subsidiary of Hodder and Stoughton, and ran to five editions before they finally stopped selling in the 1960s.

Dad typed the first on an 'invisible' Remington, so called because you had to lift the heavy carriage to see what you were writing. It had a two-inch-wide ribbon and was one of the first practical standard office machines. He bought it second-hand for about 3 in 1921. His second and third books were done on an A.M.C., a flimsier German machine that cost 7 new because of the fall in the mark, and I was given the old Remington.

My father drew all his pictures, with motor cars travelling at 60 miles an hour, illustrated with a bullnose Morris and everyone holding their hats on, and beautiful Shire horses pulling weights to show horsepower. The books were based on his teaching methods and he had a genius for teaching and explaining, which he never valued. The royalties those books brought saved our family financially many times, for my parents had a rare handicap.

My father could not fight but served his country in two world wars with his inventive ability, unrewarded by royalties because he was a Government employee. Although other schoolmasters, who served in the armed forces, had their war service counted as teaching experience, after 1918 he actually forfeited four years' salary increases. This also reduced his pension, curtailed still further by inventive service in the Second World War, in the field of hydraulic equipment for tanks and aircraft. My father had always been on the staff so had no stamped insurance card to entitle my mother to any form of old age pension later. She was one of the last of her generation to suffer this injustice.

2

Teenage Gardener

I GOT my first job at 16 by catching more than two thousand minnows to stock the lily ponds at Central Park, Dartford. When I last saw them more than thirty years later they had grown to a huge shoal which included several seven-inch specimens, showing that the entry in my father's 1924 edition of *Chambers Encyclopaedia* was correct.

My first meeting with Mr Dudman, the Park's superintendent, was on one of my visits to the Dartford library that stood in Central Park. A large but harmless wood wasp (*Vespa austriaca*) was alarming the borrowers. The library girls appealed for my help, so I captured it against a window in a glass and an index card slid under it, for safe release. Mr Dudman arrived to change the flowers during the excitement. He was a very large and dignified man, who always wore a pepper-and-salt tweed knick-erbocker suit with a hat to match, and four gold watch-chains sweeping across and up his well filled waist-coat like anchor chains in the bows of a ship. Two gold watches were presented to him for long service to titled employers, the third told the time and the fourth led to a silver medal he had won at Chelsea Flower Show. He had a reddened face and a well trimmed and grown moustache that was designed to bristle with determination in the face of resistance by employers who wore merely military or legal moustaches and with fury at anyone who had left a plant unwatered or a spade uncleaned. He was a kindly man, a lay preacher and a tee totaller, who smoked a large pipe in his small green painted office shed full of seed and bulb catalogues and copies of *The Gardener's Chronicle*, which carried a column charting the progress of head gardeners from one stately home to another.

After that I used to meet him frequently, usually up a ladder pruning the many hardy shrubs and climbers on the walls that kept the wind off the better tennis courts, and when he complained to me that the goldfish did not seem to be keeping

11

down the gnat and midge larvae I offered him all the minnows I could catch. I had his permission to ignore the signs and cross the sacred grass to tip in my almost daily catches, supplemented with netted ramshorn pondsnails as additional scavengers, from the ponds on Dartford heath.

I caught my minnows with an eight-foot length of stout cord tied to the neck of a two pound jam jar smeared generously inside with a stiff paste of flour and water and thrown in the river. As the paste dissolved slowly it brought minnows in quantity, drawn by the food drifting downstream. I would watch till I could see the jar full of fish tearing at the pale lumps, then pull in the cord fast. The minnows pointing to the mouth of the jar shot out, but I caught all those that faced the sides and swam fast but fruitlessly to reach the freedom they could see through the glass.

I usually caught up to eight minnows a throw and often brought back over a hundred a trip, always with some Canadian pondweed to provide a supply of oxygen, in a 14 lb. sweet tin, to which I had fitted a stout wire handle. My fishing beat was on the river Darenth where it flowed through Mill Farm, Sutton-at-Hone, owned by Henry Widdows, a farmer who had a beard like an Old Testament prophet and carried a double-barrelled muzzel-loading gun with percussion caps that fitted on nipples under the hammers, though I never saw him fire it because he was more interested in natural history than shooting. His stories of wildlife and the way he told them served me in the 1950s for the 'John Greenway' articles in *The Farmer*.

When, in April 1928, my father offered Mr Dudman a premium to start me on a career in horticulture, Mr Dudman said he would be delighted to have me as an unpaid pupil, and to see me started on the matriculation-free road of apprentice, improver, journeyman, master, that could, with the hard work and determination demonstrated by my minnow-catching marathon, lead to my becoming a park superintendent. At least this outdoor life should serve to build up my strength and health. So Mr Dudman saw the Parks Committee, and at 16 I became a pupil for 12 months to try out how my health stood up to the work.

My parents bought me a new outfit. It consisted of brown corduroy breeches, buttoned at the knee (18/-), a brown tweed sports coat (12/6d), a khaki shirt open at the neck (4/6d), black lace-up boots (9/6d), and a brown felt hat (10/6d). I wore variations on this cheap and warm 'uniform' for many years.

Central Park had 20 tennis courts, one clock-golf green and two bowling greens, which earned considerable sums in fees, banked by Mr Dudman in a brown Gladstone bag, together with the pennies from the lavatory locks, almost every day. It had a large 'Recreation Ground', surrounded by shrub borders with rough grass for children's games, plenty of seats for watching, and a fine display of bulbs and bedding plants, plus over a thousand feet of dry wall planted with alpines which Mr Dudman built with my help as a replacement for grass edgings which needed mowing and trimming on both sides.

Against weeds we used old-fashioned lawn sand, made with sulphate of iron, sulphate of ammonia and dry sand, sea sand to encourage the fine grasses, and quantities of sifted leafmould which the worms took under, building up humus and adding top dressing with their casts which we broke up with a 'Selley brush' about eight feet wide that had whalebone teeth. In the late 1920s — long before selective seedkillers — we grew as good grass, especially on the bowling greens, as in any park today. Modern chemicals had not been invented, and Mr Dudman preferred to use bonemeal which lasted in the soil longer than chemical fertilizers, with leafmould from leaves that had to be swept anyway, and nicotine as our only insecticide. In fact we were 'organic' before the term was invented as were all the great gardens of the past.

During this year I joined the Dartford Technical College for an evening course in Matriculation English under Miss Browne, a splendid teacher, who taught me to read Shakespeare for pleasure. Later I came to *Falstaff* 'a babbling o'green fields'. The first essay I did, on 'A Country Walk' had to be 500 words. I cut and cut till it was exactly that, foreshadowing the future when I once pleaded for 'just 20 of the words in *The Observer* that do no work today'. She raised my style from the impossible, like the three novels of childhood I had written, to the rejection-slip-worthy, but my handicap was my complete lack of ability to draw characters and my inexperience of life, except in a very limited field.

I had another handicap: constant spells of quite high temperatures, as well as diarrhoea. So I gave up my English classes, though I might have become a better writer more quickly had I continued, but it was clear, as Father said, that I could never get matric.

When my year was nearing its end, my mother took a hand, for she could not see me as a park keeper, even as a park superintendent. On our trips by tram to Woolwich Free Ferry, on the way to our family voyages in the *Golden Eagle* and *Crested Eagle*, the paddle steamers that took us to Margate or Clacton, she had noticed a nursery garden at the end of Upton Road, Bexleyheath. She took a tram there, and met Alfred Parris of 'A. Parris & Sons, Wreaths and Crosses made to order, Floral Tributes sent, Bedding Plants in Season'. He was then about 82, and his two sons, Mr Fred and Mr George, were in their sixties. They wrote my indentures not so much on Mr Dudman's testimonial as the fact that Mr George's son, Godfrey, was at Dartford Grammar School and knew my father as 'Tubby Hills' — the only master who knew *exactly* how aeroplanes flew and wireless worked. The indentures were simple enough. They bound me for three years at 6 shillings a week the first year, 9 shillings the second, and 12 shillings the last, and concluded 'We will do our best by him, if he will do the same by us, and we will learn him all we know'. They certainly carried out their part of the bargain, and I did my best to do mine.

There were two nurseries. One was run by Mr George together with the shop, where Mrs Fred Parris and Hilda her daughter made up the wreaths and crosses and the 'floral tributes' which covered wedding bouquets and buttonholes. There were ten greenhouses of varied size, including a fern house, an orchid house, and a propagating house with bottom heat, frames for bedding plants and alpines, beds for herbaceous plants and shrubs, and an acre of apple orchard at the back.

The other nursery, where I first worked, run by Mr Fred, up a turning off the main road, consisted of 11 newer and larger greenhouses, some 14 feet wide with raised beds each side and paths down the middles, and the others 21 feet wide and about 12 high, with level soil, which had formerly grown grapes for market and were now cropped with tomatoes and cucumbers. All were 100 feet long, and were heated by a Bisson and a Rochford boiler, with a 'Twelve Hour' which had extra fuel in a cast iron tower above it, to provide extra heat for No. 4, the propagating house. I learned stoking on those boilers. Mr Fred used to say 'Always remember Lawrence, if those boilers burn more than three pounds ten worth of coke in a week, they're taking more out of the business than I am myself.' Both brothers used to draw this much, so did their father, and they had a 'divvy up' at intervals when profits allowed.

14

Teenage Gardener

I have never been a small nurseryman myself but what I learned at Parris's gave me material for many articles in *The Horticultural Advertiser* and *Nurseryman and Seedsman* in the 1950s. I had only to think of them talking with their blend of horse sense, small-scale commercial ability, and horticultural knowledge, to raise in my readers' minds the image of the 'Old Guv'nor' to whom so many nurseries owed so much.

A landmark was passed when I entered my last year as an apprentice, and tore my ten shilling note in half when I opened my first 12 shilling pay envelope (1/6d came off each week for my Health and Pensions Insurance).

I took it into the local Lloyds Bank branch in distress, and the grey-haired cashier gave me a brand new one instead. Since then I have always banked at Lloyds, though it was very many years before I had money enough to need a bank. I celebrated by buying myself a new bicycle, paying 2/6d a week instalments for an Elswich with 'North Road' handlebars, an all-weather touring bag from Buckleys for 12/6d, and joining the Cyclist's Touring Club.

This gave me part of what I had missed. I had very rarely played with other children. I had never run shouting round a playground, or argued and crossed mental swords with my contemporaries. Apart from my sister and a few of her friends on very rare occasions I had hardly spoken to girls of my own age. I knew of schools only from school stories, and life only from books.

The West Kent District Association of the C.T.C. started its 'club runs' mainly at the War Memorial in Bexley about two miles from Tower Road. I just turned up on a Saturday afternoon at 2.15, and went for a ride with about seven other cyclists, four male and three female.

I then took to visiting the clubroom, a shed in the grounds of the Bull Inn at St Pauls Cray, on Tuesday evenings, and going for all-day runs on Sundays. There were two Sections, the Fast, riding from 90 to 100 miles a day, and my personal choice the Loiterers who rode from 60 to 70. We would meet at 8.30 or 9 a.m. carrying sandwiches, and with yellow oilskin capes, leggings, and sou'wester hats in case of rain. We stopped for 'elevenses' when we drank tea, usually costing 3d. or 4d. each from large shared pots. We ate our sandwiches with more tea about 1 p.m. and stopped for a full tea at about five, a long way from home. Those studying for exams or working would ride direct to the tea venue. We rode back in parties and couples. The total cost in modern money for the whole day varied between 15 and 20p.

As a 'new boy', I learned fast. My 'corners were rubbed off', and I became an accepted character in my own right. Wherever I went there was the companionship I so much needed, in District Associations all over Britain. Soon I found myself on the committee and editing our magazine *Winged Words*.

This taught me not only what prefects and monitors learn at school, but also about proofs, deadlines and advertising. My first success was to get a half-page advertisement out of Messrs Buckley who made my bargain touring bag, and we seem to have about broken even on a circulation of around 1,000, a great many selling to neighbouring District Associations and clubs through the cafés. My first and only short stories to appear in print were in *Winged Words* under the pen name of 'Loiterer'. They were appreciated, to my surprise, which should have taught me what I took so long to learn. It is always best to write about what you know.

The marriage rate among members was probably about the same as in a modern Young Conservatives Association, but on a lower social and income level. We provided a vastly cheaper way for boy to meet girl, in the open air, among their contemporaries, than on the dance floor or at the tennis club. Unlike the cyclists of the cycling craze of the 1890s, we did not drink beer and very few of us smoked, for neither go with long distance cycling.

We were all young, all learning, all enjoying ourselves, with war waiting just round the corner.

3

Up the Long Green Ladder

A. PARRIS AND SONS did not have land enough to grow the bush and tree fruit, roses, climbers, flowering trees, and shrubs they sold to customers from the new housing estates springing up all round them. These were bought from Messrs Stuart Low of Enfield, whose traveller, Mr Lawrence Cooke, was small, neat and birdlike, and kept a sharp eye on all his best customers. It was a tradition that every apprentice who completed his time and served a year as an improver should have the chance of an interview that could lead to a job with this leading wholesale nursery.

This gave the firm first pick of keen young men who knew enough to be useful quickly, and — even without matric — who had fathers likely to be able to raise the money to buy them small nurseries later on, when they knew enough to become customers of Messrs Stuart Low. Already eight improvers had taken this road successfully from Parris's.

When my turn came, Mr Cooke fixed the date of my interview at Bush Hill Park, Enfield (now built over like almost every nursery I have ever worked on), and I was told to ask for 35 shillings a week: lodgings with full board would cost 25 shillings and all a young man needed for pocket money was 10 shillings a week. I cycled over, wearing my best 'plus four' suit.

Old Mr Low was white haired, wore spats, and rode a Singer bicycle on which he shot from one end of the nursery to the other. The Cambridge Arterial Road went straight through it, and he had an unnerving habit of forgetting this and would go straight through the gates with the heavy lorries standing on their brakes as he rode across the road in front of them.

As he walked round with me, showing me some of the activities of the firm, I ran my hands through some very good soil and remarked, 'That's good stuff. For cyclamen, Sir?' He replied, 'Yes, my boy, plenty of coarse bonemeal, they last longer for seed with it.' I had potted hundreds, all growing

17

from Stuart Low seed for which they were famous, and I knew what the soil should look and feel like. We went back to the office and I met the 'Young Guv'nor', Hugh Low, who said, 'The question is, what money does he want?' As instructed, I said, 'Thirty-five shillings, Sir.' 'No,' said the 'Old Guv'nor'. 'We cannot afford more than two guineas.' The young Guv'nor shouted 'He said thirty-five shillings, Dad.' 'No need to shout,' said his father sharply, 'he may be worth it, he looks like a hard worker, but we can't afford more than two guineas.' I then shouted, 'I said THIRTY-FIVE SHILLINGS, SIR'. The old Guv'nor then smiled and said, 'Yes, but I *said* two guneas. So two guineas it was. That extra seven shillings made a very great difference to my life in 1932 when millions of men were bringing up families on such an income, and millions more of them on even less, with more than two million of them on the dole, for this was in the big slump of the 1930s.

So I set off on my bicycle to find myself lodgings, having told Mr Low I could give a week's notice and start on Monday week. I went to the local newsagents and studied the cards in the window. The advertisements were written by the shop owner, who also numbered them, so the neighbours would not recognize handwriting or addresses and see who was having to take in a lodger. The usually middle-aged and motherly woman behind the counter would look in her book and give me a rapid commentary.

My first landlady was a motherly soul, who considered I needed 'feeding up' and called me 'sonny'. I had to reach the nursery by 6.30 a.m., then back to breakfast from 8.30 to 9 a.m., and again from 12.30 to 1.30 for the dinner hour, and finally home at 5.30.

In our pay packets each week we had a set of six perforated cards with our numbers on (mine was 59) and one of these had to be handed in each morning to the timekeeper who turned them over to the office at 6.40. He was there again at 7 a.m. and 9 a.m. but you lost the time difference, at overtime rates, time and a half. After 9 a.m. you lost a whole day. The 20 field men clocked on separately. With the office staff, the 'Carnations', the three horsemen, and four motor lorry drivers, we totalled about 100 people. Including the main orchid nurseries at Jarvisbrook near Crowborough in Sussex, the very large fruit tree nursery at Benenden in Kent, and a further 30 acres at Carter Hatch, about three miles up the arterial road towards Cambridge, we were one of the biggest general nurseries in Britain.

It was organized like a 'county' with 'market towns', like 'The Cars', indoor carnation houses, or 'The Cycs' where cyclamen were grown for seed and pot plant sales. Nearly 20 villages were under a grower and his men, with a general foreman in charge. There were 32 stokeholes, with a boiler at each end of all of them. Two men spent their whole day going from one to another stoking and clearing clinker and ashes, with two more taking it in turn to work overtime replacing them at the weekends.

My grower was Tommy Gant, an ex-soldier with grey hair and a blue vocabulary. We grew ferns, clematis, and hydrangeas in those seven 100-feet long greenhouses and nine cold frames with sliding 'lights', six feet long and four feet wide which took two men to lift and carry. There was also an open-air pot-standing ground that stretched out into a rose area, all roses being rotated because of the baffling condition called 'rose sickness', now known to be caused by one of the eelworms, *Pratylenchus pratensis*.

The 'we' were Tommy, young Syd Phillips the foreman's son, Robin Cooke, the son of Mr Cooke the traveller, who also organized the shows and attended them, the other improver, and myself. Robin and I were known as 'The Young Gentlemen' and we were moved about to wherever anyone was getting behind with his work. This widened our experience but did not make us popular with growers who deliberately got behind in order to earn overtime catching up.

Robin had trained at Wye Agricultural College, had worked on nurseries in Holland, France, and Germany, and had a straight road ahead to a directorship, but after I left Stuart Low's he went to 'The Cars' and liked it so much he started his own carnation nursery, which was a great success. Promotion ladders are short and slow in the nursery trade because senior staff live so long. He was able to marry his girl, Phyllis, after borrowing a large sum, and so by-passed the ladder in the only possible way to reach an income large enough to marry on. Skill in growing plants and an affection for them are not enough. You need organizing and business ability too, and these Robin had, as well as a father who knew the trade.

Robin and I had the job of repotting 30,000 hydrangeas from 60s (2½ inches diameter across the rims) into 48s (3½ inches), averaging 1,000 a day, including mixing our own soil, setting the potted plants up in the open, watering them with a rosed hose, and plunging them in ashes to keep them from drying out.

Souths and Sankeys were the two big pot makers, both near enough, at Tottenham, to deliver direct to us by horse and cart. Robin and I caught them, stacked one inside the other in 'hands' of a dozen. Unloading and soil mixing made welcome breaks that allowed our hands a little time to recover from the cruel wear of the rough pots on our fingers.

All the clay from tunnelling out the London Underground was dumped at Tottenham by special trains that ran at night, and fired by coke. The over-burned and misshapen rejects were crushed, and made the red hard tennis courts of the day.

The long and monotonous haste of so many jobs on this huge nursery made me appreciate my weekends and bank holidays. I had a choice of C.T.C. District Associations to ride with, and I could be doing 90 to 100 miles on Sunday and as much as 150 over a weekend. I was working in the open all the week, and every weekend cycling in shorts and a short-sleeved shirt with the sunlight fixing my vitamin D and my calcium absorption, though no one (least of all I) knew it, and I had persuaded my landladies that though very thin I was fit and did not *like* steak and kidney and roly-poly suet puddings.

Thirty years later, my mother went through all my old letters and traced my worst 'attacks' to when I had motherly land-ladies who were ex-cooks. There was no excuse but ignorance for not curing me easily and cheaply by a special diet, and there is none today.

I rode with the Metropolitan Loiterers, who met at Totten-ham, and organized weekends, which gave them time to get well clear of London. Once I took a party of them down to 'The Ladies' Rally', organized by Molly Hunt of the West Kents. That would be impossible now. Traffic has made cycling a solitary rather than a social recreation. When I began, a cry of 'oil up' meant a stray motor car approaching, perhaps a Clyno, or a Bean, or a Bullnose Morris, with a red triangle on the back to warn that it could stop suddenly because it had brakes on all four wheels.

We used to meet at Green Street Green near Farnborough, Kent, about 500 cyclists of both sexes, including tandems with sidecars to hold young children, and pillion seats on the back for older sons and daughters. Mollie had laid on Petronella, the only lady cycling journalist, the faithful Kuklos, making sure of a report in the *News Chronicle,* and *Pathé Gazette* ('Presenting the World to the World') to film us.

Her organizing secrets were to agree the route with the police, and have plenty of marshals. They would wave the great chain of cyclists round the corners, mend any punctures, and sell the printed programmes, paid for by the advertising on the back, that covered the costs and even made a profit (because so many motorists, held up by the crowd, bought them to see what was happening), and arrange for the meal stops at two large picnic spaces, where the surrounding cafés did a roaring trade. The event was a gamble on weather, but Molly had insured against a wet Sunday through a member whose father was a Lloyds underwriter. The local papers did us proud and Pathé did their best filming us coming down long hills.

Before Christmas I had joined the Youth Hostels Association, subscription 5 shillings a year under 25, and 10 shillings (50p) for the wealthier and more mature members, and a shilling a night for dormitory accommodation, 'bring your own sleeping bags'. The hostel at Hildenborough, near Tonbridge, Kent, was staging a special Christmas weekend, and my brother Geoffrey, who had married his tandem partner Jean and was living in a flat at Bromley, was joining me there with my West Kent friends Cyril Hayward and Hugh Carey for a cheap and festive gathering.

I felt I was coming to a crossroads. I had landed a job with one of the biggest of all British nurseries, but all it offered was monotony and no ladder of promotion of the kind my contemporaries enjoyed. My only chance was to run a nursery of my own, and I had no more chance of running one on Stuart Low lines than a boy who is keen on model aeroplanes has of some day owning his own aircraft factory. I felt I was on the wrong track — one that led to living only for the weekends.

What I secretly wanted was to explore the wonders of photosynthesis, as revealed by Brownie my stone loach. I was interested in plants and how they grew, in trees, and in wildlife generally and I talked of what filled my mind as the young do, which is probably why I never married any of the pretty, cheerful, and kindly girls I met in the C.T.C. and Y.H.A., and why they did not want to marry me.

At the gates of the great green and exciting garden I wanted to explore was an angel with a flaming sword bearing in letters of fire the words 'No Matric'. In the autumn of the hydrangeas,

I saw an advertisement in *The Gardener's Chronicle* for 'six student gardeners' at the John Innes Horticultural Institution at Merton, where John Innes potting composts began, and Malling-Merton 106 apple stock that carries immunity to American Blight (*Eriosoma lanigerum*) was bred. Someone must measure the tall and dwarf peas and pot the primulas, for the work on genetics by Crane and Lawrence, or chromosomes by C. D. Darlington. Perhaps there existed an outside ladder, like the one my father took. So I put in my application for studentship and failed to get one. I tried four times until at 25 I was too old. Had I succeeded I might have gone far further in another direction (if my 'attacks' had allowed) but I would never have become an organic gardener.

When we finally reached the Youth Hostel, we found a huge house, looking more like an R.A.C. than a Y.H.A. establishment, for in addition to the Y.H.A. part of it was a hostel for international students. Dormitory accommodation was provided and the charge for three days of Christmas festivities was £1.87½ p. Even at 1932 prices that was cheap. It was called 'The Oaklands International Hostel', one of a chain run by the A.P.A., (All Peoples Association), 'a non-political movement designed to bring the ordinary people of all nations into contact with one another, through exchanges of families, and International Hostels, the publication of a magazine in English, French and German, spreading the idea of World Peace and the support of all movements tending towards International Goodwill'. Sir Evelyn Wrench was Chairman of the English branch, and Arthur Henderson was Joint President with four others — French, Italian, German, and Danish.

It is hard for anyone in the 1980s to share the hopeful innocence of an age which imagined that goodwill between young people meeting in a friendly atmosphere would have any effect on what we had coming to us. After World War II and still more wars since then — though *Cyclamen persicum* grows on Iranian fields like poppies in the fields of Flanders — a war that has produced books and films with a faint and profitable flavour of G. A. Henty, but never an *All Quiet on the Western Front*, we can feel only envy of this more hopeful past, and having once looked round, we turn no more our heads, on our lonely road towards a nuclear winter.

The proprietor of the Hostel was a Mr Udell, an L.C.C. schoolmaster. His staff consisted of Mrs Udell, Enid his daughter who was 24, and his son Oswald, about 17. At the end of the weekend Mr Udell offered me a job. He wanted me to run the glasshouses commercially and grow vegetables in part of the kitchen garden in return for my board in the Hostel and 10 shillings a week.

I took the job, partly because I was fed up with the driving monotony of Stuart Low's, but mainly to work with congenial people for what I felt was a worthy cause. It would be an extra experience and among the overgrown shrubs in the garden I had noticed Forsythia, Weigelia, Tamarisk, Philadelphus, Dautzia, and *Spirea arguta*, all of which are easy to grow from hardwooded cuttings, as I remembered from Parris's. So I gave in my notice at Stuart Low's, strongly against Robin's advice but with the approval of my father. He took to heart Mr Udell's idea that with more vegetable experience — so far I had worked on vegetables only with my mother at home, which in fact had given me a very useful grounding — I could get an R.H.S. Teaching Certificate followed by a job as a school gardening master. I never went on to do this. All the advertisements for these jobs in *The Gardener's Chronicle* were from approved schools and, after reading a book called *Borstal Boy* by an expupil, I decided that there was no career, at any rate for me, in teaching budding burglars to grow their own food.

Then Mr Udell began to get behind with my weekly pay packets (less 1/6d for Health and Pensions Insurance) for the Hostel was going down hill. I had found that the greenhouses I could use were the most dilapidated. All the glass panes were non-standard size and had to be cut to fit. I could get no tools, and not even seeds, because these could not be afforded, and I was learning the salutary lesson that large gardens are liabilities, not assets. No nursery can prosper if it has mowing, edging and weeding tied round its neck, and above all, the worst millstones are broken down lean-to greenhouses with rotting rafters and frames with the lights decaying at the corners.

I could cycle home easily at the weekends and when there was nothing special on I used to go home to ride with the West Kent D.A. I told Molly Hunt and Norman Coles about my problem. Molly lived at Chislehurst and had been at school with the daughter of George G. Whitelegg, the landscape gardener and hardy nursery firm there, and knew that George G. was looking for a salesman to start immediately at the Daily Mail Ideal Home Exhibition. My father promptly bought me a new dark brown worsted suit in Dartford, I went for an interview, and got the job at two guineas a week again, plus 1 per cent commission. My father paid for a monthly season ticket up and down to London each day, so I lived at home. Iris lived at home, for she was still at the Royal College of Art, and Geoffrey was working in Victoria Street. He was designing, among other things, a railway engine for Brazil to burn wood, coal, or coffee berries, a great many electricity pylons, and the aerial masts for Sydney Radio Station, which still stands, or did in 1976 when I photographed it.

Back to Hildenborough I went by train, collected my belongings, told Mr Udell to take half what he owed me as notice, and went home with two pound notes for the rest in my pocket. I think the A.P.A. changed to helping Jewish refugees, and Oaklands closed down soon after I left, leaving my hopeful rows of cuttings in the neglected garden.

At Olympia, Whitelegg's had a formal garden, all flagstones and steps, with a long oblong pool in the middle containing a leaden statue of a cupid, holding a large fish in a position so uncomfortable that it was jetting a fountain of water out of its open mouth. The stonework was all cemented over to take the wear of the many people walking over it, but it could also be built 'dry', with soil instead of cement, and plants sandwiched between the courses as I had built walls with Mr Dudman at Central Park. On the stand were George Whitelegg himself, Harold Whitelegg, (the Young Guv'nor), Marcel de Smet, a former Belgian refugee boy who was now building rock gardens and formal layouts, and myself. The others were there to sell replicas of the stand at £200 each (the statue cost £15 on its own), and to land other orders for layouts.

My job was the humble one of selling Japanese flowering cherries, *Daphne cneorum, Dicentra spectabile* and assorted spring flowering trees, shrubs, alpines, and herbaceous plants, but I did clock up £8 in commission in the whole month I was there, which went on shirts, shoes, and my general extra expenses from living in London.

Next to Whitelegg's stand at Olympia was the exhibit from Hillier and Sons of Winchester. They showed a mass of spring flowering trees and shrubs, grown in pots like those on our stand, and replaced each weekend if anything which had been forced to bring it into early flowering had dropped its bloom. All the pots were hidden with damped peat so the effect was of a weedless garden. Hillier's stand had a hollow centre with a large pool in the middle, flat Westmoreland limestone rocks set to overlap the three-inch deep galvanized iron tray in which waterlily leaves and flowers floated artfully, and one magnificent flat rock, lined up like a diving board.

Hillier's had only two salesmen. White-haired Mr Sanders and Sydney Weaver, a tall, thin, curly-headed improver with an impish grin. Both of them were working a 12-hour day, from 8 a.m. to 8 p.m., but old Whitelegg let me off early if things slackened off after six as I had a long train journey to get back to Dartford.

One morning, when I had been over the stand picking off dead blooms, I saw a strange little procession approaching Hillier's stand. It consisted of the Manager of the Gardens, in striped trousers and black morning coat, who was an employee of the *Daily Mail*, a photographer with a large reflex camera and a belted raincoat plus trilby hat, his assistant with a shabbier raincoat, a plump middle-aged lady in a grey coat and skirt, a large hat and an air of great dignity, and a tall blonde in a voluminous black mackintosh. Syd Weaver came round his stand to meet them just as the tall blonde slipped off her mackintosh and handed it to the dignified lady who was a professional chaperone. Then she walked on to the Hillier stand, in a dark blue, one-piece bathing costume that had a kind of very short skirt across the front, with the deliberate glide and fixed smile of a fashion model who knows she earns more in an hour than everyone in sight earns in a week.

Syd started to protest that the rock was only propped up but the *Daily Mail* man cut him short. 'WE have the photographic rights, it is in your firm's contract that WE have the right to take what pictures we like, WHEN we like...' The photographer raised his camera, his assistant thrust high in the air a black painted tray about a foot long on a stout handle, and the model switched on her smile which hit me full in the face. The assistant gripped the trigger in the handle, and shot a cigarette lighter flint spark into the pile of magnesium flash powder. There was a blinding flash and a cloud of white smoke went billowing towards the Olympian heights of the roof. 'OW GAWD ,' screamed the poor model in pure cockney as she fell flat on her face in three inches of water and waterlily leaves.

As the bathing dress gripped even tighter, the chaperone wrapped her quickly in the mackintosh and led her away squelching, dripping, and weeping, and Mr Sanders arrived, almost weeping himself at the thought of the shock and horror that would be felt by the directors of Hillier's, all very godly Quakers, at the shame of this disaster. There was no time to waste, for the public were already queueing to get into the gardens. The *Daily Mail* man held them up as he sent some porters with brooms, buckets, and sawdust to clear up the mess while Weaver, Sanders, and I fetched replacement water and salvaged the waterlily leaves. Old Whitelegg arrived just in time for me to ask him if I could give Hillier's two of our spare waterlily blooms from our bucket in the store. 'Certainly Hills, always help another firm on a show. Never know when we might want help ourselves.'

From the Ideal Home Exhibition we moved straight on to Chelsea Flower Show. In fact, during the last week of the month-long show, George Whitelegg was building his rock garden there. It had to win yet another of the Gold medals he won year after year in the face of hotter and hotter competition. The rock gardens at that time swept from the end of the Sundries Avenue to the Embankment gate, then began again beyond and extended to where the police caravan now stands. The two ends were used by the R.H.S. to try out new firms, who had to have shown at the fortnightly shows at Vincent Square about six times to prove they were good enough to be allowed into Chelsea at all.

In the middle of the great rock garden bank there were four key sites, deeper and wider than the others, which were drawn for by the leading rock-garden builders of England who could be relied on for a virtuoso performance. They were George G. Whitelegg, A. R. Wallace of Tunbridge Wells, Gavin Jones of Letchworth, and Hocker Edge Gardens of Cranbrook, each with their own style.

Whitelegg had three stands at Chelsea, 1933. Apart from the rock garden, in the central position as in 1932 by the luck of the draw, he had a large stand of irises in the marquee, and an even bigger one of azaleas beside one of the entrances to the largest tent in the world.

My first few Chelseas showed me the fearless nimbleness of the men who 'crewed' this tent, swinging hand over hand up the ropes and sliding up and down the hills and valleys of snowy canvas. They were from the crew of the *William Mitchell*, the last British square-rigged sailing ship. Some day, no doubt, the R.H.S. will just blow a huge, expendable, weatherproof, plastic bubble over the whole Royal Hospital gardens, but until then strong, skilled men will need to wrestle with the strength of the wind in iron-hard fighting canvas.

Motor lorries there were in plenty. These had a tendency to backfire with loud bangs that alarmed the waiting horses, tossing their heads impatiently while chains of men passed towering antirrhinums from hand to hand. I remember seeing old Peter Barr, of Barr and Sons, the big British bulb firm, wearing a grey top hat and full morning dress complete with a giant red carnation, leap to the heads of four frightened and plunging horses, to comfort and soothe them to safety.

There was a personal problem I kept to myself. I found I was not to be on the rock garden, where I knew all the names and habits of the more usual alpines from reading and working at Parris's, but with the azaleas in the company of Mr Baverstock, Whitelegg's alpine man, a gloomy character in his fifties, and I knew nothing about these lovely lime-haters. I was, however, staying at the London Youth Hostel in Great Ormonde Street, which was cheaper than travelling up each day from Dartford or Chislehurst, so I took a chance to visit Charing Cross Road before the bookshops closed, and picked an elderly, battered gardening book from a sixpenny box.

It was called *Azaleas and American Plants*, for most of the hardy azaleas come from the USA and the hardiest of the lot was *Azalea coccinea speciosa*, of which we had two big groups, one each end of the stand. The book was published in the 1890s, the hybrids on the stand were mainly new, but a number were of 1890 vintage and, assessed on Mr George's principle, these were likely to be the best and hardiest if they were still in cultivation.

The idea being that Baverstock should train me, we had staged the stand together. Then he took one end of the stand, I took the other, and he left me on my own. His habit was to put his pencil in his mouth behind his drooping moustache, hold his order book behind his back, hunch his shoulders, and complain, 'No money about, no money about, only sight-seers.' Mine was to 'tackle' anyone who looked interested, and to keep talking to everyone, giving sound advice on azaleas dating from the 1890s, helped by the blazing orange scarlet *coccinea* which was very 'speciosa' (the most striking or beautiful) because the Dutch supplier had sent us larger specimens of this old, cheap kind.

The second day was, and still is, the fashionable one. When it used to cost 10 shillings to come in and was part of the London season, at least one-quarter of the men wore black or grey top hats. Early in the day I saw Winston Churchill, MP, walk straight through the entrance by our stand smoking a cigar. Lord Aberconway, the President of the R.H.S. happened to be strolling by. He raised his topper and said, 'Sir, your cigar. No smoking in the marquee.' The crestfallen MP raised his topper and said, 'Sir, I am sorry' and threw away an almost whole three-and-sixpenny cigar. Baverstock started after it but another salesman beat him to it, not as a link with fame but to smoke later in the exhibitors' tent.

As we stood behind the white ropes on the grass with yet another Gold medal card displayed on a well-placed rock, a charming, elderly Duchess in grey silk, wearing long kid gloves, came up to us. 'Mr Whitelegg, may I go up into the bushes at the back of your stand?' 'Certainly, my lady,' said the Guv'nor, hardly raising his eyebrows. She opened her matching handbag and secured at least a dozen R.H.S. fellow's passes it contained with rubber bands to the tip of her neatly furled parasol, marched up between the beautifully set rocks, thrust the parasol through the Embankment railings, and called, 'Maud, Maud, Maud.' Maud at once slipped the cards off the end, and trooped in through the Embankment gate with the rest of the 'girls', who came to our stand in a bunch. Her ladyship then collected up all the passes, re-fastened them, and repeated the process, then placed quite a good order with de Smet, the Guv'nor having gone to lunch.

The relationship between customer and nurseryman (as distinct from the sundriesmen, and machinery and gadget salesmen) is rather special, perhaps best summed up by a grey-haired lady to a newly acquired daughter-in-law a long time after my first Chelsea.

'Always choose the sunburnt salesmen. The most sunburnt is probably the foreman and he will know most. The well dressed pale one is probably out of the office for the show and knows nothing, neither does the pretty girl who is the typist. If you can find one who is both sunburnt *and* well dressed, he will be the managing director and will know more than anyone.' I was the sunburnt salesman, and Chelsea to me still means what Wimbledon means to some and the Derby to others.

4

Tougher near the Top

AFTER CHELSEA I showed for Whitelegg's and in between shows worked with Baverstock propagating alpines. Then Whitelegg's started me canvassing for landscape jobs on my bicycle, promising me 2 per cent commission on orders I secured. On a £200 rock garden, even a £50 front garden, this would have added up to enough to replace my Chelsea suit as it wore out, but I found it a miserable job.

The best way to get enquiries about orders, I found, was to look for single large houses being put up by individual builders, at £3,000 and upwards. These were based on a plan in the builder's office, which often carried on the bottom corner the home address of the customer for whom it was being built. Architects just took my card saying they would pass it on. They never did. But, if only a foreman or a bricklayer was on the job, he would call me 'Sir' and show me the address, with a wealth of graphic detail.

I would then call on the customer and see if I could get any further, but I also turned some straight over to the office for Whitelegg's to write to them. To me this job ranked with the many door-to-door canvassers who were 'on the knocker' at that time. I might have succeeded had I stuck to it, but I was learning nothing, and I wanted to get back to alpines.

At Chelsea I had seen about 16 table rock gardens in the marquee, on staging about three feet high, six feet wide and up to 20 feet long, set with lesser rocks also on the strata line, and a range of small and lovely alpines I had never seen before. Clarence Elliot had a fine collection and I read his book *Rock Garden Plants*, and Reginald Farrar's *The English Rock Garden* and also gathered catalogues. The books were botanical and to learn more about alpines, especially about their propagation, I needed to know them with my hands. So I wrote to Major Thorpe of Orchard Neville Nurseries, Baltonsborough, Somerset, whose catalogue, called *A Book of a Thousand Alpines*, headed *The Times*

29

Saturday gardening column every week. This column was arranged in strictly alphabetical order so unless some artful dodger had called itself 'Alpines Anonymous', Orchard Neville would continue to enjoy this plum position.

When the catalogue came I found it was very detailed, being full of heights, colours, and flowering months, charging 4d each for Helianthemums, Sedums and other easy subjects. So I wrote to Major Thorpe asking if he had a vacancy for an assistant propagator and showman, at present with George G. Whitelegg. He wrote asking me to an interview.

Major Thorpe smoked more than any man I ever met, buying Gold Flake in boxes of 100 and cramming them into a huge case with his great hands. He took me round the nursery he had started in a field by Orchard Neville house, in partnership with T. C. Mansfield, a schoolmaster who much later wrote *Alpines in Colour and Cultivation* for Collins, as well as others in that series. They were pioneering new ideas for mass-producing alpines, selling them by mail order at prices far below other firms. What he wanted was a foreman. What I wanted was to learn more about alpines and to use my newly won skills to build table rock gardens as an aid to selling them. I had doubts, however, inherited from Mr Fred, about the wisdom of selling for four-pence what others sold for sixpence.

He offered me 50 shillings a week, more than I had ever earned in an age when a £5 wage meant you could buy your own house and an Austin Seven. I took it and became 'Mr Hills' with Norton the propagator, Martin the packer, Richards who drove the van and did odd jobs, and 10 boys ranging from 14-year old school leavers to Big Floyd, a gawky lad whose voice had still not made up its mind to break. I gave in my notice (old Whitelegg was very decent about it, saying I was a hard worker and he would not stand in my way), bought myself a pair of rather better breeches, sent off my bike and two suitcases as luggage in advance, and set off on my journey up the ladder.

I had fixed up digs at The Laurels, the only possible lodgings in a village of cottages, run by Mrs Reynolds, a widow who kept chickens, gardened, took summer visitors, and was a pillar of the local church. Fortunately for me she was thin, had no ambition to put weight on me, and my health held out through this toughest period of my life. Usually I worked from 7 a.m. to 7 p.m., and after that on stocktaking or on the new catalogue.

Mansfield used to come down almost every weekend, so on Saturdays I worked till 6 p.m. and on Sundays from 9 a.m. until about 4 p.m. which left me just enough time to write home to my mother after tea.

We had three 14 ft. by 90 ft. greenhouses one with a propagating frame along each side, and electric soil warming wires under the sand giving bottom heat. This worked well except for the enchartrid worms, creamy white, non-cyst-forming eelworms, about half an inch long, which wriggle along like heraldic flashes of lightning, clearing up decaying vegetation. They are harmless in a garden or a compost heap that has heated badly, but are gluttons for unrooted cuttings in heated frames. Mansfield had learned from some source or other that commercial acetic acid mixed with sugar helped cuttings to root, and this is what we were using in 1934. Indeed he was the first to apply the fact that alpha-naphthalene acetic acid (later developed as 'Hortomone A', the first rooting hormone, by ICI) was present in commercial acetic acid. I could appreciate the value of this and it drove me to work flat out in my new job.

I did my very best, but it was not good enough. I had tried for the job of an assistant propagator to learn alpines with my hands and been given the job of foreman, further up the ladder. However many hours I put in, or however hard I worked, nothing could alter the fact that I knew too little about alpines to hold down this supervisory position. So I got the sack.

It happened like this. We had a large frame full of *Sisyrinchiums* which resemble small irises, and two species appeared to have died out utterly so I threw them away to make room for plants clamouring for space. Mansfield and Major Thorpe found them and I had to turn all the boys out hunting through the rubbish to find the lost dormant roots. One was *S. grandiflorum* with large, dark red, saucer flowers among rush-like leaves that die down in winter. It comes from California and even at our prices cost 3 shillings each. The other was *S. fififolium*, with smaller, shallower, white saucer flowers and the same rushy deciduous leaves. It comes from the Falkland Islands where it is called 'Pale Maidens' and is their national flower. On these and some other islands the summer is too short for bees to gather enough pollen and nectar to keep them through the winter. If you look at the bottom of a clear British pond that has no fish, the chances are that you will see small white threads, perhaps an inch long, weaving away in an endless dance. They are gathering oxygen from the water for the larvae of Heliophylla, a species of hoverfly, feeding on vegetable wastes in the pond mud.

On all these islands there are little ponds that collect the rain and provide year-round homes for such larvae. They turn into small flies, like slender wasps, poised on wings that move so fast they are invisible, feeding on the nectar and pollen of flowers with an easy way in to the centres. On the Faroes they pollinate the clover that has seeded itself there ever since the Islands were colonized by the Vikings; on the Falklands, where our rare seed came from, they pollinate the Pale Maiden, in their short summer flying season before they go back to the mud. In no time the whole nursery knew I had thrown away the precious, small, dormant, root crowns because I did not know enough.

So I went home in disgrace. Luckily I had saved money, so was not penniless. I advertised at once for a job, knowing that these were scarce. This time I felt I must aim lower, for something nearer to my job at Parris's, where I felt there would be fewer pitfalls. I should have tried for alpines again, but I was 23 and felt my life was wrecked.

I was offered a job at Scunthorpe with a small firm growing chrysanthemums, bedding and pot plants, and blooms for wreath work, mother and daughter making the wreaths, crosses, and 'floral tributes'. I took a month on trial at 45 shillings a week, and got it on Parris's testimonial that I was a non-drinker and smoker. However, my predecessor who had fallen down the stock hole blind drunk, soon recovered and reformed, then got his job back. So I had to advertise again.

This time I got work at Maidenhead, with a firm that grew violas, dahlias, and bedding plants. They also had a team of jobbing gardeners and specialized in floral decoration — especially such expensive temporary gardens as those for the enclosures at Ascot, and the stands at the Aldershot Tattoo. Though I had enjoyable cycling at weekends with the C.T.C. my heart was not in the job. I wanted to get back to alpines again, where a successful nursery could be small, needing less capital for greenhouses, and I should be selling interesting skills. I had met Syd Weaver again at Chelsea 1935, when I had shown violas for my Maidenhead employer. We had discussed the big four of the alpine trade. He ruled out Wallaces as an old and famous firm where all the good jobs were filled by men in their forties and fifties, good for 20 or even 40 years more. Both Hocker Edge Gardens and Gavin Jones were owned and run by ex-Colonels from the 1914–18 War and were new and growing firms. First choice would be Hocker Edge, because Lt. Col. Grey had the best alpines, and a very high reputation as a botanist.

So I wrote to Colonel Grey and he replied offering me an interview for a job in his office, to include showing, serving customers, and landscape work in emergencies. It was not possible to get from Maidenhead to Cranbrook by train or coach on a Sunday, so I cycled the 75 miles each way, putting up at a C.T.C. boarding house on the Saturday night, with a pair of new grey flannel trousers in my saddlebag, so I could arrive in the morning looking suitable for office work, then change back into shorts behind a hedge for the return journey.

Hocker Edge Gardens were at Sissinghurst, near Sissinghurst Place, the home of Vita Sackville-West and Harold Nicolson. It was at the end of a road down to Hocker Edge, Colonel Grey's large house, and the nursery was in what had been a huge kitchen garden on the side of a steep valley, sloping up into woods. All the hedges on the estate were laid or pleached at intervals to keep them cattleproof and cut with hedge slashers. These were billhooks on six-foot shafts; in skilled hands they cut faster and nearly as well as shears. I ate my sandwiches under one of these hedges and arrived dead on time at 11.30 a.m.

The Colonel was standing outside his long, green shed office, tall, military-moustached, wearing a dark tweed suit, a white panama hat and an Old Etonian tie. I said 'Good morning, Sir'. He replied 'Good morning, Hills' (correct when you are addressing a servant or potential servant) and then, because I had taken a drink from my thermos by the bridge over the stream where he had built a magnificent sandstone rock garden, and it was fresh in my mind, I said, 'Your *Schizostylis coccinea* is very early this year, Sir,' which broke the ice.

During our short walk round, the fact that my stay at Orchard Neville had been at the same time the previous year made me able to recognize and name every alpine in bloom, which was a great advantage. Then he led me into the office where he interviewed me very kindly. He had a fierce temper (my predecessor had been a village girl who burst into tears too easily) but he and Commander Thursfield, RN (Retired), with whom I shared the office, made this perhaps my happiest job.

Colonel Grey offered me 45 shillings a week, to start in a fortnight's time, and I accepted at once. 'You'll require lodgings. I suggest Mrs Delves at Gatehouse in the village. She was a cook, and Delves was a sergeant in the Buffs [The Royal West Kent Regiment]. Jim, the fourth gardener at Sissinghurst Castle is there, and so is Miss Brown who teaches in the village school.'

Because George Delves, head gardener to a Mrs Alexander, got Gatehouse as his 'cottage' with free coal, light, vegetables, fruit, and butter, milk, and eggs from home farm, Mrs Delves took in three lodgers. We had free homemade cider after supper, and Mrs Delves, who was the best cook and the most motherly of all my landladies, threw in mending as well as washing.

I have never fed better or more disastrously (as I now see) than with Mrs Delves, whose perfect pastry rabbit pies appeared twice a week at least, after Delves had shot rabbits with the accuracy of an ex-sergeant and the use of free cartridges from the gamekeeper; boiled beef and carrots with dumplings, and steak and kidney pudding appeared almost as often. She welcomed me with tea and treacle-dark, raisin-haunted, egg-and-butter-crowded cake, and a graphic account of how 'Delves' organized the baths on Friday evenings with water heated in the copper and carried across the kitchen in buckets to the downstairs bathroom just outside the backdoor with the sanitation.

My first job was to file the letters and the previous day's orders, writing up the new customers' addresses in a register book so they would receive the new catalogue. A card index would have made it easier to avoid duplication, but I was new and kept my mouth shut. Then I wrote up the stiff, orange, paper labels for the plants on the orders to go that day and took them out to Tom Moody, the bulb foreman, who was also in charge of packing. Commander Thursfield arrived at ten in his Austin Seven, and the Colonel a bit later, bringing the day's post which he had opened over breakfast. This meant many a chase round the nursery for blown-away cheques and letters.

The Commander typed the letters, the Colonel wrote some in his own handwriting, and I entered the invoices in large duplicate books. I kept a postage book and a parcels book, which meant that we could look up quickly when anything had gone out but it took me a great deal of time. I was also fetched out as required to serve customers, as did the Commander, Nye the alpine foreman, and Merriman who looked after the shrubs. The Colonel went out himself when it was someone he knew.

Over the trestle table at which I worked was a long, divided shelf containing catalogues of all the alpines and hardy bulbs in the world, and a full range of everything else, for when we planted a garden we planted it with what was botanically the best. Towards the end of his life, Colonel Grey founded The Northern Horticultural Society and laid out their gardens at Harlow Carr, and these remain as his memorial, as well as his classic *Hardy Bulbs*.

We used to buy our Himalayan gentians and primulas from a firm in Darjeeling who hit on the idea of employing Indian ex-students from Kew to join the bands of nomads who crossed illegally into Nepal and Tibet to hunt for the bulbs of *Fritillaria roylei* for sale in China as a cure for impotence. These students were trained botanists, collecting ripe seeds from correctly identified plants, but they looked like the rest of the fur-clad gangs.

A professional plant hunter, like Captain Frank Kingdom Ward, would advertise in the *Gardener's Chronicle* and the *Journal of the Royal Horticultural Society* that he was organizing an expedition to a district where he hoped to find a list of species and their possible unknown relations, offering shares for between £100 and £500 — the fee varied according to the reputation of the collector. Many of them made a good living out of it, even though the travel books they wrote rarely sold well except to botanists because they were almost entirely composed of plant names.

A single share brought a packet of seed of everything the collector found, labelled with its genus or family name, and the collector's number, which was the initials of his name, followed by a number. The one I remember best was Cynanthus K.W. (Captain Frank Kingdom Ward) 4959, which was allotted a second name by Kew after being grown for about 10 years under the botanical equivalent of 'L' plates.

The Colonel gambled many a £100 on taking 'packet luck', knowing that whenever you climb a mountain anywhere in the world the plants that grow near the top will grow in a temperate climate like ours.

Our most successful venture in this field happened soon after I arrived. A cousin of the Colonel's who was in the Diplomatic service wrote suggesting he might be interested in bulbs of very small daffodils, about a quarter inch across the flowers, which had been offered by a Syrian he knew. The Colonel sent his cousin four large, white five pound notes (the first I had ever seen), and the result was box about half the size of a shoe box, full of tiny bulbs.

The Colonel took them to Kew to have his opinion confirmed that these were *Narcissus wateri*, the smallest and most rare daffodil, selling, if they could be found, at 6 shillings each or more. Then another box arrived, and another, and another, all containing the same species, as the faithful cousin doled out the fivers. We got a letter back from the worthy Syrian when we asked how he found them. 'I visit Mohammedan graveyards at night with an electric torch. The natives are frightened of djinns, ghouls, and affrits and dare not penetrate these places in the dark. But I am a Christian and climb over the walls with my ladder which I pull up after me, and take what I like with impunity.'

The Commander sent some bulbs to J. C. Van Tubergen, the largest Dutch wholesale bulb supplier, from whom we bought our bulbs, offering him *Narcissus wateri* at £15 a hundred, and got an order for 500 at once and a request for a price by the thousand. I never knew what we finally made on the deal but Tubergens sent a special offer round the nurserymen of Europe and sold all but the few large ones we kept to plant in pans. The undersized bulbs went in a raised bed to grow to saleable sizes, but they attracted slugs and we lost them, but we paid for our 1935 bulb order in *N. wateri*, and became perhaps the only firm exporting daffodils to Holland.

I no longer had watering to worry about, so I could enjoy my weekends, but in the office, as in all offices, there were long-term events that had to be organized ahead. The build-up to Chelsea starts in the spring, with plants to grow and price lists to print. For me, Chelsea 1936 began with the delivery of some rather good oval seed pans. We had gathered a number of old stone sinks from local builder who had pulled down cottages, and the Colonel had the idea of planting these up with alpines, such as the small *Kabschia saxifrages* and other miniature species, to show at Chelsea. I suggested (via the Commander, the official channel) that it would be a good idea to make up very small gardens in the oval pans, using rock chips from the dump where we had rock delivered for nearby or small layout jobs and shows.

The idea took off and after I had made one, setting the rock on the strata line so it would echo our big rock garden, Nye took over and made them fast and well. The Colonel worked out what we ought to charge, timing Nye with a stopwatch, and costing up the small portions of miniature Sedums, the rooted cuttings of *Polygala calcarea*, *Rosa pumia*, and other quickly grown treasures.

He arrived at the figure of £5 each for the 12 big sinks, before the fashion for these began — our big display under the trees facing the rock gardens probably started it. The pans worked out at 15 shillings, which was far too cheap, for it allowed nothing for the knowledge that went into selecting the plants so they would flower from about February to October, choosing only species that would not swamp each other.

This, my third Chelsea, was perhaps of the greatest personal importance to me of any, because my first book, *Miniature Alpine Gardening*, grew out of those pans. I sold all the sinks in the first two days and by the last day there was not a pan left. I was selling the idea of the sinks (which of course were then easy to get) and pans, and also collections of suitable plants. The pans were delivered by District Messenger Boys. The problem of how to deliver the heavy sinks and awkward pans was solved by leaving them labelled for delivery by Carter Paterson. This method was suggested by a determined lady who said firmly, 'Young man, I will have these two. Send them round by Carter Paterson. I'll pay the carriage on delivery.'

We were greatly overstretched that Chelsea, with a stand of hardy bulbs in pans in the marquee, our big rock garden, and my sinks and pans under the trees facing it across the space now filled with folding chairs for sandwich eaters. We had Nye, Moody, Merriman, and Austin the packer, with the Commander dashing from place to place relieving us for meals.

This was my busiest Chelsea. We could have sold at least twice as many pans at double our prices. The last day was simply murder, with all the labelling and tying up and the fact that there were not enough District Messenger Boys and I found myself at 7 p.m. with 15 pans still to deliver. I went out to the Embankment and took a taxi, driven by a whiskery old cockney, inside the Show. I called out the destinations and we stowed the pans on the seats, on the floor, and beside the driver. He took me to blocks of flats, mansions, up mews and to hotels, and I nipped in with them while he worked out the next one. I had charged 5 shillings carriage each, and I finished up 10 shillings ahead of the game after tipping the driver 10 shillings and having him drive me to a hotel in Southampton Row because I was too late to book in at the London Youth Hostel.

That summer I showed at the R.H.S. Hall, and built a sandstone rock garden and a dry wall garden in Surrey, as a landscape foreman under the direction of the Colonel, with two men from the nursery under me. I founded a local Section of the East Kent D.A. to give me cycling company, and folk danced, Youth Hostelled, and rode tandem with a small and charming village schoolmistress, who, wisely for us both, rejected my calf love and married someone else.

All through these halcyon days, there was a hidden war going on between Mrs Delves's cooking and my insides, where my long suffering villi were under increasing strain. As Dr Sanders had predicted from practical experiences of coeliac children, long before the condition was named or recognized, my health had improved in seven year stages, and there were three to go before the final stage ended at 28, and I was as fit as I imagined then I should ever be.

I was getting plenty of vitamin D from sunlight on my skin from cycling up to 150 miles a weekend, and cycling was ideal exercise for me because it developed my leg, thigh, and arm muscles. I was very thin because however much I ate I could not absorb certain vitamins and minerals or essential fatty acids. I was enjoying both my work and the leisure I gained from giving up writing short stories as my Remington rested at home, unused as well as 'invisible'. Increasingly I began to suffer from my 'attacks' which I held down with mixtures of kaolin, bismuth, and bicarbonate of soda.

Then I started getting temperatures with the diarrhoea. This made me feel really rotten, till one day the Commander told me to go home early and 'report sick'. I went to the doctor in Cranbrook, who decided I had a 'gastric infection'. He prescribed a powerful laxative, to 'clear it out of your system' and told me to go to bed on a light diet, so I bought three packets of cream crackers to go with unlimited milk from Mrs Alexander's cows, while my prescription was being made up. Then I stocked up on library books, which was almost a reflex action when I knew an attack was going to get out of hand and I had to have a few days in bed. I rang the Commander from the 'phone box. He said I had been 'looking like a job for the bosun' all week, and that he would tell the Colonel, and look in to see me next morning. It was the job of the bosun to sew up corpses in canvas for burial at sea.

I wheeled up the long hill from Cranbrook, which I usually rode, and broke the news to the Delves. He went up with a barrow and fetched a commode dating from the 1880s from Mrs Alexander's box-room, and entertained us with memories of dysentery, cholera, and other Indian intestinal afflictions. I had a very bad night with the doctor's prescription intervening as a Third Force in the heavy fighting between my long suffering villi and Mrs Delves's diet for disaster.

The Commander arrived during the morning. His first words were: 'You look properly in the Bay' (the ship's sick bay). 'You can't stay here with the heads [toilets] in the back yard. Are your parents on the telephone?' They were not, so he rang my father at the Dartford Grammar School from the office. My mother, with three brothers in the 1914–18 war, dreaded tele-grams, so I did not want to send one when a letter would get there next day. He called on the way home to collect and post mine to Mother.

I only saw him again once, at a Chelsea after the war, which he spent back in the Navy, in delightful semi-legal activity in small craft off the west coast of neutral Ireland. I met the Colonel again in 1953, looking very bent and elderly, also at Chelsea. When he shook hands and congratulated me on my book *The Propagation of Alpines*, which took four years to write, it was the proudest moment of my life.

The Commander's telephone call brought down my parents in Puddleduck, the 1935 Hillman Minx — a family friend who served us faithfully and well for 15 years. She gave little trouble except for a mysterious noise that my father finally traced to his pipe tapping against Mother's cigarette case in the dashboard pocket.

Delves helped my father tie my bicycle on the luggage rack, Mother packed my two suitcases, and I came shakily across the wavy floor boards and down the crooked stairs for the last time. Mother had telephoned Uncle Gordon with big-sisterly deter-mination, and he located a specialist, a Dr Maxwell at Barts, and started the first of many investigations to find out what was wrong with me. Uncle Gordon paid the very substantial fees for the specialist and a consultant surgeon, and sent his new Rolls Royce to take me to hospital in state.

For six weeks the Commander sent on my pay, and then my father wrote and told him it was unlikely that I would ever be able to return to Hocker Edge. I was not too badly off because I belonged to the now departed United Horticultural Benefit and Provident Society (Motto: Unity is Strength)which, for 14/6d a quarter, paid me 27 shillings a week. This generosity was possible because they took only gardeners, unlike other Friendly Societies who admitted more unhealthy trades. With 15 shillings a week from the National Health, I was saving money for a future that I hoped would lead to a complete cure for whatever it was that struck me down so often and had cost me a job I enjoyed. It was hard enough to climb the ladder without a hidden enemy inside.

The investigation took so long because the consultant surgeon wanted extra tests, and at one time there was a strong possibility that I should have a section of my large intestine removed and the rest rejoined. It was agreed that I had diverticulitis (pouches in the intestine wall), and inability to split fats, and a low level of hydrochloric acid in my stomach. They decided finally against surgery to the relief of my parents, and probably Uncle Gordon's bank balance. I was rather fed up at the time, because I was under the innocent impression that all my problems would vanish once the defective section was removed.

I was still more fed up when I learned what the treatment involved. I was to have olive oil enemas twice a week which I had to retain for an hour, for it was supposed I would absorb more fats from a whole quart of the oil than if I tried to make up for my defective digestion by drinking this much. I was to eat powdered glucose after every meal, and take a medicine containing dilute hydrochloric acid. In addition I was to have a low-residue diet.

This restricted me to chicken, rabbit, and fish, plus rice, semolina, tapioca, sago, milk, and eggs, but no fruit and vegetables unless rubbed through a sieve. Jelly and blancmange were allowed, and white, but not brown, bread. The idea was to avoid putting a strain on my defective intestine with the 'roughage' cherished today. I was calculating the chance of finding landladies who would cope with such a diet, and the difficulty of explaining it to them.

Uncle Gordon sent the Rolls Royce again and I glided home to Dartford with my mother who did her best, as mothers will, to comply with the direction supplied by the hospital dietician. It was an honest attempt to solve my health problem without surgery, using the knowledge and fashions of the time. I had to suffer the consequences. Fortunately, the diet left out suet puddings and pastry, for, as the dietician explained, it was a 'light diet' and so it spared me the risk from motherly ex-cooks, if I could find landladies at all.

Mother and I decided that in future I must have a job nearer home, which ruled out advertising and just taking one anywhere I could find. I knew of one local nursery large enough to employ me and growing the plants I knew.

I wrote for the one possible job, at Redgrove and Patrick of Sevenoaks. It had started as two firms, one at each end of the Greensand Ridge, good, sandy, nursery soil on the other side of the valley, south of the North Downs. At Seal, Mr Patrick, tall, thin, with large ears, a stutter, and a wide knowledge of horticulture, grew roses and a range of shrubs and herbaceous plants. Both nurseries had shops and had started competing with each other. They joined forces, but had always done better separately than together, for the idea that mergers produce economies and automatically increase trade is one of many modern delusions.

They took me on as a traveller and showman to increase their lagging sales. It was about the most awkward job possible for a not very robust 25-year old with a difficult diet and the complication of the wretched olive oil enemas. But needs must when the Devil or the doctors drive.

That autumn I bought myself a motorbike so I could live at home and still travel. On the advice of Ken Nichols, my closest C.T.C. friend, I got a 1934, 150 c.c. Excelsior two-stroke for £18 (new they cost £36). She would do 45 m.p.h. flat out with the wind behind her and about 120 miles on a gallon of petrol and oil, mixed by shaking her vigorously from side to side after each fill-up. My father made a box to hold my catalogues, order book, and sandwiches, that fitted on the carrier (she was too small to take a pillion seat). Redgrove and Patrick paid the petrol and I extended my range to cover Kent, Surrey, and Sussex.

I soon developed a routine. I would come purring up the drive (she had an exhaust note like a bumblebee under a glass), lift the bike on to its stand, take out my catalogues and order book, and set off in quest of a gardener. When I found one engaged in some relatively unskilled task like sweeping leaves or mixing potting soil, I would ask to see the head gardener. 'Mr Grubb, Sir? He's pruning his climbers on the south wall.' Away I would stride, in my riding mac for I never wore a motor cyclist's overalls, and march up to the head gardener, usually in tweed suit with breeches and often a bowler hat. 'Good Morning, Mr Grubb. I represent Messrs Redgrove and Patrick of Sevenoaks ...' and away I would go on my sales talk.

Head gardeners, like ship's captains, were often lonely men, and they greatly appreciated a chance to show off their successes to someone who knew what they were talking about, so we always talked gardening. Sometimes there was an order at the end, but more often there wasn't. Though I did not realize it at the time, I was having a unique opportunity. I was meeting the last of the old head gardeners in command of stately homes before there was any idea of opening them to the public. Not even the stateliest home, at the top of the league tables of attendances published in the serious press today, is kept to the standards they demanded.

The writing was on the wall, though not in the august pages of *The Gardener's Chronicle*, and very many places I called on were allowed to place only one big seed order with Suttons. Anything else had to be passed by the estate office. The owners were usually the titled, who would pay to keep their staff together, especially as they grew older, and the middles of stone steps up and down into the greenhouses wore into deeper and deeper holes where generation after generation of gardeners had trodden.

All the time I was learning the wisdom of gardeners who had gone on learning through their long lives, in the days when nicotine soap wash was the favourite insecticide and manure from the home farm the only fertilizer. They were organic gardeners from conservatism, the need to economize on materials rather than labour, and because they were observant men who had trained in an age without chemicals. They used peat only for ferns, orchids, and begonias, laid down their leafmould like vintage port, and invented their own soil recipes.

At one place I met two garden boys sorting through hundreds of shotgun cartridge cases that came down after 'the twelfth' in the large wicker baskets in which fruit and vegetables travelled by passenger train to the moors, where a shooting house party was in progress. The head gardener, who was also expected to supply the family with produce at the town house for the London season and at a house they rented for Ascot week, told me the cartridge cases made the finest of all earwig traps.

He showed me a well-filled pot chrysanthemum standing ground, as large as two tennis courts, with a cartridge case on top of each cane. Garden boys would go round lifting off the cases and shaking the earwigs that sheltered in them into a nicotine solution in a large pail or tin, so there was no risk of their eating the petals of the cherished blooms. The Ladies (he gave them a capital letter in his voice) used 16-bore shotguns because there was less recoil, although the range was slightly shorter. These smaller cases attracted more earwigs, so the boys were picking all these out; the commoner 12-bore cases he gave to several head gardener friends.

During this period, when I was living at home and cycling at weekends, my C.T.C. friend, Cyril Hayward, had the idea of starting a Kent Group of the Y.H.A., so we got a list of local members and wrote to them all. The result was that I acquired a social life ready-made. We found a cheap hall on the other side of Dartford, where we held socials, committee meetings and dances from time to time. There were about 20 of us, and our basic activity was hiking rather than cycling.

It was possible, at that time, to get a very cheap weekend return on the railways for parties of six or more, out to one station and back from another if you wished, provided you were members of an approved organization. We would go to Dorking, Guildford, or Reigate on Saturday, spend the night at Chelwood Gate, Ewhurst, Holmbury St. Mary, or any of the nearby hostels, walk on footpaths and bridleways all through Sunday, and come back by train. The railways, of course, were using space usually empty at weekends but filled by commuters on weekdays. As many of our members worked in London they used their season tickets, so paid nothing extra.

We had a committee of volunteers, including Anne Darton, a schoolmistress teaching large classes of difficult and backward children. She was our social secretary, and Lillian Booker, from the office of the Sidcup Branch of Crittalls Metal Windows, acted as Treasurer. I was secretary and we had two brothers, Jack and George Rufus, ex-Dartford Grammar school boys, who were keen organizers of hostel repair teams.

We were responsible for Ide Hill Hostel, South of Sevenoaks, and would spend weekends there redecorating it with materials provided by the owners, for this hostel was run by private people who made what they could on meals, etc., and kept half the 'bednight money'. We also used to send couples to all the hostels in Kent in turn, to spend a night and report on their treatment and the general conditions. Our report, typed by Lilian, to the Southern Regional Headquarters, then at Toynbee Hall, could get an unsatisfactory uncontrolled or private hostel removed from the official handbook.

In the spring of 1939 the alpine propagator of the Borough Green Nursery gave a week's notice in order to set up an alpine nursery on his own, and Hugh Redgrove offered me his position. I took it gladly, for I was wearing out my clothes and my Excelsior, and not getting enough orders for my commission to pay for replacements.

The new job entailed finding digs in Borough Green, which I did with a retired clergyman who still acted as a locum for colleagues with other engagements on Sundays, and his wife, a retired district nurse. Then I got back to learning alpines with my hands, and as the months went by I faced the problem of all alpine propagators — the relentless drive of the circling year. It is simple to sew pan after pan in spring of easy seed subjects, and fill your frames with dianthus and campanulas that will only have to be dumped unsold. I had suffered too recently from trying to sell these wholesale to nurseries to make the same mistake again.

The alpines that sell because they are beautiful and scarce are those that root best at certain seasons of the year, and do badly or fail at others. *Lithospermum diffusum* Heavenly Blue, for example, insists on having cuttings taken in the first two weeks in July. If those weeks are taken up with agricultural shows the plants are gone for ever. Today, when T. C. Mansfield's mixture of acetic acid and sugar has developed into rooting hormones, propagators use these, but I had not even electric soil-warming wires.

Chelsea began the real show season, but this year after each one I had to race to catch up on my cuttings. That lovely mutation from Miss Willmott's garden at Great Warley in Essex, *Aeth- ionema* Warley Rose, like a minute pink hydrangea that flowers all the summer, will root from tiny cuttings which I took with a safety-razor blade, slicing off the lower leaves and inserting them with dibbers made from the points of wooden knitting needles, ring after ring, in pans of packed sand. Let the cuttings grow too long and they will flower and fail. Another slow and small trial was *Wahlenbergia serphyllifolia major*, with very lazy-growing, dark red cushions of leaves and rich purple bell flowers, producing only a few small cuttings from each cushion every week or two, depending on the weather.

I took to coming back in the evenings and working while the light lasted. Unfortunately, Redgrove also used to come back. He would talk over his problems and we got to know each other rather well in consequence, but it wasted time, and when I had, at last, got my hands on alpines instead of just selling them, seeing them, and reading about them, I wanted to make the most of it. There would be dodecatheon, primula, and gentian seed to gather, watching till the seeds blackened and then sowing these as soon as ripe, still sticky from the pod, to ensure 100 per cent germination, instead of buying two and even four-year old seed and having barely a dozen come through in each pan.

After Chelsea, we followed the 2–3 day shows held at many seaside places — Eastbourne, Bournemouth, Blackpool, and our furthest of all, Southport — working all day getting it ready, driving all night to get there, our little trailer, full of rock, peat, and plants, roaring and rattling behind Redgrove's faithful Morris Major, then staging the show and selling all the next day. This meant about 42 hours without sleep, except for about two hours by the roadside dozing in the car. We won a silver medal at Southport 1938 for a really splendid table rock garden, swept up high to show above the crowds in the tent, with the strata line followed through right down to the fragments set among the flowering carpeters at staging level.

In the 1930s, agricultural shows did not stay on fixed sites, but went round the county towns and cities, with a fresh crop of customers in each. At Tunbridge Wells Agricultural Show I recall especially two horsey ladies in jodhpurs and riding boots with weather-reddened faces under their caps, followed by a girl of about nine, dressed in exactly the same outfit on a small scale, fresh from the pony competitions. One lady smacked her boots with her riding whip and exclaimed: 'Aggy, I've just discharged my pigman. A pigman who won't sleep with his pigs is no bloody good to me!'

It was the custom for pigmen to sleep in a large square tent at the end of the long double row of styes, full of trusses of straw, sacks of pig meal, primus stoves, sleeping bags, crates of

45

beer, and pigmen of all shapes and sizes. If a pig woke in the night with a nightmare or wanted a drink of water, it had only to squeal and its very own pigman would get up to bring comfort and reassurance, wearing the old overcoat with the familiar smell, with soothing words for lonely pigs in unfamiliar styes.

Any pigman who stayed in a hotel would cut himself off from the fraternity of his colleagues, who suffered no more hardship than I did on a camping weekend. When we arrived late and had to sleep on the staging we often heard them enjoying convivial evenings. Later we heard both pigs and pigmen snoring.

Stockmen and herdsmen usually slept in their lorries, and all had a separate canteen, after run by the Salvation Army, with lower prices but no bar. Salesmen could also use it, and we went there to get good food cheaply. Often I escorted timid goat girls (goats always had female attendants and owners) to the canteen.

Unlike machinery firms who never have to sell off wilting combine harvesters cheap at the end of the show, nurserymen do not have to pay for space, for they are providing part of the attraction, and the public are charged extra to go in the flower tent, thus avoiding crowds of mere sightseers who would block the gangways, and making room for interested gardeners who might place orders. This applies also to the Dairy Show at Earls Court or Olympia, which gives free space in central London. In 1938 it was held at Earls Court, and it hit the September Crisis.

I was there, with the last of the gladioli and a good show of herbaceous blooms, ready to take orders for autumn delivery and dahlias for the coming spring, but there were very few, for everyone talked of the coming war, anticipating gas and air raids that would destroy London. Our stand was next to Yokohama Nurseries, with Bonsai — Japanese dwarf trees. Mr Oyano, in charge, was terrified that Japan would come in at once on the German side.

He only sold three of his trees during the whole show. Each had its own name, being sold as an individual not as species or varieties, like 'Tree from the Garden of the Tea House of a Thousand Elegant Delights'. 'Tree from the Garden of the Contented Spirit', and 'Tree from beside the Pool of Tranquillity'. He would write the name in Japanese on the pot for each customer. When I remarked that the names did not take him long to write, and asked whether Japanese was quicker than English because each character was a word, he gave me a beaming oriental smile. 'I write my telephone number in Tokyo each time. The customer never knows. If they buy two I write the number of our Yokohama Head Office.'

5

Journey through a War

AFTER the 'September Crisis' came Munich and 'Peace with Honour' on a soon-forgotten scrap of paper. Like the famous headline in the *Daily Express*, 'There Will Be No War This Year or Next Year Either', these served to keep up trade. Despite the Air Raid Shelter trenches in Hyde Park, the R.H.S. Autumn Show at Olympia was surprisingly good, and as the rush of alpine propagation died down I went travelling again on my Excelsior, even gathering in several layout jobs.

I had to decide whether, if there was not going to be a war, I should carry on for a third round of shows, or even a fourth, and a summer of driving haste to keep on top of the propagation. Though I was very thin, my health was as good as it ever had been. I had given up the olive oil enemas after a long spell of doing shows and moving digs had shown me there were no dire consequences from getting rid of this burden. If I stayed where I was there could be no promotion because I was at the top of a very small tree. If I met, and won, the right girl, I might well be able to start a small alpine nursery or take a partnership in one.

Then I ran into Syd Weaver at one of the early Spring R.H.S. Shows. He was very pleased with himself, having just been accepted as a student at Edinburgh Botanic Gardens. He had heard that Messrs Wells of Merstham, with three quarters of a mile of nursery beside the Brighton Road, wanted a rare plant foreman. Though they were most famous for introducing Korean chrysanthemums, they were also remembered for *Gentiana macaulayi* Wells Variety, the magnificent August-flowering, royal-blue cross between the early, but difficult, pale blue *G. farrari* and *G. sino-ornata*, with deep blue trumpets in October. Ben Wells, it seemed, wanted to build up his alpine collection and was looking for someone who could not only propagate but control other propagation, and the money was good — three pounds ten shillings a week.

So I wrote for the job, asked for this princely wage, went down to see Ben Wells, and got it. I would have seven girls working under me (it rose to 18 at one time) and because the main outlet for the alpines and herbaceous plants was sending out orders for Suttons, Carters, Harrods, and the Army and Navy Stores, who took a 25 per cent profit on each order that they never saw, there would be no showing. They did show at a month-long exhibition, staged in the food hall at Harrods by all the firms who supplied their customers under this arrangement, but the main job would be to propagate, and first of all I would have to divide and take cuttings from thousands of delphinium in named varieties.

I found myself lodgings in the village, gave in my notice, and my parents moved me in Puddleduck, bringing with them the elderly Remington, for I was determined to have another go at writing.

Ernie Rowe, the manager, and I shared a potting shed, connected by telephone with the office like all the other potting sheds that studded the mile long, about a quarter-mile wide strip behind the houses on the Brighton Road. Ben Wells could talk to all the potting sheds via the switchboard in the office, and the office could ring up with queries on the range of plants that came under each shed. The girls were very largely those who had got fed up with working at the large local laundry where the forewoman was reputed to be an ex-prison wardress, and they were hefty and hard working.

All soil was steam-sterilized and brought to us in a battered van. I was mainly cutting up the more expensive plants, which produced the fewest cuttings. The girls potted up the rooted portions of the stools from which the cuttings had been removed. The cuttings themselves were potted in sandy soil, made by adding extra sand to the standard mixture. We came to the end of this job and I got down to my alpines.

I had a whole greenhouse 120 feet long and 14 wide, one of a block of five, which took herbaceous plants and ordinary alpines, under Nobby Wallis and Jack Partridge, who became my good friends. I filled pan after pan with ring after ring of gentian cuttings, 500 to 700 in each, especially *G. veitchiorum* from Tibet, with its glorious, pure, deep blue, of which I had about 1,500, and nearly 2,000 of the cross between this and *G. sino-ornata*: *G. stevenagensis*, a purple-blue. As they rooted, my girls potted them on and we filled frame after frame, watered with overhead irrigators that would do four ashbeds at once, all in sterilized soil to save having to weed.

The most personally important event at Merstham was when I noticed that our stock plant of *Polygonum vaccini- folium* was completely covered with its pale, rose-pink flowers. When I got home that evening, instead of starting another short story to add to the small fleet my landlady put beside my plate at breakfast time as they came back in my stamped addressed envelopes, I wrote a 500 word article on the plant and sent it off to *Popular Gardening*. By return I got a letter accepting it. At last I was on my way as a writer.

I bought *Popular Gardening* and two weeks later it appeared. 'Insist on seeing the Stock Plant' had been changed to 'A Beautiful Trailing Plant', cut down to a bare eight lines. All my sound advice on buying from a firm with a really good form of this hardy, easy alpine from the Himalayas had been removed. I still have the cheque from the Amalgamated Press stating that endorsement of the cheque grants them all rights in the article, including translation rights into all known languages, film rights, broadcasting rights, and of course television via Alexandra Palace. The cheque was for 1/6d, or $7^1/_2$p, the exact sum for the words they had used. I never cashed the cheque, which is gummed in our family photograph album, so I still hold those rights in the first material I ever wrote and was paid for.

Through the second weekend in August, when I was finishing the last short story I would ever write, I noticed increasing traffic on the Brighton line that ran along the back of the nursery and past my lodgings, and on Monday the trains were even more frequent, for extra services were put on to get holidaymakers back from the Continent. Everyone knew war was coming; for us it arrived that day at 2 p.m.

Ben Wells came out of the office and went from potting shed to potting shed telling all of us that he had received his call-up papers and had to join his ship within three days, for he was on the Reserve of Naval Officers. There would be a pay envelope for everyone on Friday and if anyone wanted to leave without working out his notice they could. Ten of us were to stay on, including Ernie Rowe, Nobbie Wallis and six of the packers, plus a few in the office, to cope with the trickle of orders still coming in.

I rode on my Dawes up the back roads behind the villages to where there was rumoured to be a Militia Camp site. According to the *News Chronicle*, the Militia Camps, to take the about-to-be-called-up 20-year olds, were so desperate for carpenters they were paying as much as £8 and even £10 a week for them. The *Daily Express* said £15 a week, but this was hard to believe.

I got there to find a couple of small green sheds being connected to the telephone, two big lorries, a strange yellow vehicle, some cars parked by the hedge, and about 20 men putting in pegs while others sighted with dumpy levels. By the gate next to the sheds was a stout man with a face weathered red, in a blue suit with a bowler hat on the back of his head. I parked my bike in the hedge, marched up to him and said 'Are you the foreman?'

'I am that.'

'I want a job as a carpenter.'

'And how long have *you* been a carpenter?'

'I'm a foreman at the big nursery on the Brighton Road. The Boss has been called up for the Navy and we've all got the sack. I can handle a hammer and saw and fit greenhouse boilers and piping.'

'When I start a carpenter, he's a CARPENTER. He'll have his tools, and know his trade and get on with the bloody job. But as you don't sound as though you know how to fiddle a time clock you can start as time-keeper and storekeeper at 7 a.m. sharp tomorrow morning, and if any of your men want a job, they can start as labourers. Tell them to bring picks and shovels.'

I rang the office, asking for Mr Edwards, the grey-haired accounts clerk, to pass on the offer. I learned afterwards that he rang all the potting sheds, and though Ben Wells gave permission to take tools, there were only four picks and six shovels. Someone drove the soil van around Redhill and Reigate, buying up picks and shovels in the ironmongers. This was not legal, for the old van was not licensed or insured, but, as was said for the first time: 'There's a war on.'

Next morning I was there at 6.30 to find the foreman getting out of his Morris Cowley carrying a battered tomcat in a new wicker basket. 'I always have my cat Jenkins on the job, it makes a site more homey.' He released Jenkins, who went straight to a clean folded sack under the table with the telephone on, and then told me how to write the details on the long cards the men put in the clock that stamped the time on them. A wages clerk would be arriving on Friday to add up the times and make up the pay packets. He also showed me how to enter up the insurance cards and addresses in the record book which I could do when I had time.

Soon after that the first arrivals from the nursery turned up, about 40 men, all with brand new picks and shovels. Their job was to dig the trenches for the sewer and water pipes leading to the ablutions and lavatory blocks, the two-foot square, foot-deep holes that took the short brick piers supporting the huts, and to square up the sides of the excavations for the cookhouse and other buildings with concrete floors. These were made by the big yellow machine and two more which arrived later that morning. They were 'scrapers' and planed off the surface down to a foot, filling themselves full of the lovely loam, which would have made beautiful potting soil, then dumping it in long piles by the hedges.

Our three greenhouse repair and construction carpenters were putting up the shuttering of sawn timber to hold the concrete bases of some of the buildings, and sides of the roads, for the traffic was tearing up the grass and one good wet day would make the site a sea of mud. With overtime they were getting £15 a week, showing that even the *Daily Express* can be right sometimes. I got £7, plus £3 more for working each weekend, but I would return to my lodgings each evening at 6, sometimes as late as 7 p.m., exhausted.

I heard about the bombing of Poland over the telephone from Head Office, for a clerk there put the mouthpiece of his telephone next to his portable wireless so we could hear the news. I heard Chamberlain's speech on the Declaration of War on September 3rd from this portable.

Nearly three weeks later I was replaced by an experienced timekeeper from one of the other Wates's estates for as these finished off their houses they shared their labour round the R.A.F. and Army Camps, cramming men into those sites where the authorities clamoured loudest. The new timekeeper, another wages clerk, and a storekeeper shared my bedroom when I moved out. I was not sorry to go for I had one of my 'attacks' coming on, not from overwork but from eating at least two sandwich meals a day. No-one realised, of course, that the bread was my enemy. Of course it was white, but even brown, organically-grown wholemeal would have been just as bad for my disability.

My father was busy teaching, so I sent off my two suitcases by Carter Paterson, who took my typewriter, with a sack tied over, generously decorated with 'Fragile' labels, and delivered it safe and well to Dartford in three days. I rode home on my faithful Dawes with over £20 saved out of my high-wage period.

When I tried to join the R.A.M.C., I discovered that the industrial letters on my insurance card, ZN, meant I counted as a farm bailiff and was heavily reserved, so could not join the forces, yet my health would certainly not stand the harder physical work of a farm labourer.

I had hoped to get a job as a full-time Air Raid Warden at £3 a week like my sister. She had graduated from the Royal College of Art and was at the Bromley Incident Control Centre, industriously controlling dummy incidents. My brother, a long way up the ladder, designing chemical process plant with ICI, was heavily reserved. But he finally got his release, joining the Navy as an Engine Room Artificer, and finished the war as an Engineer Lieutenant.

Dartford did not need any more paid Wardens, but Joyce Green Hospital, out on the marshes near the jetty where my brother and I once played our model submarines on fishing line reels, wanted an 'intelligent and well spoken man' as a tele-phone and messenger porter. So I rode out there, and got the job at £4 a week.

My hours were 2 to 10 p.m., 10 p.m. to 6 a.m. and 6 a.m. to 2 p.m., a week of each at a time. The telephone exchange was in the Gate Lodge where a senior porter booked the nurses in and out in a register that went up to Matron each morning, with dire consequences for nurses without late passes who were not in by 10 p.m. During the day, from 9 a.m. to 6 p.m., two telephone girls worked alternate days. We telephone porters did the night shift, and meal periods, and spent the rest of our time in the Messengers Office, with the non-telephone messengers.

The night shift was important to me, so by arrangement with the three other telephone porters, I used to swap shifts to get more of them. I would bring reference books for checking the spelling of plant names and write articles in long hand, then post the final copies to a Mrs D. A. Drowley, who advertised as a copy typist in *The Writer*, a monthly I had bought when look-ing for new markets for short stories. She sent them back, beauti-fully typed for 3/6d a thousand words, all through the war. I met her only once, a plump, middle-aged housewife, who told me she regarded typing for me as her special piece of 'war work'. When she typed my first book I dedicated it to her.

On 'quiet' nights I got in three hours before the 1 a.m. meal, with the tea kettle boiled on the Gate Lodge gas ring, and the night gate porter and the night watchman, and sometimes patrolling policemen and 'Parashots' (as we then called the Home Guard) for company. So here I had another long spell learning the writer's trade, sending articles to *Amateur Gardening*, *Popular Gardening*, *Garden Work for Amateurs*, *The Smallholder*, *Gardening Illustrated* and a monthly, *My Garden*, and getting 80 per cent of what I wrote accepted at 21 shillings a thousand words.

On Messenger's Office shifts I sorted the letters for patients and staff, collected 'specimens', delivered Path. Lab. reports, and took stationery round the wards in a dark green, rubber-tyred handcart. To start with, only about 10 wards had any patients; the rest were empty, waiting with bedding folded back lengthways to take helpless patients, who seemed to be a long time coming, straight off the stretchers.

But it occurred to Authority, after Narvik, that evacuating elderly patients from London to South Coast seaside resorts could have drawbacks, so back they came in Greenline buses converted into ambulances, and we used them to fill up the Orchard Hospital. Joyce Green grew a Military Wing, with an R.A.M.C. major in charge, about 30 N.C.O.s and other ranks, and khaki envelopes of case papers of incredible complexity, which fortunately were handled by them, not us.

Finally, on May 31st, at 5 a.m., when I was on night shift, we were warned by Sector Ten to expect 150 B.E.F. from Dunkirk and that no one was to leave the hospital. Spending 42 hours on duty, not working, just waiting, I learned to smoke. Finally they arrived, hundreds of them, in double-decker buses from Margate and Ramsgate, in hospital ambulances, and in a stream of Army ambulances with camouflage netting and bren guns in the cabs. Some had been dive-bombed and had been shooting back at the Stukas.

The buses were full of 'walking wounded', and we got them into the wards as we could. At one time I was taking men on stretchers into the anteroom of the operating theatre, but I was mostly helping the men off the buses and carrying their kit.

You could tell the Guardsmen as they lay on their stretchers, not only by the extra weight of the six-footers, but by the fact that they had all shaved that morning on the beach at Dunkirk. They remained longer in our hospital than men from other regiments, for we had half a wardful of them, their faces painted with gentian violet, who all caught some skin infection from shaving in dirty water from Belgian ditches.

By this time my parents had moved to Surbiton. My father's younger brother (Uncle Kenneth) was with Fraser--Nash B.M.W. sports cars. Once they had used up the stock of engines from the Bavarian Motor Works, the firm had turned over to making parts for tanks and aircraft, and he offered my father a job designing hydraulic gear. So for the second time my father served his country at the expense of his pension.

I went to live with Mrs Gale, our next-door neighbour, an elderly widow with a rather less elderly maid, and rigged up a battery-powered lighting system in the air raid shelter in the cellar. When the raids really started and I would ride back in the morning with the 'All Clear' sirens sounding triumphantly all round me, the ships on the Thames joining in joyfully with theirs, and unswept broken glass in the Dartford streets, I just had my breakfast and went upstairs to bed to sleep thankfully.

It is hard today to realize that many of my generation joined up hoping to roll Hitler back, and to achieve a stronger League of Nations with an International Police Force to back it up. It was to fight for this unfortunately still unachieved war aim, that on December 4th, 1940, I became 1221280 AC2 Hills L.D. at Cardington, managing to pass the mathematical questions for air gunners, with a number of tricks of mental arithmetic my father had taught me to help in landscape gardening estimates. But I failed on eyesight. Though I hadn't known it I had a 'lazy eye' and air gunners need perfect eyesight. So, lacking the mechanical aptitude for servicing aircraft I became an Aircraft Hand, General Duties, an ACH/GD, the lowest form of life in the R.A.F., with the option of remustering to any trade I thought I could do after training.

Issued with a vast quantity of kit, I was taught how to cram it into my webbing packs and straps, how to march in column of three, how to salute officers, but not warrant officers, and how to clean buttons and boots. After 10 days we were sent to Morecambe and billeted in seaside boarding houses, while our N.C.O.s taught us to handle the short magazine Lee-Enfield Mark 3.

We were also given a whole cocktail of injections, and this, combined with the cold, shot my temperature up to 103°, so I had to pack my 'small kit': shaving gear, toothbrush, button-cleaning material, mug and 'irons' (issue knife, fork, and spoon), plus pyjamas, into my grey webbing haversack and 'report sick'. Fortunately there was just room for a Penguin, a small, dark blue Kipling, or an Everyman edition to read while you wait, for the waiting rooms of service doctors do not provide reading matter.

I was sent to the local hospital, where I was kept for ten days and came out only just in time for the rehearsals for the passing-out parade. I was so far behind I was like a lost dog on a football field. When the 'Great Day' came, they hid me behind the Winter Gardens theatre with all the other 'odds and sods', while the billet orderlies stood in for us.

Nevertheless, I was placed in charge of the draft of five ACH/GDs for No. 150 Squadron, Bomber Command, at Newton, near Nottingham. Our corporal, a firm friend by now, told the others I was in charge and responsible for their good behaviour, and gave me a railway warrant and a Route Form, which began 'We, George VI, by the Grace of God' and ended with a squiggle in green ink from a pilot officer. I was chosen not for qualities of leadership, education, or intelligence, but because I was the 'senior man'. We all joined the R.A.F. within the same half hour, but I had been the first to be listed, so I had several minutes seniority over the second man, who would take over if I became a casualty on the journey. He was Elisha Hicks, a poultry dealer, so fat that he had to have an overcoat made specially for him and until this arrived was known always as 'You in the civvy overcoat'.

My responsibilities weighed on me seriously. It was a long slow journey with four changes but I did get 'my men' across England without losing one of them. There was a lorry waiting for us at Bingham, the nearest station to Newton, and we bumped our way through frozen fields to a snowed-up aerodrome studded with Wellington bombers, standing huge and black, canvas covers flapping round their engine cowlings.

In the morning we all had to report sick, to ensure we had brought nothing infectious to the camp. The old patients were treated first, grimy men in battered caps and tunics mended under the armpits with copper wire, usually with knuckles gashed from slipped spanners. By virtue of my number I went in first, had my chest sounded and temperature taken by a young doctor, and was told to wait.

Then I overheard him on the telephone. 'They're all right, just want their arses kicking to stop them swinging the lead

— all except for that poor bugger Hills.' A sergeant came out from the surgery and told me to follow him upstairs to the sick bay and get into bed. There were four other men up there in a small ward with a radio going full blast, three playing cards on the fourth's bed. Presently lunch arrived, mince, to which the left-over porridge from breakfast had been added, followed by suet pudding and custard. My 'irons' had pink adhesive plaster stuck to the handles, to be washed separately so no one else should use them. The doctor had diagnosed me as a T.B. case since I was emaciated, had a chest infection and a temperature, and would be better off away from a snowed up 'drome where the C.O. was leading all hands, including officers and my four new recruits, on clearing the runways to get the aircraft flying again.

It took a medical board to get me out of hospital, because the doctor had diagnosed T.B. and sent me there for discharge, which was why I had gone to a hospital that also took cases suspected of 'working their tickets' (faking illnesses to get discharged). I was reduced to Grade 3 and returned to 150 Squadron, where, after a spell of sick leave at Surbiton, where my parents had been bombed out of their first house and just moved into their second, I started work in the orderly room.

Here I used an elderly Underwood, which was a vast improvement on my old Remington, and generally fitted in with Corporal Smith, Cyril Jones and George Murray, under Alice the Adjutant, a flight lieutenant who had been in the diplomatic service and at 40 was the oldest man in the Squadron.

Soon I was put on typing a massive movement order and so was Murray, for the rumour that we were to move to a new aerodrome at Snaith, near Goole in Yorkshire, and eventually to be rearmed with American four-engined Liberator bombers, turned out to be true. We avoided all 'Careless Talk that Costs Lives' but despite our precautions, the W.V.S. canteen in Bingham had laid on a farewell supper of rabbit pie baked by the ladies of the village with rabbits supplied by local poachers, followed by a concert. The honorary secretary, a plump contralto, sang 'Three Fishers Went Sailing Away in the West', the vicar, who had a good bass, gave us 'Down, Down, Down, Down, Down among the dead men let him lie,' and then there were calls for the R.A.F. to sing something. One of the Sergeant pilots, whom I hardly knew, suggested 'The Professor' should 'do something'. This was my nickname and the cry was taken up.

So I went up on the platform and recited G. K. Chesterton's *Last Hero*.

'I shall not die alone, alone, but kin to all the Powers,
As merry as the ancient sun, and fighting like the flowers.'

They clapped and clapped so much that I gave them Chesterton's *Second Childhood* as an encore. The party ended with a spirited rendering of *Jerusalem*, in time for a drink at the pub, where one of our corporals said to me, 'Professor, you're a bloody marvel! How you make it up so fast as you go along I cannot imagine!'

Snaith was a large new 'drome, with the barrack hut sites dispersed and well camouflaged in the fields; there was no booking in and out, giving us a freedom that would last till it was abused. There was room for us to have a squadron operations room, and I was transferred there with LAC Ken Holmes and Pilot Officer Jimmy Derrett, the navigation officer.

My work included keeping the big wall map up to date with the latest positions of the rescue floats, both British and German, which could mean life or death to wounded aircrew in rubber dinghies. These were constantly changing because German E Boats came across and stole ours, while our MTBs stole theirs and recaptured our own. Each float had an automatic radio which transmitted to listening stations as soon as someone landed on the stern ramp, then rescue launches went racing out to collect the 'catch', either for return to their squadrons, or to P.O.W. camps.

I also had to set out everything that would be required on each aircraft, such as coding machines, like small grey attache cases, with the code card for the night in each for wireless operators, and large Very pistol cartridges which discharged coloured stars in combinations that varied through the night according to a card carried by observers, again altered each day. These were to be fired to tell our over-enthusiastic A.A. batteries that they were shooting at 'one of ours'.

Though I could not fly, I could help the men who did, and I found it an interesting and satisfying task, so I put in to remuster to Clerk S.D. (Special Duties) to be permanently on this kind of work. If the war lasted long enough I might become a corporal.

There was a very good W.V.S. canteen in Snaith, and there I met Harry Senior who farmed a 200-acre mixed farm with dairy cattle, pigs, sheep to tread and dung the light barley land, and grain, mainly wheat for seed and malting barley. His wife and farm workers' wives ran the canteen. He invited me to the farm to stay for official and unofficial weekends on 'sleeping out passes'.

Harry was a much younger, North Country version of Mr Widdows on whose farm I had caught the minnows that landed me my first job. Mary and George, their two children, were there on holiday when I first went to the farm. There was a small brewery next door, and a number of by-products from converting barley into beer made it possible to feed extra pigs, and as Mrs Senior had bought a large stock of the spices, herbs, saltpetre, and other requisites for curing bacon and hams, there was no shortage of food. It was glorious to wake up on a Sunday morning and hear the farm noises, have a leisurely breakfast of non-cookhouse food, and best of all take part in Harry Senior's Sunday morning walk.

Suddenly my posting came through. I was to report to Digby, a fighter station, as an 'Under Training Clerk S.D.', and to my surprise I was invited to a farewell 'booze-up' with the aircrew. During the three months I was in the Ops Room I had lost 36 friends, some of them P.O.W.s shot down in Germany, and others 'missing believed killed'. Three of the ACH/GDs I had 'commanded' from Morecambe were still with the squadron, and Elisha Hicks, once 'You in the civvy overcoat', was now a sergeant. His hobby had been pigeon keeping, and he was now in charge of one of the first R.A.F. pigeon lofts.

Digby was an old station, and I was to be trained in plotting enemy fighters located by radar, and guiding our own night fighters to them. We were billeted in the stables of a large country house, and here I caught scabies. All our sheets had been collected, for issue to the W.A.A.F.s, and we slept on blankets like the Army, but the Army organized blanket steriliz-ing. Before the R.A.F. got found to doing this there was an outbreak of the skin disease produced by the itch mite (*Sar-coptes scabici*).

I spent Christmas 1941 — the most miserable Christmas of my life — in the station sick quarters, another converted country house, having baths in which I scrubbed off the scabs, and then smeared myself liberally with an ointment based on sulphur. While I was in there, my medical records caught up with me, and it was discovered that I was Grade 3 and unfit for overseas posting. As I was being trained to plot aircraft in Malaya, a job that was done by W.A.A.F.s in Britain, I was transferred at once to the Orderly Room.

I now became a permanent UT/Clerk SD, because I could not go back to ACG/GD without failing the trade test, which I could not take because I was not fit for overseas.

I settled down and made friends, especially with 'Doc' Dockrey, who was a Doctor of Music and played the organ in Lincoln Cathedral after completing his duties of cleaning the lavatories as an ACH/GD, and John Fassell, who described himself as a 'good 10th rate violinist', counting Kreisler as a first rate one. He used to play the two parts of Bach's Double Concerto separately, and was an armourer, whose job was testing the cannon in the wings of the Spitfires. He was terrified the noise would destroy his ear for music, and I put him up to remustering as a ground wireless operator, listening to enemy Morse code transmissions.

In 1926, Rudolph Steiner had started the Bio-Dynamic Agricultural Movement, and early in 1942 I read a copy of a quarterly *Tomorrow* published by the Bio-Dynamic Farm and Garden Association, which also covered Rudolph Steiner's Educational ideas and his philosophy. In it was an advertisement from Maurice Woods, Sleights Farm, Aislaby, Yorks., a pioneer of stone-ground wholemeal flour and one of the very first organic farmers. I wrote to him asking if I might visit his farm on my next 48-hour pass, and got an enthusiastic letter back.

I spent a delightful weekend walking over the farm, feeling for the first time the springiness of the living soil of the first organic pastures I had ever trod. He had problems with the War Agricultural Committee. They insisted on his accepting chemical fertilizers, but he left them unused in his barn. When they congratulated him on the improvement in his wheat crop, he showed them the still unopened sacks. As fertilizers were then scarce, inorganic farmers decided to let him alone and use the chemicals on their own land, for his yields were no lower than theirs.

I got home leave in the spring, in time to prune the bush roses at 29 Pine Gardens, where Mother had persuaded the road men who mowed the wide verges to use a grass box and give her the mowings for her compost heap, as they did the dead leaves for her leafmould. She had been using Adco, the inorganic activator invented at Rothamsted, but turned over to the horse manure from the milkmen and other tradesmen, and poultry manure from one of my father's fitters. It was from him that she learned that run-to-seed salsify is a splendid poultry green food.

On my leave I went to London and hunted through Foyles for Everyman editions and Kiplings. While there I looked through the alpine books, new and secondhand. They struck me as mainly expensive, padded, and short on practical information. So I telephoned Faber and Faber, whom I knew as the Siegfried Sassoon publishers, told them I wanted to write a book on alpines and that my articles had been appearing regularly in the gardening press on this subject. I asked for an appointment and got one for the following day.

Marching into the soon familiar office in Russell Square, I saw Miss Swann at her little reception desk, where she must have spent about 50 years. She showed me into the long, narrow, waiting room with a framed page of *Memoirs of a Fox-Hunting Man* corrected within an inch of its life on the one wall that was not filled from top to bottom with bookcases.

Soon she told me to go in. In a lofty room like a headmaster's study, but with many more books, at a long, Chippendale table covered with manuscripts, was Richard de la Mare, a tall, dark-haired man with a moustache and a lazy Old Etonian voice. I never met his father, whom I knew only by his poems, but a friendship started then that lasted until 1986 when Richard died, aged 84.

I had in my haversack a photograph album, gummed full of my published articles, written in those quiet nights at Joyce Green, in Gosford Hospital, and at Scopwick Hall sick quarters through my scabies-scarred Christmas. The guineas these brought in uncrossed postal orders, which I could turn into cash in the N.A.A.F.I., had paid for many a meal for me and my hard-up comrades. The evidence they supplied, that I could write, gave Richard de la Mare something to show his co-Directors to justify his offering me a contract for *Miniature Alpine Gardening*, about the pan gardens I had shown at Chelsea 1936 and alpines for small gardens. My hope was to replace the plant killing 'rockeries' of the suburbs with outdoor versions of the table rock gardens I had built at flower shows all over England.

It takes privacy and quiet to write a book, and these are the rarest of all commodities in a serviceman's life. It took me over two years to write that book, in N.A.A.F.I. quiet rooms, Toch H, W.V.S. and Salvation Army canteens, and, above all, in hospitals.

61

When I got back to Digby I had some real luck. I was sent to Wellingore, its satellite Station, which had a grass 'drome that was having concrete runways built to take four-engined bombers. The empty station buildings were used to accommodate squadrons before they went overseas while they shed their problem people, and those who were medically unfit, were brought up to strength, sent on embarkation leave and finally packed off on troop ships.

The station used to hold two fighter squadrons, but as they were posted to us one at a time we were never more than half full. The long hut, divided into single rooms for the sergeant pilots of the missing squadron, was always empty, so I got a room of my own with a far more comfortable bed, an easy chair, and a good table where I could spread my books and papers.

My luck ended when the adjutant at Digby found a way of getting me out of my 'Catch 22' situation. The R.A.F. wanted groundsmen to make aerodromes and station buildings blend into the English countryside, by spreading fertilizer, mowing, and spraying a black dye to imitate the shadows of hedges to make a wide expanse look like a patchwork of pastures. They wanted experienced gardeners and, as I was one, I was sent for a trade test.

Warrant Office Crabbe of 52 Works Flight told me I had passed the exam with 98% of the possible marks, making me an LAC, and that he was recommending me for promotion to corporal. I would be posted to his flight at Linton-on-Ouse, a large bomber station on the other side of York.

The Works Flight was in a hutted site that had once housed a battalion of the R.A.F. Regiment. It had a vegetable garden between the huts, piles of ashes all round it, and it was so far away across the 'drome we had to commute to work by lorry. As there was no groundsman's work available, I was put in the office in the main camp but after a few weeks our flight and six others were formed into a detachment to cope with an emergency.

A number of contractors had skimped on the concrete in the runways put down to take the great weight of the Halifax and Lancaster bombers, making them break up. Our job was to smash the defective runways with pneumatic road drills and load the fragments on to dumpers, to be piled beside the runways and tipped back into the deepened excavations, with more hardcore on top and thicker concrete.

My wrists gave out after two days, and I went to hospital to have them put in plaster because I had synovitis in both of them from lifting heavy lumps of concrete on to the dumpers. I came back to 'light duties'. However, there were none, so I was sent to the cookhouse on the washing-up machine, with three men from station headquarters who were there as a punishment. When asked what my crime had been, I told enquirers I was on *light duties* — when we got 'Jankers' in the Works Flight we had to bite out the concrete with our teeth.

When I went back to full duty I had the same job as on the Militia Camp, collecting and entering in the payment register the load tickets from the lorries that brought in the sand, ballast, hardcore, and concrete. This was complicated by the number of lorries that brought in poor quality sand and hardcore. These were sent back after I had taken down their numbers to show which tickets to return as rejected loads.

Then I went down with an 'attack' and they sent me to Naburn Military Hospital where at least I was warm and had a chance to get on with my book. They again X-rayed me from all directions, but could find nothing to justify invaliding me out, the comment of the R.A.M.C. doctor being, 'A man of good intelligence but poor physique. Recommend clerical duties.'

By the time I came out and had taken some sick leave, at least our share of the emergency was over, and I went back to Linton, where Warrant Officer Crabbe appointed me permanent orderly corporal on our hut site. I was in charge of the billet orderlies, low medical category men, who kept the place clean and looked after the vegetable garden.

We had bucket sanitation and had to bury the contents, for providing water sanitation for about 200 men, including a septic tank, is too big an operation to wangle. I had bought a second-hand copy of *The Waste Products of Agriculture* by A. Howard and K. Wad, dealing with the experiments in composting human wastes carried out at Indore Research Station in India. I wrote to Albert Howard (later Sir Albert), the father of the compost heap as we know it, and of the organic movement that today includes the Soil Association and the Henry Doubleday Research Association.

He sent me a nine-page letter of advice (which unfortunately I lost in my subsequent service postings) on how to compost our bucket contents with straw from local farmers. This would have been possible to follow had I been a group captain, or ideally an air vice marshal, but as I was only the R.A.F. equivalent of an acting, unpaid, lance-corporal, I could do nothing at the time. But his letter marked an important day in my life for it became the date of my entry into the organic movement. An aspect of the greatness of Sir Albert Howard is shown by the fact that he took the time to write that long letter in his own handwriting, with sketches of the layout of the composting unit, to an unknown man in the R.A.F. who asked a complicated question.

However, I was able to get on with my book in comfort. Unfortunately, I went down with another 'attack' and was sent to Naburn Hospital again. Here the medical authorities decided that I was unfit for the tough conditions of a works flight, so I was sent to West Drayton, where the R.A.F. were sorting out their misfits and unwanted tradesmen.

We were all put through a medical check and given an intelligence test. It included, among other questions I thought rather obvious and silly, a trick one. This was: 'All conifers are evergreens, therefore are all evergreens conifers?' I answered: 'All conifers are not evergreens. The Common Larch, *Larix decidua* is deciduous. The Holly, *Ilex aquifolium*, and the Holm Oak, *Quercus ilex* are examples of non-coniferous evergreens.' At the interview afterwards I was told that only two of us, a B.Sc. Forestry and myself, out of about 300 men tested that day, had answered that question exactly correctly. Both our I.Q.s were registered as high, but he, being fit for overseas, was sent on a course to become an anti-gas officer, while all they could make me was an equipment assistant.

So I lost the room of my own and was posted to Weston-Super-Mare, on the equipment course and became one of Flight 423F, which included a director of a brewery, a juvenile court officer, an expert on bee keeping, and a man whose job was faking antique furniture. We were in civilian billets, and I managed to get on still more with my book. Again I passed out as an LAC, reaching the opulence of 5 shillings a day, plus threepence for one good conduct stripe, worn at the bottom of the left sleeve, having completed three years without a single charge on my conduct sheet.

At Weston-Super-Mare I gave my very first gardening lecture, to the largest audience of my life. It was at the end of the course and we had several days to wait before going on leave for Christmas 1943, so our class sent those of its members who had unusual jobs around giving lectures to the other classes. There were several Army units there, also training, and an A.B.C.A. (Army Bureau of Current Affairs) lecture was arranged for them all one afternoon in the biggest cinema in the town. More than 5,000 men came to it because, of course, they had been ordered to attend. We four from Class 423F, plus the head kennelman of the Battersea Dogs' Home, gave them half an hour each. The ex-kennelman got the most applause.

Afterwards, I was downstairs in the gents and the man next to me said, 'That was a good lecture, Hills.' I looked sideways to see the group captain in charge of the equipment course. I said, 'Thank you, Sir,' standing to attention.

'Anywhere you want to be posted?'

'As near London as possible, Sir. My parents live at Surbiton.'

Sure enough, when my route form and railway warrant came round next day, 'Lossiemouth' had been crossed out and 'West Drayton' inserted by the officer who signed it. In our billet there was a man named McGregor, also wild with delight, because he lived in Lossiemouth and on his forms 'West Drayton' had been crossed out and the name of his home town had been put in its place.

So I went home for Christmas and finished my book, posting off the last pages to Mrs Drowley, who returned them in time for me to post it complete to Faber and Faber.

Back at West Drayton I began to think about photographs for my book, then wrote to Orchard Neville to see if I could borrow the blocks of the small coloured illustrations of alpines from their catalogue, because I knew that new blocks were expensive. This brought T. C. Mansfield round to my home address, which I had given in my letter. He told my parents that when I left the R.A.F. he wanted me back to manage Orchard Neville again. He told them that Major Thorpe had retired, married an ex-nurse who had kept him in order and stopped him smoking, but he had died.

I settled down in the stores, mainly doing the clerical work involved in invaliding people out of the service. Then I got another 'attack', just as I was waiting for my galley proofs, and went into the station sick quarters and then to Hillingdon County Hospital. I was there three weeks, then sent back to wait to see a specialist at the Royal Free Hospital in Gray's Inn Road, where R.A.F. medical mysteries were sent. Doctors, in or out of uniform, strive to do their best for their patients, and while I had been writing my gardening book in hospitals, a medical detective story was being written in my case papers, lavishly illustrated with X-ray films.

They sent me back to West Drayton with, I learned later, a report that said I had 'idiopathic steartorhea', meaning, roughly, 'inability to digest fats, peculiar to himself'. I got some sick leave at Surbiton where I corrected my page proofs and made out the cards for the index which I wrote out and sent to Mrs Drowley. Then I went back to West Drayton to await events.

I was summoned to Uxbridge for an interview with an elderly R.A.F. doctor looking like a moulting eagle, who began by telling me that it was lucky I had never had any money, because had I been rich I would have been a gold mine for quacks. Then he told me that a report would be sent to the civilian doctor I should later acquire, recommending that I should have liver injections and an extra milk ration. So I was discharged as unfit for further service in the armed forces, but with no pension because I had joined the service with the same condition I still had. When he asked me what I proposed to do, I said, 'Go on writing gardening books and articles, Sir.'

'Good luck, Hills, as a second Mr Middleton. I hope you become as famous as he is.'

6

A Gardener's Peace

I ARRIVED home at Surbiton in my grey, chalk-stripe demob suit and brown trilby hat, and on the afternoon of my very first Sunday out of uniform there was an immensely loud explosion, a sudden tower of black smoke, and a swift rush of air through the leaves of the sapling street trees of Pine Gardens. It was the first of the V1s, 'doodlebugs' or 'buzzbombs' to arrive in Surbiton. These did not make much crater, but a fearful blast that smashed windows, swept tiles off roofs, and could kill and injure over a wide area. They were very roughly made and their remains looked like smashed metal dustbins.

My trips to London to see Faber and Faber, and round Surbiton to the various offices involved in fitting 122180 LAC Hills, L.D., back into war-time civilian life, were punctuated by watching these wicked little daggers flung at London high across the sky, hearing an engine cut out, then waiting for the thunderous explosion that could be near or far. They were kept on course by gyroscopes and once the fuel finished these ceased to spin and their final dive could be in any direction.

I had just over a month before I should be off to Somerset, to take on the job of managing Orchard Neville Nurseries where I had failed 10 years before, at the war-inflated wage of £7 a week. I had fixed up to lodge with Mrs Reynolds again and I would be fighting to get a nursery that had once grown a million alpines in a thousand varieties back into production. It had sunk to less than half a million a year, but was growing vegetables for the Somerset School Meals Service.

My mother was now in her fifties, and was feeding a husband working long hours and children on leave, while coping with everything that came. She once entertained my Aunties Chrissie and Daisy to lunch, on salsify roots cooked by her own recipe, later given in my *Grow Your Own Fruit and Vegetables*, when the meat ration was finished and the most beautiful words in the English language were 'Offal Today' outside a butcher's shop.

We had a large allotment as well as the garden, and I did my best to get both plots well ahead. They were highly productive with compost and manure, including poultry droppings from my father's chicken-keeping fitter at the factory, with ample leafmould from leaves the road men dumped on the allotments. There were, as yet, no organic gardening books, but my mother's 'Bible' was *Kitchen Garden and Allotment*, published by *Amateur Gardening* in 1916.

I left Surbiton on July 8th with two heavy suitcases, luckily getting a taxi from crowded Waterloo to an even more crowded Paddington, where I queued for half an hour for my ticket to West Pennard, the station for Baltonsborough.

Ten years ago I had taken on that job, done my very best and had failed, because my best was not good enough. Now I took it on again, armed with knowledge, but still with the hidden enemy inside me. Again I did my best, and this time *it was enough*. But I worked harder.

I put my luggage in my old bedroom. Mrs Reynolds had tea with two eggs for me, for she kept chickens, and by hook or by crook she fed them well enough to feed her lodgers plenty of eggs. It is hard for anyone under 50 to remember what eating two eggs at a time once meant. Then I walked up to the nursery. Mansfield was still there, and we went round together. He had bought the stock of R. W. Millard's nursery at East Grinstead and wanted to go up in about a fortnight with Day to pack it up and send it down. I would have to mix all the potting soil I could and be ready to get it all potted. I would probably have trouble with Jenkinson, the propagator, but Jose, the son of the Gibraltarian widow Major Thorpe's batman had married, was his assistant and very good. I would share Mrs Long, his secretary, and dictate my letters to her. Osbourne drove the van and took vegetables to greengrocers in Glastonbury and Street, and I should probably also have trouble with him. Mansfield drove me back to my digs at 10 p.m.

So the day that had begun in Surbiton at 6 a.m. ended at The Laurels, in my old bedroom, with time only to unpack and get to bed.

Orchard Neville House had become a Women's Land Army hostel, and the rock garden was three feet high in weeds and brambles, but I took the propagator down next morning and showed him where there should be a large plant of *Androsace semperviviodes.* There still was, ready to divide, and one of *A lanuginosa* with plenty of cuttings on it just asking to be taken.

The big pasture field that ran down to the pond was under vegetables, of which the most paying crop was sweet corn. It paid because a corporal and three G.I.s came over in a jeep twice a week and picked the cobs as they were ready, spending most of a day heaping soil and manure round the bases of the plants, weeding between the rows, and making nearly an acre look like home in far-away Georgia. The corporal even wrote out the bill and we got paid by the U.S. Army base.

Up on the hill, looking towards Glastonbury Tor, over the *Lonicnera nitida* hedges I had planted as tiny cuttings all those years ago, and now four-foot high windbreaks, there was a water tower and pumphouse in which was a one-cylinder engine that started on petrol and ran on T.V.O. (Tractor Vaporizing Oil) which was unrationed. The well would only give 10 to 15 minutes pumping in an hour, to run the irrigators for the alpines, water newly planted vegetables, keep the cutting frames moist, and soak up full trays. We got 5 gallons in petrol coupons for starting it every quarter.

Mansfield's Ford V8 did about 12 miles a gallon, so we started our engine on cigarette lighter fuel so he could use the coupons. My habit of constantly looking at my watch, that I still find myself doing, dates from 1944 and 1945. Then I would come back evening after evening, taking or putting in special cuttings, sorting out mix-ups in alpine frames, or working in the office on a catalogue, then checking if it was time to go and tip a measure-full of lighter fuel in the little green-painted tank, fitting the big rod in the hole in the flywheel, then throwing her round till she fired and the familiar dum-dum-dum and the suck and gurgle of the pump brought the healthy swish of water in the tank.

I had only two weeks to take hold of the new job before Mansfield was away, with a hoard of petrol coupons and a full tank acquired mysteriously (after 50 years I feel it is safe to say that the U.S. corporal was even more helpful than usual) towing the big trailer. Before he left he told me that he had never left the place before with such an easy mind, which I took as a great compliment.

The staff was what we could get against the pull of White-head's torpedo factory at Street, and Clark, Son and Morland at Glastonbury making R.A.F. flying boots. There were six men, apart from Day: Osbourne, aged about 50; Jenkinson; Jose who was officially Spanish and 'neutral'; Jack Squires, an ex-mill-stone dresser of 80 who was the hardest working of any one I had; and a perky little man who had been a jockey and did the odd jobs.

I also had about sixteen 14- to 17-year-old boys and girls, who were good if you kept them working, plus Mrs Day who did the packing, and another three girls under her. Mrs Long, and a copy typist made up the office staff, a second, separate department under me.

I kept the ex-jockey running the soil sterilizer flat out on loam, fetched in by the lorry driver who brought our plunging ashes, using coke breeze from the gas works to run it. This inferior-grade coke was unrationed, unlike the anthracite for the greenhouses, and both the sterilizer and the jockey grumbled about it, but I had to have ready a real stack of John Innes Seed Compost, an excellent alpine mixture, sterilized to kill all weed seeds: the peat and sand, being weed-seed free, needed no steri-lizing.

Mansfield and Day came back after a week, at 10 o'clock at night with the trailer full of pans of seedling rhododendrons, gentians, androsaces, campanulas, and rarities I had last seen in 1939. They had taken out the car seats and filled up with clumps of division subjects that could be split, and of pot and rooted cuttings wrapped in newspaper. We spent the next day, which was Sunday, unpacking. I dashed round the village on my Dawes, which had now arrived, and brought the girls and boys in for a potting marathon, and I worked with them and drove them hard.

Again I had the sore fingers from rough new pots that I had experienced at Stuart Low's, but I learned to spare my hands and to think ahead to keep everything moving, with nothing done that could wait, nothing mixed, and nothing left to spoil. For about three weeks I worked all the hours God sends. If the Devil himself had turned up on the nursery, I should have told him to tuck his tail through the tapes of his gardening apron and get on with the potting. Mansfield and Day drove back on the Monday to fetch more.

After that three week marathon, working till eight or nine each evening and every Saturday and Sunday, I had a week's holiday with Ken on his Model 18 Norton, based at a boarding house at Porlock Weir with a red geranium with a wrist-thick stem spread over its whitewashed walls. Mansfield, out of the generosity of his heart, gave me a whole five-gallon coupon, which we deposited at the local garage, as we had to take it in instalments, for even Norton tanks held only two gallons. It was delightful just to talk and talk, play chess, and do nothing at all.

When I got back the pace had slackened, but we were still potting steadily through the pans of seedlings. Our problem was labour, for though we got conscientious objectors on the vegetables and our other nursery over at Street — the alpines had to take what we could get.

Then Mansfield advertised in *The Times* and got two pupils, Noel Andrews, whom everyone called 'Andy', 22 with a weak heart, slow but willing, and a retired squadron leader who had white hair, and was also trying to learn enough to start an alpine nursery. I think they both paid premiums and had capital behind them, but lacked the drive to start successful businesses. They lodged with Mrs Reynolds and were good company for me. I shall always remember the squadron leader throwing his copy of *The Times* across the room, exclaiming indignantly 'The paper's nothing but a socialist rag. They've moved the crossword puzzle *again* .'

Slowly the war ground to an end in Europe, while we were beginning to sell off our bonanza of rare alpines that Mansfield's (and my) hard work had got potted in July and August rather than October or November, when they would not have had time to take hold of the soil and grow. Then, on the 5th May, it was V.E. Day. The Surbiton celebrations were decorous, though bonfires were lit on the well-mown turf of Pine Gardens, and there was some thin community singing. Those at Baltonsborough were far nearer the tradition of the West Country Carnivals.

When the news came through, we all went down to the Greyhound, and I drank rather more than I should have of sweet cider and peppermint cordial, because I hated the taste of beer. The next day we went to work as usual, and I turned a blind eye to lateness. As the news came through on the radio, Mansfield told me to announce a day off next day, and give everyone the rest of the day off.

Mansfield invited Andy, the squadron leader, and me to dinner and we stayed on listening to the radio. On the way home late we drove through Glastonbury Market, a wide street with cobbled areas each side where the cattle enclosures once stood. The manager of the local cinema had rigged up the loudspeakers and was playing popular dance music at full blast, and there were at least two thousand people dancing, and flags were strung across the street.

Baltonsborough had spent its time decorating, and there was a note for me from Bill Brougham, a retired London policeman who organized much of what went on in Baltonsborough, to tell me that a decorated lorry would call for me at 9 a.m. the next day. 'Please wear fancy dress.'

All I could think of was to put on a pair of pyjamas over my suit, supplemented with large black pom-poms in place of buttons, and an old straw hat Mrs Reynolds found, but I joined the jazz band on the back of Bert Dodge's lorry, playing a kazoo, an instrument that was hummed through.

We spent the morning serenading lonely farms and hamlets. My staff, especially the girls, sang surprisingly well. I felt we were exorcizing the Spirit of War as we hurtled down the lanes, leafy with the bright new green of a Somerset May, the cattle stampeding in the fields at the noise.

The little valley was full of cheerful and healthy children, evacuees from London, by now all speaking broad Somerset, snaring rabbits, and scrumping apples with their village contemporaries. Everywhere mugs of cider were passed up (tea was rationed, cider home-made) and in the course of the morning we collected nearly £10 for the Welcome Home Fund, for the lads of the village in the forces. We got back in time to lead the fancy dress parade of the children from the village square outside the Greyhound to the school, singing 'Shine on Victory Moon'. It was almost more than I could bear after all the years of refugee women and children plodding along the roads of Europe, to think that at last the killing had stopped.

We provided the music for the children's tea, for the ceremony of burning Hitler in effigy on the sports field, and finally for the dance outside the Greyhound which finished at midnight.

Soon after the July 5th election I had a welcome surprise: Faber and Faber sent me my six free copies of my first book. I had been dealing with proofs of the line blocks and their captions, the captions of the photographs, the preface, the index, the dust jacket and all the delaying details that make it a lucky writer who has only to wait a year from the date when his book is accepted to the date of publication. Now in 1944 it was really out, at eight shillings and sixpence. The first edition sold out in six weeks and there was a second large printing in September 1945 and another in September 1946.

My first fan letter arrived a fortnight after publication, four pages long, full of detailed questions on alpines, and ending with congratulation on writing such a useful book. It was post-marked Wells. Mansfield told me that as most of my letters would be from people wanting to know where to buy the alpines I wrote about, I should dictate replies to Mrs Long as part of my job, sending a catalogue with each.

About three weeks later I received an income tax demand for £500, signed with the same electron-orbit-like signature, from the local tax office at Wells. The local inspector of taxes, a keen alpine gardener, had read my book, thought it excellent, and got me to answer all his outstanding queries. Then, in his official capacity, he demanded far more than my royalties had yet totalled. Mansfield, from experience with his own book, put me on to his own accountants.

Since then I have always employed an accountant, whose fees are a tax-deductible expense. Fifteen books later my advice to any author is to have your income tax handled by the Trust Department of your bank. Let this expert do the arguing with the authorities, pay nothing until he says you have to, and remember that you employ him at the expense of the Government.

After V.J. Day, Powered Mountings (my father's firm) at Surbiton closed down, and he, retiring on his schoolmaster's pension, sold No. 1 Tower Road for far too little (about £700), to the tenant who had rented it through the war, using it to take in boarders very successfully. The Surbiton house was rented and he had never taken up the offer from the landlord to buy it for £400 at the height of the buzzbomb period. We decided we should look for somewhere that my parents and I could share down in Somerset, with a garden, where I might perhaps run an alpine nursery.

Mansfield solved our problem by finding us a house lease-hold at £150 a year for five years. Called 'Farm House', it was in Wells, with a walled garden most of which was taken up by two hard tennis courts, an orchard, two more hard tennis courts, a small kitchen garden and a quantity of lawn. Judge Jeffries had lodged here when his Bloody Assizes visited Wells after the Monmouth Rebellion. The house was old and lovely with a big *Wisteria sinensis* on the front, a cobbled courtyard, and

what had been a large, long barn and was now The Barn
Theatre, holding audiences of up to 200 and run by a Miss
Carritt, in her eighties, and Miss Hollins or 'Holly', an ex-Wren
in her forties. The rest of the farm building held vast quantities
of 'props' and costumes, with the wicker baskets to pack them
in when they went to amateur dramatic societies all over
Somerset. The theatre was usually used for competitions,
rehearsals, and classes, which Miss Carritt took with professional skill and fees.

Managing the garden and tennis courts was too much for her
— a five-year lease would see her into her nineties, and keep
the house in condition to sell separately if she then wanted to
retire. Mansfield offered to release me to start what I could at
Farm House with my parents as he could take on Millard's
foreman as manager in my place. From Mansfield's angle, the
chance of my health giving out remained a risk, and the older
man would probably be better at running the expanding
business.

I had done the hard work, pulled the nursery round and got
it going, wiping out in my own mind the failure of the past, and
I felt I had done enough. There is a limit to the time a man can
work flat out, week after endless week, with hasty holidays and
not even evenings in which to write. So my parents came down,
fell in love with Farm House, and we signed the lease, though
we had to wait several weeks in lodgings while Miss Carritt
and Holly moved out into a cottage they had bought as a
retirement home.

My father took on rolling the hardcourts and booking and
charging for them, which more than covered the rent each
week, and mother and I attacked the garden with the help of
Piper and Mrs Piper. Piper was a pensioned farmworker who
scythed with speed and grace, cutting down the weeds along
the disused lane that gave us a back way, for compost material,
at intervals so timed that he killed out everything but the grass
in two years. Mrs Piper was small and bustling, and cleaned the
house from top to bottom with great grumblings about the state
'them two' had let it get into compared with what it was 40
years ago, releasing mother for the gardening she loved.

Every path and border was edged and overlapped with great
clumps of Mrs Sinkins pinks. It was just the right time to root
them so I advertised unrooted cuttings in *The Horticultural
Trades Journal*, calling our new enterprise 'Farm House Plants'.

The result was a flood of orders, including one for 10,000, and all three of us cut back the clumps, counted and packed. We must have grossed about £600 on them, and the only expenses were postage and packing. Piper fetched us barrowloads of boxes from a sweet shop, and as unrooted cuttings are lighter than plants, was able to wheel the packages to the post.

As they flowered I labeled the Aubrietias, and sold unrooted cuttings. I split up the herbaceous plants, especially a vast clump of *Iris siberica* that had flourished through the War on a leaky shed gutter, and cashed the post-war shortage.

Our worry was that though I could build up a small wholesale nursery business, post-war shortages would end, and so would our lease, so we had to find something we could sell to 'take away'. My first idea was the 'Man' tool cleaner, a traditional wooden tool used by the 'navvies' who dug the navigation canals across pre-railway Britain to clean their spades. I found a local firm willing to turn these out as blanks, and my father finished them off in his workshop in one of the ex-stables. These sold well.

Our next idea was the 'Slopemeter', which was the curved spirit level from the dip and bank indicator on a Hawker Hart fighter, which was obsolete even in 1938. I bought up all the spares from an advertisement in *Exchange and Mart*. Mounted in a piece of wood it could be used to test the slope of a drain. I advertised them quite expensively in a surveyors' paper and they sold well, especially a six-foot long model of which ten went to the Sudan Plantation Syndicate where I had failed to get a job all those years ago. Unfortunately, in the end we ran out of dip and bank indicators.

The real success that grew out of these non-gardening enterprises based on my father's ingenuity and my horticultural trade knowledge was the garden label venture. From October 3rd, 1939, to November, 1953, soft wood timber was rationed, because it took shipping space, and individual citizens were allowed £1 worth a month for personal use. Even then that was not enough to build a chicken house or dog kennel. Industry was also rationed, so no allowance was made for garden labels.

We heard of a firm at Avonmouth that had a huge dump of Douglas fir strips, used for separators that went under the lead plates in the accumulators that drove submarines under water. Dad and I went over in Puddleduck and Dad sketched out a gadget that would chop a point on one end and cut the label off the strip adjustable to four, five, or six inches long. The strips were about an eighth of an inch thick and three quarters wide, rather dark coloured, but a gardening pencil wrote well on them. Dad designed the machine, to run off a belt from the timberyard shafting, and away we went. Our bottleneck was getting the labels bundled, for we could not get cardboard boxes made for them and we had to bundle them ourselves after they were delivered to us in very greasy boxes that had held lard from America.

We started advertising in the trade press and built up a trade. We could have shot ahead had we been able to produce them in quantities enough to get a wholesale sundriesman handling them, but my parents had a great objection to employing labour. This was quite right, for we had little capital and could do only what we could fit in to Farm House. Timber rationing would not last for ever and we should spread our effort over enterprises we could manage ourselves.

One of these was cut flowers, which I grew in a bed between the Barn Theatre and the orchard, not to send to market, for even to Bristol the rail rate would have killed it, but to sell in mixed bunches first to the tennis players and then their friends, until Mother built up a steady backdoor trade at half-a-crown a bunch. They were mainly hardy annuals, some autumn-sown for earliness, chosen to last well in water and also for unusualness, such as *Malope grandiflora*, *Phacelia tanacetifolia*, *Gilia capitata*, Annual Scabious, and some of the less common everlastings for drying, such as *Rhodanthe carneum* and *Ammobium alatum*

I also planted up what we called 'The Fold' because we kept alpine phloxes there in a raised bed with a dry wall round it, and the 'Ben Bank'. This was a long, sunny, sloping bed beside the hedge that divided the kitchen garden from the lawn, planted solid with Helianthemums, so christened because the leading varieties were called after Scottish mountains — Ben Dearg, Ben Hope, Ben Vorlich, Hen Heckla, and Ben Nevis. In all I had 25 varieties to be sold, like the *Phlox subulata* and *P. douglasii* hybrids, as rooted or unrooted cuttings, advertised at the exact time to put them in to catch the eye of alpine propagators who never had enough of the best varieties.

Then disaster struck. The factory dump of battery separators caught fire, together with a great pile of beautifully smoothed hardwood sticks 16 inches long, each with a hole near the top to take white tape for marking cleared paths across landmine fields, which I was selling for flower stakes. All we had left were in the shed for immediate use, a mere 20,000 labels, and that was the lot.

To replace our stock I advertised in *Exchange and Mart*, and had replies from a toy-making firm in Birmingham willing to use their offcuts, a beehive maker in Bath, a joinery works in Bristol making something that left them with offcuts exactly 15 inches long, 2 inches wide and half an inch thick, and a wood-working factory near an L.C.C. depot where they could get unlimited cut-down plane trees. My father investigated their sample of London Plane (*Platanus acerifolia*), a very close-grained, white timber that can be cut with a high-speed circular saw so it is beautifully smooth to pencil on, designed a gadget with a gang of little saws and sent it to them. They became our main supplier.

The Bristol firm had only to point their offcuts and they were ideal for the large nursery labels for roses, fruit trees, and all growing stock. The problem was that they had only about 300 of these offcuts a week, which they sent us once a month when their lorry came our way, so I found another firm who had unrationed poplar wood. It did not make such a lovely label, but I could have 18-inch lengths, making them handier but less lasting.

Throughout this period, when I was enjoying a happy family life with my parents, and because of Mother's preference for giving us fruit rather than puddings and pastries, my health remained good, and only two events were of permanent importance, both connected with Richard de la Mare.

He sent me a manuscript, written in long hand on both sides of the trade notepaper of an asparagus grower, W. F. Kidner, asking me if I thought it a book or just a long, rambling letter. I read it and replied that Kidner was a genius and the best asparagus grower in Britain, but his manuscript was muddled. He then asked me to advise the writer on how to make it a better book, saying, 'Never mind about spelling, typing mistakes, poor punctuation and grammatical errors. I can get plenty of M.A.s of Somerville at £700 a year to correct those. What are scarce are good books by writers with something to say that is interesting and original.'

So I began my 25 years as a publisher's reader for Faber and Faber. Faber and Faber subjects ranged from art and architecture, through biography, history, medical subjects and nursing, to theatre, ballet, and travel. My field — farming and gardening, especially organic — was only a small part of the work of a large and famous firm, and as Richard said once when I was in his headmaster's-study-like office, 'We do not really like losing money on a book, but we will if a book is good enough.' I was what would now be called an editor, and so many of the writers whose books I helped have thanked me in their prefaces that I think I must hold some sort of record.

Richard (it was 15 years before we were using first names, moving slowly from 'Dear Mr Hills' to 'Dear Hills' and 'My dear Hills') asked me to undertake the hitherto missing book on the propagation of alpines, and I spent the next five years writing it. The reason it had never been written was that anyone qualified to write it knew how much work it would be. You can look up descriptions of plants, but to give practical information on how to propagate the 2,500 alpines my book covered, you had to know your plants with your hands. I knew only the easiest 1,500. For the rare and difficult 1,000 I was helped by Mr G. H. Preston, curator of the Rock Garden at Kew, and Mr Peter Benton, his assistant, with Jose Perez, my one time propagator from Orchard Neville.

I always read manuscripts looking for where a book 'came alive' and took hold of the author, for inside every fat mass of dull words, clichés, and quotations may be a real book struggling to get out. My *Propagation of Alpines* took on a life of its own, attracting the help of men greater and more knowledgeable than myself and demanding the best I could give, like a talented child, for a book is a writer's child and only mothers know how demanding children can be.

As the book began to grow, so did the business and so did the garden. We were now half way through our lease, and to write that book I had to be near London, Kew, Wisley, and Faber and Faber as well, and to get to nurseries for photographs. Farm House Plants had grown out of shortages that would pass. We had to sell the business while they lasted, for a sum that would give us enough capital to buy a house — and house prices were rising all the time. So we advertised our garden sundries business and quite soon a small saw mill up in the Mendips agreed to buy our stock and goodwill, plus files and ideas. I think we got £1,200 for it and though we had all three put a great deal into it, the work was getting us down, for

Mother and Dad were feeling the strain, apart from my need for time to write.

The 'business' became 'Mrs M. A. Hills, Alpine Cutting Specialist' — which she had become — and she and my father ran the tennis courts, sold the cut blooms and unrooted cuttings from the Ben Bank and the Fold, while I chased my photographs, took Maurice Wilson who did the line drawings to Kew and Wisley, and made trip after trip to Barton St David, near Baltonsborough, where Jose lived, to ask him about alpines.

During these weeks of 1947, I saw an advertisement in the H.T.J. offering *Phyteuma comosum* at 10 shillings a dozen, which was the alpine equivalent to seeing a Stradivarius violin advertised for £100. It was advertised with a number of gentians, meconopsis and primulas, all brutes to raise from seed. I knew I could never succeed myself in growing that Phyteuma from the Tyrol, with its lovely, almost stemless, blue bell flowers and rather fleshy leaves. It is the most slug-beloved of any alpine, so difficult that really keen Alpine Garden Society members are reputed to yodel at it to make it feel at home. I ordered a dozen, adding 2 shillings extra for postage, expecting to get *P. scheuchzeri* which is tough and easy but not so lovely.

When they arrived they were *P. comosum* all right, and very good plants too, so I sent them straight off to G. H. Preston at Kew. You can acknowledge help in a preface, you can arrange for your publisher to pay a fee out of your royalties; but if you take help and advice from the curator of a rock garden, you cannot possibly give him a tip however much you appreciate the trouble he has taken. But it is perfectly correct to send a dozen rarities as a present to an alpine man who had everything until the slugs ate it.

I immediately wrote to H. G. and P. M. Lyall and asked how they raised it and the other rarities on offer, and fixed up to visit their nursery at Bricket Wood, near Watford. Instead of a car to meet me at the station was a tall and sunburnt girl with a lovely voice, who arrived riding a heavy trade bicycle and towing a lady's light-weight beside her. Riding two bicycles can be done, but it does take skill.

She was 'P. M.', for Phyllis Margaret, a graduate of Swanley Horticultural College, in partnership with her father. She told me he had been crippled by polio and spent his time either in a wheelchair or crawling round the nursery. I insisted on riding the trade bike, which I hadn't done since Parris's, with my suitcase in the big front carrier.

H.G. was a small, Scottish, dynamo of energy, who had run what was probably the first public relations agency and certainly the first opinion poll, long before Gallup. He wore trousers reinforced with leather so he could get out of his chair and crawl about on the paths, weeding and inspecting his seed pans. He was a genius at raising things from seed, and was making a good living selling the really awkward species to the trade. His secrets were good drainage, careful watering, and the energy that determination to overcome handicaps can bring. I took copious notes, he took photographs, and we built a friendship, or rather two friendships, that day. They also added priceless knowledge to the book that was growing into my life.

In November, 1948, I stayed for a weekend with my mother's brother, my Uncle Gordon, who was managing director of John D. Wood, the estate agents, at Hadley Hurst, Barnet. He had invited me because he had an idea. He wanted me to grow him a million celery plants a year to plant on 50 acres of his fen farm, on a nursery he would start on his land, building a bungalow for the three of us, at Southery in Norfolk, between Littleport and Downham Market. Until it was ready we could live in the empty top flat at Hadley Hurst. I could build the nursery round this main crop including experimental crops for his grass drier.

I insisted that if I was to grow celery plants on that scale I wanted electric soil-warming wires like those in our propagating house at Orchard Neville, not manure hotbeds without any control over the heat, and precast concrete frames that would not rot, with dutchlights that one man could handle, not heavy six-foot pitlights. He was all for it, and promised me Ted Reed as a foreman, the best celery plant grower in Southery, and only Ted and the vicar would know that I was nephew of the owner.

It was then that I saw my first comfrey — the plant that was to change my life. It was in the form of a steel engraving from Sutton's *Farm Seeds Catalogue* for 1879 which Uncle Gordon showed me, illustrating a single sheet advertising handout from Websters Nurseries of Stock, Essex. 'He's rather a naughty old man,' said my uncle. 'He's given the analysis of marrowstem kale on a fresh weight basis and his Russian comfrey on a dry-matter one, so it looks is if it had about eight times more protein. But suppose it really *does* grow a hundred tons an acre?'

So we added Russian comfrey to *Lathyrus sylvestris* (a fodder pea from the U.S.A.), a set of the 'Grunder Grasses' which were pure clones of cocksfoot (*Dactylis glomerata*) raised by a Dr Grunder at Beltsville, roughly the U.S. equivalent to Rothamsted, an acre of celery to grow blight-free seed by spraying it with Bordeaux mixture once a fortnight, and some special peppermint plants Uncle Gordon had found in Germany when he was there just after the war with a party of British industrialists to look for any inventions worth taking as reparations.

My own more modest contribution would be Gypsophila Bristol Fairy, the double white, which was then expensively grafted because it would not root from cuttings, but I now knew that beta-indole-butyric acid would root it fast and well, and as time went on I would add other ideas. The beauty of the scheme, in Uncle Gordon's eyes, was that he could run a research nursery, give his nephew a chance to show what he could do, and provide a retirement home for his elder sister Mabel, and William her husband whose knowledge he respected, all at the expense of his farm income tax. He could even get the bungalow off it as a 'tied cottage'.

7

The Coming of Comfrey

I PLANTED the first comfrey in my life in February, 1949. Hodson, the best tractor ploughman on Manor Farm, Southery, Norfolk, deep-ploughed, cultivated and harrowed the five acres of good, light loam for the new nursery, then asked me where I wanted the comfrey row. We bolted a steel stake, shaped by the local blacksmith, to his tool bar, then drove his giant yellow crawler to make me a single furrow straight as a garden line up my land for the comfrey, two more for my stock plants of gypsophila, and another two for the standard briars on which to bud our roses. Then he roared away singing *Lili Marlene* at the top of his voice.

He had been the best horseman on the farm and was rumoured to hiss through his teeth still as he cleaned his tractor. Certainly he sang to it, as his 16-year-old son Eric did to Daisy and Blossom, the last two horses, which I borrowed for jobs on the nursery. Ted Reed, my foreman, the last man alive in the village to have harvested wheat with a scythe, and still capable of reaping an acre a day where a field was too badly laid by the wind for the combines to cut, made up the rest of my staff. He, Eric, and I put in the hundred comfrey offsets from Websters Nurseries, three feet apart along the 320-foot-long furrow.

My temporary lodgings were with Mrs Jeffries, a widowed ex-ladies maid, who owned the cottage by the corner the lorries went round to the sugar beet factory. If they rounded it too fast they shot some of the load, which she collected. With the red salad beet from her long and crowded garden they made a powerful vintage that looked like a claret but was nearer an undistilled rum, with an after-taste of her fertile soil and a kick like a colt's. New curates were urged to visit Mrs Jeffries who was such a pillar of the church; then the village watched to see if they had to wheel their bicycles home after two glasses of the brew she remained convinced was entirely non-alcoholic.

My permanent lodgings in Southery were with Mrs Hobbes, who owned six acres of fen land, where she kept pigs and raised sugarbeet, chicory, and potatoes. The family consisted of Tobe (Tobias) her husband, her 20-year-old son, Effie her 15-year-old niece, plus 'Pop', not her father as I imagined but a 90-year-old retired grocer, another lodger, and Waggles the dog. Once I gave Tobe a pair of my old green breeches but she would not let him wear them; they were 'unsuited to his station' — being gamekeeper's breeches, and he was a pigman.

In Southery almost every family owned or rented some land. They started work at 6.30 a.m., stopped for a sandwich meal at about 10.30 and finished at one. Men earned £1 for this 6-hour day, five days a week, and women 12 shillings. They then went home, had a cooked meal and a rest, and started work on their own land. It was quite common for two men to work for each other on the same day, cancelling out their money. I have never known harder and better workers. Where smallholders all grow the same crops the labour peaks come together. Southery Nurseries would add extra crops with different seasonal demands. I started by 'demanding' Tobe whenever his land could spare him, and whoever Strawson could spare from the Manor Farm.

The nursery consisted of four acres of back land and an acre of frontage which gave us a way in from the road, and barely enough to fit a bungalow, for Mrs Jeffries's cottage and garden took the lion's share. A straw bale wall about 12 feet high and two bales thick, built and bonded like bricks, ran across the top of the frontage land to shelter the seedling celery. Behind it were two small wooden sheds over 10-feet-deep pits for 'Ladies' and 'Gents', and in front a straw bale-walled shelter roofed with corrugated iron. There was a stand-pipe to which we could connect the hose coupling for an overhead irrigator, consisting of a number of sections of galvanized iron piping with nozzles at intervals, which fitted together and oscillated with the pressure of the water. This was for watering celery seedlings for which the land had been ploughed, cultivated, and harrowed. Otherwise there was nothing. Nowhere dry to keep seeds, nowhere to lock up the tools, and no electricity.

I spent the first two days with Ted, Tobe, and Eric, digging out four inches of top soil to lay the foundations of three concrete frames each each 104 feet long and 5 feet wide, wheeling and stacking some of this first class loam for potting soil. Then we dug eight inches deeper for 25 feet of each frame, to fill with coke ashes for extra drainage under the cutting section. The soil-warming wires went on top of this, to have four inches of sharp sand on top, while the rest had good top soil over them for celery sowing.

I had not even a telephone to curse through about the delays on the wires and transformers, dutchlights, the soil-warming apparatus, and finally the poles, the cable, and the electricians to connect us to the mains. I had to go up to the Manor Farm House to abuse, threaten, beg, coax, and implore the makers of all we bought to deliver in time to sow those million celery. In desperation, we carried the least rotten of the old frames down, walking across the fields from the Manor Farm, with five borrowed farmworkers inside it because it was too awkward to carry by tractor and trailer.

This of course brought the electricians, with their cable and poles, the day after we had piled in the manure from the farm to start the traditional hot bed. Ted started sowing thinly and well, with a screen made of barrage balloon cloth on six-foot stakes, in place of traditional sacking, to keep the wind from blowing the seed away. By then the frames were up, and the slopemeter I had brought from Wells (a 'master tool' in the opinion of Ted, who had vast experience of land drainage) came in very well for setting the concrete frame sides on bricks to follow the slope of our land.

As soon as we got our frames going, I took on more women, all recommended by Ted for celery skills. They were Mrs Jeffries, her friend Miss Porter, Mrs Worledge, and Mrs Whitehand. The last lady was famous for having once earned £2 in a day pricking out celery plants. When Ted pointed her out to me as she bicycled down the village street, I thought she was a large black bear. Her husband bred Norwich Roller Canaries as a hobby and promised her a fur coat if ever he won a first prize at Norwich Show. He did, too, but its value was only £10. He bought one probably dating from the 1900s, made of black bearskin. She wore it every winter as she cycled to work and home again on piecework jobs on windy fen farms. Her sail area was considerable, so battling against a wind coming straight in from the North Sea must have been gruelling, but she worked hard, fast, and cheerfully.

My team of women had only to be shown a job and they would go straight at it, because the work was new and interesting. They planted 5,000 briars for bush roses, got my stock

84

delphiniums, phlox and physostegia into the frames, and when I showed them how to take root cuttings of the last two, they tucked in over the warming wires with flying fingers. As soon as my gypsophila Bristol Fairy started to make new shoots, I taught them how to take cuttings with razor blades and insert them in the sand frames after dipping each into Seradix B, strength one — the mixture of beta indole butyric acid in talc, tinted pink to show it was for use with soft cuttings, which they called 'face powder'.

Ted sowed his Waring's White celery seed, which would grow so large on the fen farm that most went to Glasgow for making tinned celery hearts at a special contract price. His batches kept pace with our pricking out and planting. In the intervals he sowed Blackmore- and Langdon-strain delphiniums and Velocity cabbage, which I knew from Baltonsborough would grow from sowing to eating in 10 weeks. This was the first crop we sold. I advertised it in the *Horticultural Trades Journal*, sold the lot at £3 a thousand, and so impressed Uncle Gordon that we decided to grow other brassica plants in the Manor Farm celery frame when it was empty.

My parents were now living at Hadley Hurst, where my father was using his ingenuity to help Uncle Gordon with various ideas he had as part of the work he was doing for the Ministry of Agriculture and the N.F.U. As chairman of the Crop Drying Committee he was behind the great expansion in dried grass for cattle food, and many less successful ventures.

In March I took an afternoon off and went down to an open day at the ICI grass driers at Wissington Farm. The object was to show how beet tops, chicory tops, and above all brussels sprout tops, had been converted by that special drier into a high-protein, high-carotene meal for pigs, poultry, and milking cattle, saving imported cake and using existing grass driers when there was no grass to dry.

All the farming press sent reporters, as well as several nationals including *The Daily Telegraph*, and our agent from Norwich was busy taking orders for tons of brussels sprout meal. Claude had cleared all the sprout stems from nearby growers without having to pay for them, the trick being to put the stems through a shredder. When the Captains and Kings had departed, I rode home on my bicycle. I had been introduced as 'Mr Hills, Manager of our Research Nursery'. After the open day the farms bought me a 125 c.c. Royal Enfield two-stroke (1948) to use between the two farms, for part of the nursery would be down on the fen land. The War Agricultural Committee did not recognize motor bikes, so I got the allowance for an Austin Seven, depositing my coupons and drawing a gallon at a time, for trips down to Hadley Hurst.

On one of these trips I came back with German peppermint clump in a sack tied on my carrier, and sliced the long white roots into inch-long sections, as well as taking two jointed cuttings all down the stems. Then the Grunder grasses arrived by air from Beltsville, 25 of each, numbered individual 'clones' — the term for varieties of anything propagated vegetatively, ensuring that every plant is identical. I set them out in the frame and they grew and grew, needing splitting about once every three weeks. I remember I.34 was the fastest in the race to grow enough for a set of replicated plots on the land behind the straw-bale wall.

A hundred plants, cut and weighed to give an absolutely fair comparison, would be planted to find which was the best to try growing from sections of their couch-grass-like roots. My job was to grow enough to find the best for trials at research stations against the various strains of seed-grown cocksfoots, like those bred at Aberystwyth. Uncle Gordon had seen Dr Grunder's work in the USA and had volunteered to try the idea in the hope of starting fields of identical grass on the fen, where couch grass grew well enough to hold the black and blowing peat. Soon I had five times as many I.34s as H.9s, the slowest of the batch, and solved the problem by planting specimen plots of the strongest, which would obviously be needed in greater quantities.

I carried on with these, and the peppermint which was doubling and redoubling ready to fill a trial strip, while the celery campaign raged. Trailer loads of fen peat had arrived and been dug in by Ted to make up four-foot-wide beds. Tobe, Eric, and the women arrived with their 'dockey bags' for their mid-shift break, and their tools — small bricklayer's trowels, with which they took out straight lines across the beds, each holding 500 celery seedlings. They had rag-stuffed sacks to kneel on, and never stopped gossiping no matter how fast their hands flew at their skilled but monotonous task.

My three men were 'flopping' the seedlings in thin spadefuls into potato-chitting trays to keep up the supply for the swiftest celery women in Southery who were breaking records because, thanks to the soil-warming wires and Ted's thin sowing, the seedlings were a level batch so little time was wasted on throwing out small plants. Even the relatively slow workers were earning 35 shillings a day and Mrs Whitehand topped £2 day after day. As soon as the transplants were growing ahead fast under irrigation, I had the team on day work filling my frames with cuttings and root cuttings.

The estate handyman had laid us a nine-foot square of concrete for mixing soil and converting it to hexagonal soil blocks with our two hand 'block' makers. Ted and Tobe became very fast at this, keeping pace with the women potting our well-rooted gypsophila cuttings, and setting them out in the frames. All too soon it was time to lift the now 4 to 6 inch high celery plants, count and cram them into chitting trays, and load them on the lorry for the fen women to plant on the ploughed ridges of black peat in the huge flat fields of the two fen farms. We also planted an acre of the nursery with celery for seed.

When the celery rush was over, Ted and I went up to the far end of the nursery to see how the comfrey was getting on. The furrow we had planted with three-inch-long, brown-barked root sections, each with a growing point, had become a three-foot-high row of inch-thick stems and small, purple, hanging, bell flowers above clumps of large leaves up to 30 inches long. It was now mid-June and the leys of pedigree Aberystwyth grasses were at their best and, as Ted said, 'If Strawson's cows will eat comfrey when they have all that good grass to go for, that'd be a fair test.' I went up to the farmhouse and arranged to borrow a milk-recording balance, some sacks, Daisy, and the tip cart for the next morning.

Ted scythed 50 plants at ground level, and we stuffed the fresh foliage into sacks totalling 200 lb. Planted three feet apart each way, 4,840 plants go to the acre, and at 2,240 pounds to a ton, our first cut would have given eight tons an acre. We loaded the sacks on the cart and Eric drove us from field to field. Old Strawson was amazed at the spectacle of his Friesians heaving themselves up to come across for the comfrey. A single cow would come over to the cart out of curiosity, and then the others would follow and clear the ration we threw in. Though Daisy and Blossom did not fancy it at first, Eric fed them some each time we borrowed them and they liked it when they knew it better. The next day we cut the other 50 and the cows were waiting for the cart which we took round at roughly the same time in the morning, and finished all the comfrey before they went back to the grass. The pigs ate it most greedily.

Most of the Manor Farm fields were sown with single Aberystwyth numbered varieties, so that crops of expensive seed could be harvested from them in rotation, and all were generously fed with nitrogen fertilizers for high yields and a high carbohydrate level. Even inorganic farmers today use ley mixtures that include deep-rooting herbs to add variety to a grazing diet, but the farming fashion then was for a nitrogen-forced 'early bite', and for growing four identical blades of grass where two different ones grew before.

Organic farmers rely on deep rooters such as chicory, and lucerne where this will grow, to bring trace elements and minerals into circulation from the subsoil. Comfrey roots penetrate four feet and even 10 in some cases, and are fast and greedy mineral gatherers. Cattle, pigs and horses, especially when pregnant, crave mineral-rich food, and the cows on Manor Farm, grazing only shallow-rooting grasses went for the comfrey as they will for wild garlic if they feel unwell.

In June we had enough peppermint plants for a trial row, while still increasing them in the frames for our target of two acres by the spring of 1950. As the leaves began to darken and flower stems to start, showing that the oil level was rising, I wrote to Messrs W. J. Bush who supply oil of peppermint for making sweets. They asked for a sample and we sent a sackful by passenger train. They sent us a cheque for £30, the value of the oil in the sample, and asked for all we could supply, offering to send an expert to help with the harvest next autumn.

By the end of August the gypsophila planted out in its soil blocks had begun to flower, growing almost as fast as the comfrey, far faster than the stock plants. I sent for flower boxes from George Monro, who told me that the market liked large bunches, eight to a 'trunk' as they called the biggest size. Luckily it was dry and sunny, so we rigged up a table with straw bales and corrugated iron sheets, and I taught my remaining women, Ted, and Eric, bunching blooms for Covent Garden. Ordinary gypsophila has single flowers, but our Bristol Fairy, with double blooms, making far better 'floral tributes' with carnations or orchids, is always scarce. So we cut and cut till the price fell and Ted was cutting the last of the crop with his scythe before it went over. Then I made my first commercial size compost heap, with pig manure as activator, slaked lime layers, and a tarpaulin rick sheet over the top to hold the heat.

When we came to dig the plants in November we found the reason for this extraordinary bloom bonanza. Normally, roots of gypsophila Bristol Fairy are like slender parsnips, and as the hormone which directs their growth is weak, they have to be grafted. If their cut stems are dipped in a far more powerful artificial hormone, they grow fine roots first then, when the effect wears off, convert them to their natural, small parsnip type. The result is a magnificent root system, a mass of bloom, and a plant as hard to pack as a frozen octopus.

We sold most of our plants to Bloom's Nurseries near Diss, who took them away in the gross cornflake boxes we got free from grocers, hoping, but failing, to get root cuttings off them. In 1950 we solved the problem. We grew the cuttings in tarred paper three-inch pots which constricted the roots and sent them twisting down in a corkscrew shape so they fitted easily into boxes.

Mrs Hobbes was, unfortunately, an excellent orthodox cook, so in the winter of 1949 I went down with a high temperature 'attack' and had to go into Addenbrookes Hospital in Cambridge. To explain my 103° F. temperature, malaria was suspected, though the last case of malaria from the fens was in the 1900s. I got out in time to spend Christmas at home, now Hadley Hurst, then saw another specialist who suspected Addison's Disease.

In January I was back and took the nursery round another year. The Estate carpenter had built me a small but beautifully made shed as an office, with a telephone at last, and we now had a 20-feet-long bloom-bunching and packing shed. As the frames were ready, we got the peppermint planted on about two and a half acres of fen where it raced ahead as the sun warmed the black soil, with the weeds racing too. We did not need the old frame from the Manor Farm, so I planted it full of comfrey root cuttings, obtained by digging up 20 of my plants, with care to get up every fragment, and slicing them into inch-long sections to sow in rows like broad beans. They swarmed rather than grew in the spent hotbed from the celery and brassica plants.

The 1950 crop was at the rate of 45 tons an acre, so we had enough to put through the shredder and into the grass drier. Unlike dried grass, which is high in protein and carotene in the spring but falls in July and August, dried comfrey maintained very nearly the same analysis through the season, though the fibre increased as the flower stems grew. The following table, on a dry matter basis, shows the pattern:

	Protein	Fibre	Ash	Oil	Carbo-hydrate	Beta carotene
	%	%	%	%	%	p.p.m.
Comfrey (Southery)	21.80	14.00	13.60	2.10	37.40	122
Beet Tops "	16.23	11.18	9.44	0.92	48.92	14
Dried Grass (spring)	24.80	22.20	—	—	—	438
Dried Grass (good)	20.3	14.0	8.0	5.8	41.9	—
Dried Grass (poor)	12.1	22.4	9.0	2.2	42.3	—

Dried grass and meal such as that from sprout stems was sold on the protein level. Though comfrey meal came out a rather dark brown instead of the bright green the market preferred, Claude, the farm manager, saw a great advantage for it. If it would produce a 21.80 meal when the grass protein fell, just enough could be added to a poor sample of grass meal to bring it up to 15 to 18 per cent — meaning a better price for the whole batch. So he planted a wide strip near the drier with offsets from my ex-celery frame.

Ted's scythe came in again for harvesting the peppermint on the fen that August. The expert from W. J. Bush was a short, round little man who wore a tie with black and white diagonal stripes like a 'bulls-eye', and kept nibbling leaves of the crop, because the flavour baffled him. It was good, and extra strong, which would mean less expensive oil to the 'humbug'. He kept trying to find where we had got it, but we were not telling. His directions were to cut it when the flowers were open exactly halfway up the spikes, and to leave it drying until it was as dry as hay that is just too wet to stack without heating.

It took Ted two days to cut the hectare of peppermint and though it was much easier than wheat the strong scent made his eyes water, so he borrowed a civilian gas mask which was most effective. We turned the crop and raked it with Daisy and Blossom, who did not seem to mind the smell, though dogs hated it, and when we had it finally tied up in the special fine-mesh nets supplied, and stowed these in the hay barn, no dog would willingly cross where it had been stacked. A week after we got it away to W. J. Bush I was on holiday, camping with Ken, and he tasted the peppermint on the bread and butter I had just spread for him.

During this period I was reading manuscripts for Faber and Faber, including that of *Fertility Farming* by R. W. Newman Turner. He advocated a minimum-ploughing system of ley farming with tripod hay, self feed silage, and kale, which produced ¾ d a gallon extra profit for organic methods than inorganic.

Like most of the pioneer organic writers, he was preoccupied with arguing with orthodoxy, using a wealth of quotations from other books, newspapers, and magazines. None of the 'authorities' he quoted were as good as he was, for when he wrote of his own farm from his own experience he wrote like William Cobbett.

Farmer's Weekly, the leading inorganic farming weekly, bought a farm at that time and ran it out of their profits. Out of the profits of his organic farm, Newman Turner ran *The Farmer*, the first and perhaps the best organic farming publication among the many that sprang up in the post-war years. It had a section called 'The gardener' where my first article on comfrey was published. This drew enquiries for plants from organic farmers, and I sold plants from that crowded frame.

The late Mrs P. B. Greer was one customer. She farmed near Colchester and had marched in the first suffragette procession beside Elizabeth Garrett Anderson, Britain's first lady doctor, carrying a very tall banner with: 'Lady Farmer. Votes for my Labourers, but none for Me?' sewn on it in large letters with the help of those labourers' wives. She was the first to buy 4,480 plants and put in a whole acre. Others were Ian G. Macdonald of Goudhurst, Kent, who put in a thousand for his pigs, Jim Lackenbry of Middlesborough, Yorks, also breeding pigs, and Paul Weir of Alton, Hants. He had been an agricultural college student before the war and had started a smallholding in a derelict wood, living in a converted railway carriage with his young wife, near a Ministry of Food depot full of condemned dates. He was not allowed any pig food because he had not kept pigs before the war, and hoped that comfrey would provide the protein in an all-date diet. I saw his holding a few years later, with sties made of date-box wood and land carpeted with date stones that had passed harmlessly through the pigs, and fortunately do not germinate in Hampshire. Paul was an example of how far up the farming ladder training, youth, ingenuity, and energy will take you.

At Southery I had no congenial cycling or youth hostelling company, and my outings were limited to Saturday shopping and library book changing trips to Downham Market or Kings Lynn. I wrote and wrote, keeping pace with the manuscripts and pouring out articles, including three that appeared in the *Evening News* and earned 10 guineas each, and later led to the features editor nominating me as a freelance member of the N.U.J. I wrote of alpines, of natural history, including 'The flight of the water beetle', based on the day when a swarm of water boatman beetles took the dutchlights for a new pond and hit them with a noise like a hailstorm. I got into all the gardening papers, including *The Smallholder* which took one article on comfrey that started us digging up more of the original stock plants.

Finally, just when I was counting the days to Christmas, 1950, Mrs Hobbes's cooking caught up with me, and I got a diarrhoea and high temperature attack of powerful proportions. Willing though Mrs Hobbes was to nurse me — her council house at least had an upstairs water-powered lavatory — Dr Burnett sent me to Addenbrookes Hospital again, by ambulance.

I think I went up to 104° because I was delirious and kept hearing the engines of Wellingtons taking off with a full bomb load. I was then caught up in the festivities of Christmas in hospital, with a tree in each ward, presents for every patient, choirs singing carols round the wards, and a pantomime to which patients were taken in wheelchairs or stretchers on trolleys — as I was.

Claude had, of course, told Uncle Gordon what had happened. He had telephoned my cousin Cicely (now Dame Cicely Saunders, founder and director of St Christopher's Hospice, and originator of the Hospice movement in many countries) who had laid on a friend to nurse me privately, and then sent up the Rolls, bringing my parents. I was a long time recovering, and we finally decided that I could not carry on managing nurseries any more, for either my own capital or someone else's was at the mercy of the unknown factor inside me. The best thing I could do was to try to live by writing, a decision that was easier because I received my six free copies of *The Propagation of Alpines* while I was at Hadley Hurst.

Uncle Gordon kept on my pay during my convalescence, and for a few trips to Southery where Ted was steadily filling the comfrey orders my articles had brought, to wind the nursery down. I had also saved about £350 from writing and reading fees which would give me a start as a full-time writer, typing his way to fame in a bed-sitting room. I chose Blackheath as a site for the new enterprise, because Ken lived at 99 Shooter's Hill Road in a bedsitter, which would mean motorcycling and camping weekends when I could spare the time from earning a living.

I stayed with Ken while I hunted the cards in newspaper shop windows, and quite quickly located a boarding house full of young engineers working on a local power station, plus two Chinese and one Ghanaian student. My room contained a chest of drawers, a curtained-off recess with hooks behind it for suits and coats and shoes below, a dressing table with jug and basin, a bed (which was comfortable), two chairs, a gas meter with a gas ring for boiling kettles and a thirst for shillings and pennies, and a very flimsy bamboo table.

This would not take the kick and weight of a hard working typewriter, so I went to a second-hand furniture shop and got an ex-L.C.C. desk, made of solid oak for 5 shillings, and because I had spent a whole £15 of my capital on an elderly Barlock typewriter, both were delivered free. They served me long and loyally, with the desk becoming first a potting bench and then the table by the gate of the Bocking Trial Ground to hold the cash box and tea tickets on open days. The Barlock was the last all-British machine, built like a battleship, which hammered out the words as blacksmiths hammered horseshoes, rather than 'processing' them. It died from irreplaceable essential parts wearing away, as all good typewriters do.

It earned my living for the next seven years, typing three books, perhaps half a million words in articles, and countless manuscript reports. These were vitally important because Faber and Faber sent their two, four, and even seven guinea cheques by return, when editors could take three months to use an article and another to pay for it. I had to earn £4 a week to pay for my room with breakfast and evening meal and two to three shillings for lunch in a working man's café. If I felt broke, I would lunch on bread and Oxo heated on my shilling-swallowing gas ring.

Freelancing meant that I was not risking an employer's capital, or my own, if my health collapsed. If I had an 'attack', however, I stopped earning, and though I could have gone home to Barnet with my tail between my legs, this was the last thing I wanted to do. I had 'attacks' at intervals, and found that Mrs Joslin and Mrs Brown, the two widows who ran the boarding house, would put up with bringing me meals upstairs, and the two Chinese students were helpful with shopping. Ill health is the curse of the bedsitting classes, because if you get ill too often landladies give you notice. My advice to every struggling freelance is don't throw a celebration party but stamp up your self-employed N.H.S. card every time you get a big cheque.

Before I went to Blackheath I had agreed with the Lyalls that I should do their showing often enough at the R.H.S. Hall to entitle them to space at Chelsea. I used to go over to Watford on a Monday by bus and tube, pack the hired van with the plants, rock, and peat, and drive up with Phyllis and Alan Hinchelwood, their new young partner, who had grown what was the second beard in the Trade — the late Harry Wheatcroft, the rose king, having grown the first — so I wrote an article for *The Horticultural Advertiser* on this called 'Whiskers as a crop'. It was the first of my many humorous articles in this late lamented nurseryman's *News Chronicle*, which led eventually to my four and a half years as gardening correspondent of *Punch*.

I would stay on late to finish the stand with Phyllis, going home with her and returning on the Tuesday and Wednesday for the show, giving me two nights away from Blackheath. Mrs Lyall insisted that I brought mending and darning which she did for me, and I was given expenses and £5 a show, which was generous, because I enjoyed it so much as a contact with the world of growers. Lyall's plants were first class and at the Hall shows we took orders for plants in bloom from Chelsea. We put on such stands with glorious primulas, meconopsis, and gentians, that we were given an island site 16 feet long and six feet wide at Chelsea 1951, 1952, 1953, and 1954, after which I moved to Bocking, and Hinchelwood took over as a trained salesman.

My *Propagation of Alpines* was getting excellent reviews, but these could draw no fantastic sums from Hollywood for film rights, and though *Miniature Alpine Gardening* was in its third edition, no one invited me to dine at the Savoy to discuss making a musical out of it. On the other hand, my books and articles drew an ever increasing fanmail. So I acquired a very part-time secretary who would call, take shorthand, type my letters, and retype the articles I bashed out on my Barlock.

She was a Mrs Dawlish, who had advertised on a newsagent's board for part-time work because she worked for the
managing director of a Finnish timber firm who was away for
long periods, leaving her nothing to do but knit. He came back
and caught her once with one of my articles in her machine, but
all he said was, 'As long as you are free immediate I want you, I
haff no mindings.'

Whenever I wrote a comfrey article my fanmail soared. I still
had a large comfrey plant on the flat roof outside my window,
and passed on orders for plants to Southery where I knew Ted
would come in and clear them at intervals from the plants still
coming up. He still grew celery there, but the peppermint had
died out, smothered by the fearsome weeds of the fen soil that
it hated. Today, oil of peppermint is mostly imported from
Germany.

Among my fans was E. V. Stephenson of Hunsley House
Stud, Little Weighton, near Hull, who wanted me to visit him to
talk about comfrey which he had grown for many years. I took
a coach from Victoria, into a different world where man was a
noble animal and a friend to horses, the Stud Book was the
standard reference work and Surtees the best-read writer.

Vernon Stephenson (a great-great-nephew of Robert Stephenson who built the Rocket) had been a younger son, whose only
real interest had been hunting, but he started a hay and feed
business about 1912. A worthy Yorkshireman in the feed business, who was then too heavy for any hunter, offered to look
after the business while Vernon joined the Yeomanry on the
gallop to Berlin that seemed so near in September, 1914.

When Vernon was demobilized, he he found that the worthy
Yorkshireman had made so much money for him by selling hay
and feed for the horses (a greater tonnage of horse feed than of
shells crossed the Channel in 1914–18) that he was able to buy
Hunsley House, built by a pupil of Wren's from local stone and
estate timber, and start his own stud. He had ridden in 11
Grand Nationals and finished three — the other eight he had
come off and broken something. In his last he rode a stallion
called Anatom, and both horse and rider broke their shoulders.
As was then the right of the rider, Vernon bought Anatom, for
£5, had him taken home in slings, and with skilled treatment
brought him back to health. Though he never raced again, Vernon still rode and hunted, rising to M.F.M. of the Beverley and
providing those who suspected that their jockeys were 'pulling'

their horses, or thought of buying one, with the equine equivalent of my skilled reading of a promising manuscript for Richard de la Mare. This was a flat-out gallop in the grey of the morning round the small race course at Beverley with no spectators, and Vernon's daughter Crowe (a family name she preferred to her own) on Vernon's hunter to provide competition.

Horses need minerals to build their bones and give them speed. Mares in foal need calcium and phosphorus to build up the bones of wobbly-legged foals which must soon follow the herd. All through the crucial year and months up to the date of the Derby, these minerals must be available to the young animals as they are needed to strengthen and make even more dense the bones which take the shock of the thundering hoofs as the favourite pulls ahead of the field and into the straight. Cattle take mineral licks; mineral supplements can be added to pig feeds, but horses seem to take their minerals only from plants, and do best on organically-grown grazing and feed, not artificially-made substitutes. This is why studs are always on chalk or limestone or other mineral-rich land, and there has never been a stud farm in the fens.

Vernon Stephenson planted his acre of comfrey in 1942, in part of his farmyard faced by his corrugated-iron-roofed looseboxes, buying his plants from the late Kenneth Crawley of Lockerbie, Dumfriesshire, who grew a different set of variations from those I had at Southery — the mainly large-leafed, heavy-stemmed, Webster strain. His had a high proportion of a thin-stemmed, early variety with the same magenta flowers, and he had planted them as a means of getting over war-time regulations restricting feed even for racehorses. By the time I visited him, 10 years later, he had learnt a great deal about feeding comfrey to both horses and pigs.

A daily ration of about 14 lb. of comfrey per horse was cut by each groom with a sickle and gathered on canvas sheets to carry in and feed to them when they were in their looseboxes. The elderly Anatom, who died aged 22, sireing winners up to the last, during the show-jumping craze of the 1950s, got arthritis in his shoulder as he grew older, which made him bad tempered. Vernon increased his comfrey ration with the idea of increasing the soporific effect of an all grass diet, which is the reverse of the liveliness of a horse 'feeding his oats' from concentrated food.

He also found that it prevented 'scour' (diarrhoea) among the foals, and when mares and foals are returned to a customer scouring there is just cause for complaint. Middle Piece Farm, which he also used for grazing, had no comfrey, and constant scour problems, Home Farm, where the plot was, none. So he ended this problem by establishing a second comfrey plot.

In the summer, with no mares and foals, he fed comfrey to Essex pigs in harness which he tethered on his constantly-used horse pastures to prevent the risk of a build-up of parasitic worms. This cut down the food requirement and, because he was feeding more protein, produced leaner porkers, which he sold at a special price to butchers who wanted leaner pork. He kept no records of what they made, but considered they always paid for his two days a week hunting out of their profits. He also made hay from comfrey throwing the summer cuts on to the corrugated iron roofs and covering them with pig netting to prevent the dried stems blowing off. Slow drying and rain produced a black hay looking like dry rubbish but the horses loved it and flourished on it.

When this experienced enthusiast suggested I would write an article on comfrey for *Horse and Hound* and then undertake a book on the crop, for there was a wealth of material in past publications if I could find the time to search for it, I jumped at the idea. It had been at the back of my mind ever since I had seen comfrey grow 'with the muscular, thick-necked fury of the kind of bull who needs watching,' as I said in an article in *The Farmer*. Then he offered to test on his own stock anything I found relating to horses.

I told him I was passing on orders to my Uncle Gordon's farm at Southery and when he asked if I was getting any commission, I had to admit 'nothing at all'. Vernon replied 'Mean old sod. I'll send you 20 per cent on all the orders, which will help pay for you to stop writing articles and get on with the book. You will need the money running round and seeing people.'

I caught the coach home on the Monday morning, feeling comfrey had found me a friend indeed.

8

Enter Henry Doubleday

THE BEST botanical library in London — Kew is at Richmond in Surrey — is as far as the lift will go, at the very top of the R.H.S. Old Hall where, in the 1950s, Miss Edith Whitely presided over the collection of books bequeathed to the Society by Sir Joseph Lindley, with later additions. He also left money to endow the printing of the Lindley Medal cards that are awarded to exhibits of special scientific or educational interest, the only medals that can be won in the Scientific Section in the marquee at Chelsea. In 1986 they were awarded to East Malling Research Station for an exhibit on chemical weedkillers, to Gardening with *Which* for one on weeds, and to the Henry Doubleday Research Association for one on composting. It was in the Lindley Library, in October, 1952, that I discovered Henry Doubleday (1813–1902) who introduced the crop we know as 'comfrey' in the 1870s and in whose honour I named the Association in 1954, when I founded it (though it did not become a Registered Charity until 1958).

He was, I found out gradually, the son of a prosperous Quaker grocer, the cousin of Henry Doubleday of Epping, the first of the Victorian butterfly hunters, who compiled the first catalogue of the British Lepidoptera, and the brother of Edward Doubleday who was once Curator of the Botany Department at the British Museum. Their ancestors had sailed with William Penn to found Pennsylvania, the Quaker colony, and one of their descendants founded Doubleday, the famous American publishers.

I began by plodding through the early numbers of the *Gardener's Chronicle and Agricultural Gazette* which was its starting title in 1841. On April 24th of that year, the first man to feel entitled to call himself 'Constant Reader', wrote a letter praising comfrey as a cattle feed, to be followed by others attacking the crop. This went on year after year, until in a letter on October 24th, 1885, Henry Doubleday of Coggeshall, Essex, claimed that he had harvested from 100 to 120 tons an acre from between six and eight cuts a season. In one letter he gave the yields of 54 plants on a square rod (30¼ square yards) of ground for April 30th, averaging 4.08 lb. each, and June 16th, averaging 4.2 lb., a yield of 31 tons 15 cwt. an acre for the two.

The comfrey story began with Pedanius Dioscorides, the Greek M.O. to a Roman legion about 240 A.D. who described it in his *Materia Medica*, naming it 'Symphytum', from the Greek *symphuo*, meaning 'I unite' or 'I make grow together' (the word also gives us 'sympathy'). I traced the common comfrey, *S. officinale*, with its second name from the 'officina' the room in a monastery where the herbs were kept (the derivation of 'office' and 'official') back to William Turner's *Herball* (1568) which states: 'The rootes are goode if they be broken and dronken for them that spitte bloode and are burseten, the same laid to are goode to glewe together freshe woundes.' William Turner, the ancestor of F. W. Newman Turner who became President of the Association, wrote his book years before John Gerard's better known *Herball* in 1587, which mines it for information.

On the medicinal side I had the help of Dr Ronson of the Pharmaceutical Society of Great Britain, who gave his opinion that, 'comfrey was the very best weapon the past had against disease or injury. Arrows made clean cuts, but if you had one in the abdomen you would have a far better chance fasting and drinking comfrey tea than being operated on without antiseptics or anaesthetics. If "burseten" was a perforating appendix you would have no chance anyway.' The librarian of the Royal College of Veterinary Surgeons was also helpful, and the early numbers of their journal were full of references to its use for 'scour' and as leaf poultices for injuries to horses. Of course, it was all 'anecdotal'.

The library at the London offices of the Royal Agricultural Society of England was even more fruitful, especially on the upper shelves, reached from a lofty ladder and full of fat books with titles like *A Complete Cyclopaedia of Agricultlure, To Which Is Conjoined a Treatis on the Diseases of the Horse*. It was here, in *The Country Gentleman's Magazine* that I found the Reverend Edward Highton of Bude who bought 200 plants from Suttons (who sold them between 1875 and 1896), followed the 'directions on the packet', harvested 60 tons an acre, and fed it ad lib to his horses, reducing the oat ration from six to three quarts a day without loss of condition. I also found why Henry Doubleday took up comfrey.

He was a poor businessman but a great experimenter, and in the 1860s he was running a factory in Coggeshall which made starch in packets for sale by grocers to housewives, and also gum. The first Penny Blacks had to be snipped off the sheet then gummed on the envelope, and Henry invented a gum that would stay dry till it was wetted. He had a contract with De La Rue who printed many of the now valuable early-Colonial issues, and all went well until the demand for men to dig the Suez Canal at high wages took all the labour that had been earning a poor living gathering gum arabic.

In 1771, Joseph Busch, a landscape gardener of Hackney, sold his nursery to Conrad Loddige and set sail with his family to lay out the gardens of St Petersburg Palace for Catherine II (The Great) of Russia. In the 1790s he sent Symphytums back to Loddiges, as I found from the bound copy of their catalogue for 1836 in Hackney Public Library. One of these species was *S. asperrimum*, with striking cobalt-blue flowers very welcome in the borders of the 18th century before the introduction of delphiniums and other species from temperate Asia.

A Lewisham nurseryman, James Grant, saw its agricultural possibilities and advertised it as 'Prickly Comfrey', (*asperrimum* meaning 'the roughest') claiming only 40 to 60 tons for it. In Volume 7 of the *Journal of the Royal Agricultural Society* (1871) the analyst to the Society published the first analysis of this crop in which he refers to 'mucilaginous or flesh forming matter', a term often used for gummy proteins when these were little understood. Henry was a member of the Society and when he read the word 'mucilaginous' he thought, 'at last, a gum we can grow in Coggeshall', and wrote off to the Head Gardener, The Palace, St Petersburg, Russia, and the English head gardener there sent him some seedlings.

A rare chance natural hybridization appears to have occurred between the yellow *S. officinale* found all over Europe including Russia, and the blue *S. asperrimum* planted side by side in the symphytum border. Henry grew his seedlings and called his F.1 hybrid 'Doubleday's Solid Stem Comfrey', or 'Russian Comfrey' to distinguish it from the earlier introduction. Unfortunately for the gum factory, however gummy a protein you can no more stick stamps with it than you can with white of egg. So Henry lost the contract and the factory was sold.

Henry devoted the last 30 years of his life to research on his crop, leaving the marketing to Thomas Christy, a nurseryman of

Sydenham. It was his dream that his crop would feed a hungry world. We shall never know what he found, for when he died the family said, 'Poor Uncle Henry, he never made any money,' and they tidied up all his papers and burned the lot. It was to stop this happening again with my work that I founded the H.D.R.A. Even abbreviated to these initials it is an awkward title, but it honours a great and humble man with ideas ahead of his age.

I wrote the article for *Horse and Hound* and another for *Riding*, from a different angle to make sure. Both were accepted and the result was a flood of letters, which I answered with the help of Mrs Dawlish. Among them was one from Tom Hopkinson, Editor of *Picture Post*, who asked me to lunch with him to discuss an article. This was the kind of thing that happened to other people, but I rang him and met him at an expensive restaurant called 'Boulestins'. After I had talked comfrey to him he commissioned me to write an illustrated feature with *Picture Post* supplying the photographer — my best only just made *Riding*

I met the photographer at Vernon Stephenson's, and he took some lovely shots of glossy-coated stallions, all comfrey-fed, and even the roof-top haymaking and the pigs. The photographer left and I stayed the night, making the most of my first trip on expenses. Vernon was most interested in the Reverend E. Highton, who, as a fox-hunting person, would ride something like Tom Atom, a gelding sired by Anatom, which he rode to hounds himself. Tom Atom would go on ad lib comfrey, plus half oats, and his performance could easily be judged, for he was the most frequent competition provider for assessing race-horses at Beverley.

'What is he worth?' I asked.

'Oh, about £350,' said Vernon.

'Couldn't you try it on a cheaper horse?'

'I wouldn't have a cheaper horse on the place.'

The experiment was a complete success and Tom Atom looked so good after a year as the first 'C-Diet' horse that Vernon sold him for £500.

Unfortunately for my article and for comfrey, *Picture Post* never used my article, for Tom Hopkinson wrote so vehemently about the treatment of North Korean prisoners of war he got the sack. My allotted space was filled by bishops giving their views on teenage sex, but I did get my expenses and £25.

Finally, I wrote *Russian Comfrey* out of my Southery experience, and above all that of Vernon who generously poured out the knowledge that he would never aspire to write during my weekends at Hunsley House Stud in probably the last house in Britain where polished copper jugs of hot water, each covered with a clean face towel, went up to the guest's bedrooms before dinner, for the water supply was pumped up to the tank in the roof with an antique hand pump in the kitchen by Grice the gardener. Mrs Stephenson had almost unlimited domestic help because the four maids counted as stablemaids for tax purposes, and as they were mainly grooms' wives and daughters, could fairly be called on to do the odd spot of mucking out as well as hot-water-can carrying. Entertaining owners and trainers also came off tax.

Mrs Dawlish typed all my letters that drew in help from research stations and authorities that tracked down information, which I gathered not only from libraries but letters to local papers in the search for anything that might have survived from the comfrey growers of the past. She had typed the updated and enlarged edition of *Miniature Alpine Gardening* which came out as *Alpines without a Garden* in 1952. It was my third book, and I could not have done it without her.

Unfortunately, I lost my lodgings. My 'room was required', for my landladies, who had coped with three of my 'attacks' during the 2½ years I was with them, could fit three more Chinese students into my room, fed more cheaply than British lodgers but paying just the same. All were the sons of quite well off Singapore Chinese fathers, and at the local Polytechnic, quiet, tidy, polite, girl-friendless, and never in arrears with the rent. With no cassette recorders I could not tape my letters to a good typist who knows her job, as I do today. Going full tilt at my *Russian Comfrey*, writing at white heat out of what I had collected, I went home to Barnet again, to the large room in the flat where my parents lived. Here I wrote and rewrote, wrestled with long and slippery galleys, spread things out on the floor, and got through the book that was to change my life. Out of the kindness of her heart, Phyllis Lyall typed the final manuscript without charge, and I got it away to Faber and Faber.

During the years I had been away my father had a prostate gland operation, and Mother's glaucoma had grown worse. One eye had to be removed and the other operated on to relieve the pressure, which gave her tunnel vision. She could still read and get about but found pavement traffic difficult. Uncle Gordon had managed to sell my father's invention of what was perhaps the most heat-efficient electric convector heater in the world to a subsidiary of Thomas Tilling, the bus builders, which brought in royalties that went a long way to level up his reduction in pension and Mother's lack of one.

It was a garden of her own that Mother missed most at Hadley Hurst, and she hoped that, especially if the heater brought the money in, we could afford to buy a house with a garden, just anywhere so long as we three were together. We still had my grandmother's £500, held in trust for my brother, my sister, and me with Uncle Gordon as the trustee, and the proceeds of selling Farm House Plants, so we had enough capital to put down the deposit on a house. No building society would look at my parents, both over 70, but I was 42, though, apart from my health, as a freelance writer and gardening author my prospects were precarious. I aimed at Essex, both because houses were cheaper there, and it was the home of Henry Doubleday. I wanted some land on which I could grow comfrey to find out more about it.

Comfrey is unique, not only in its yield or its medicinal qualities, but in the bitter and totally unscientific hatred it can arouse in those who dislike it and the wild enthusiasm it stirs in its supporters. Following Henry Doubleday and Thomas Christy came Kenneth Crawley and Vernon Stephenson; now comfrey had taken a grip on my life. Henry was no richer than I, his religious refusal to take an oath barred him from any university, just as my health and its effect on my education barred me, and though he was awarded the proud title of Fellow of the Royal Society for his introduction of Russian Comfrey in 1875 he could never afford the registration fee of 12 guineas so could not use the letters 'F.R.S.' to which he was entitled.

At Barnet I settled down with my parents, taking on the shopping, library book getting, and other chores that my father's increasing gout and Mother's failing sight made burdens to them. On one of my trips into Barnet I found that the local branch of the Halifax would take me on as a borrower, provided I was not looking for a 100 per cent mortgage and would put down a sizeable deposit on a house that was a reasonably good buy. It meant Mother could hope for a garden and a home of her own again, if I kept on writing, pouring out the words to finance the move.

Then my six free copies arrived, with the illustration from Sutton's Farm Seeds catalogue on the dust jackets, and a price of 15 shillings, my most expensive book yet. It was reviewed fairly well in *The Field*, got a good write-up in *The Farmer*, for Newman Turner grew comfrey, and a highly critical notice in *The Farmer's Weekly*. *Horse and Hound* liked it. Though it made little impact on the literary world, to cope with the fanmail I had to stick up a postcard in a Barnet newsagent's and gather in another shorthand typist.

Then Newman Turner had an idea — the International Comfrey Race of 1954. The contestants were farmers, cutting and weighing their comfrey yields all over Britain. A plot in Kenya won in 1955 with the still unbroken record of 124 tons, 10 cwt. and 101 lb. in 12 monthly cuts. This race established that comfrey, which is dormant from about the end of October to March in Britain and other temperate countries, is in cut right round the year near the equator, where the daylength remains constant. The record for sustained production is held by Mr J. P. C. Phillips of Mteroshanga, Zimbabwe, who averaged 100 tons an acre for 17 successive years on a 25-acre field, fattening bullocks for the abattoir at Salisbury (now Harare). Unfortunately, a four-year drought dried out the root completely, the termites ate them, and the field was completely destroyed.

The 'race' began in the spring number of *The Farmer* in 1953, when *Russian Comfrey* was first on sale, and reported in the quarterly issues, which were followed with keen interest by readers who were organic farmers.

Among the letters that poured in was one from Mr A. H. A. Lasker, of Bodie Seeds Ltd. of Winnipeg, Canada, who wanted to buy 10,000 comfrey plants. One of the earliest entrants in the race was Mrs P. B. Greer, who was willing to have a go at satisfying this huge order from the stock of plants I had sent her from Southery. I left my parents on their own at Barnet and went down to Layer-de-la-Haye, near Colchester, to stay with her till I got this huge and awkward order away.

The quarantine regulations were fearsome, involving washing every plant entirely free from soil, a certificate that no vines grew within five miles of the plot, and above all inspections by the Ministry of Agriculture. This was represented by a sunburnt young man who had the misfortune to have a mother whom Mrs Greer knew, so she called him 'Billy' and bossed him. Although he know nothing about comfrey or its diseases he made a very thorough job of his grapevine hunting and we got the consignment away. It was, as far as I know, the only modern comfrey to reach Canada or the United States. The regulations insist that even if a consignment is fully documented the plants must be fumigated on arrival, which never fails to kill them. The young man must have certified that they had been fumigated for they arrived safely in Canada, and a nurseryman named Elmer Deetz bought a large load from Bodie Seeds in Canada and drove them down to Oregon over the unguarded frontier. Almost all the comfrey in the USA has grown from that one stock. Fortunately, comfrey rust (*Melampsorella symphyti*), a disease of the wild *S. officinale*, did not cross with them so American comfrey is rust-free.

Mrs Greer, her two plump women farmworkers, and I cut up, washed and packed that vast order, with Billy summoned by telephone to inspect each thousand before we crammed it into eight chests and corded them up with clothesline. We sent it air freight via Heathrow through a shipping agent, at vast expense.

When we got the last load away, Mrs Greer suggested we should have an outing before I went back to Barnet. She had checked that there were Doubledays living in Coggeshall, and we could go over and visit them in her Landrover which she drove through her own woods with the windscreen down in order to shoot rabbits with her .410 pistol over the bonnet. She would hit them too.

The grocer's shop had closed down in the 1930s and was now a very old-fashioned men's outfitter's but not even the small and sleepy town of Coggeshall had enough very old-fashioned men to keep it going. The last two survivors of a family of 14 Doubledays, plus several uncles and spinster aunts, still lived in the large and rambling house behind the shop. They were Edith, who was 96 then, large and slow, and her brother Thomas, then 94, who was small and lively. I had hoped to find records of experiments, perhaps even a manuscript about comfrey in copperplate handwriting on yellowed paper, but Edith said slowly, 'It took two days to clear Uncle Henry's two rooms and three more to clean them, sack after sack of papers they took down to the yard and burnt. There was his bedroom and the one he wrote in where all the papers were, we stuffed them in sacks and took them down to the yard to burn.'

Thomas remembered his bachelor Uncle who took him birdnesting and talked of 'Observing the works of God in humbleness', insisting that 'humbleness' meant not thinking a theory must be right because it was your own. And searching always for the Truth that harms no man. The 'murrain', the name given by Thomas to potato blight (*Phytophthora infestans*), impressed Henry very much and he tried for years to select a blight-resistant variety by looking for survivors on blight-stricken fields. He had one he grew on for years that he called 'Doubleday's Kidney': this too was swept away in a dull, humid season with the spores blowing fast and far. Henry, however, was the first man to look for it, 'Observing the works of God in humbleness', rather than joining in the furious argument in the correspondence columns of *The Gardener's Chronicle* that blamed the disease on the weather favouring the spread and increase of the spores. No one at the time observed the fields in Wales, downwind of a copper-smelting plant, that escaped the blight year after year. It was left to Professor P. M. A. Millardet of Bordeaux to give us 'Bordeaux mixture', of lime and copper sulphate which is still a good preventative for the disease which still has no cure.

Henry lost the contract with Messrs de la Rue when his comfrey protein failed to stick stamps, and his gum and starch factory was sold to a firm that still makes isinglass from fish bones. His smallholding, and his share of Thomas Christy's profits, supported him modestly while he worked away steadily at his crop. Thomas remembered him buying in stock to fatten on comfrey, and failing to drive a hard enough bargain when he sold the animals — in the opinion of the family, who considered Henry was cheated by the factory manager for years, for he was no businessman.

As we talked, Thomas gave me the only surviving portrait of Henry Doubleday. It is a Daguerrotype, taken at the Great Exhibition in 1851, where he won a bronze medal for his designs for the lace that was a cottage industry in Coggeshall, and a statuette of Prince Albert. He had to sit still for half an hour for the latest scientific marvel of 'portrait painted with light', which is why he looks so grim.

The Doubledays were organized more like a commune than a family and according to Edith and Thomas the youngest, they had 'very happy times together, without any of this wireless upsetting folks,' in Edith's opinion. They spoke as though signalling to us across a wide river of years, and beside them Mrs Greer in her seventies seemed brisk and modern.

The last memory of Henry they signalled was of a tall, thin figure in a long black overcoat walking up the Tilkey road from what is now a block of shops called Doubleday's Corner to the Quaker burial ground where more and more of his friends lay as he outlived them. Thomas remembered the village children running after him to ask the time, because for their delight he would stop and take out a gold repeater watch that chimed the nearest hour.

On the way home in the Landrover, with the empty pig swill tins fidgeting in the back as Mrs Greer drove faster and faster to reach the fishmonger, the greengrocer, and the café before they closed, and to get everything fed, including the ferrets, before we dined in the scholarly and aristocratic squalor in which she lived, I thought about Henry Doubleday and of founding an association named in his honour. I felt that he and I had so much in common that it would be appropriate. Mr Greer, an Indian judge who had been poisoned with herbal decoctions to influence his decision by both plaintiff and defendant (instead of only one or the other), and whose health had broken down forcing early retirement, suggested 'The Comfrey Club', which was short, easy, and descriptive, but would have hampered us had we wished to expand in other organic directions. He came back after taking Abraham Lincoln, the billy goat, an extra feed of cornflakes as a special treat because he had had a hard day, and said, 'Why not the Lawrence Hills Foundation?' 'I can hardly call it after myself,' said I. 'After all, it was Henry Doubleday who did the work, even if it was all burnt. I am determined no one shall burn what I find.'

When I got back to Barnet, after helping plant the surplus root cuttings and plants from the load Mrs Greer and I had fetched from Southery to make up that largest of all comfrey orders, I wrote to Thomas asking if we might call the association after his uncle. In reply came a beautifully written letter expressing his regrets that he could not manage to start us off with a large donation, nor could he or Edith attend committee meetings, but they were both very glad that Henry's work would at last be recognized, and wished us 'success in our charitable endeavours'.

I took the very first step along the road to the H.D.R.A. when I bought two machine-gun belt boxes I had seen advertised in

Exchange and Mart. They exactly fitted my foolscap files. I wrote the names of the comfrey-race competitors on file tabs on one, used the other for such subjects as 'A. H. A. Lasker', 'Comfrey — Research Stations', 'Comfrey — Editors', etc., until I had to buy two more boxes. I sat them three abreast on the wide inside windowsills to make my office.

When I told Mr Lasker what I wanted to do he offered to become our 'President', giving me a name to put on our new notepaper, and presented me with a ton of a variety of lucerne seed which was unobtainable in Britain because of the dollar shortage. Though neither of us were aware of it, this was the most awkward of gifts, for when it arrived at London Docks it hit regulation 365, which laid down that gifts from overseas must be solely for the personal use and enjoyment of the receiver, and must weigh not more than 22 lb., the maximum then allowed by parcel post.

The only way I could have used or 'enjoyed' a whole ton of lucerne seed would have been to sow it on 50 acres, and I had no land. But Twyford Mill Seeds had offered me £275 for it, enough to start the first small comfrey research station in the world. So Mrs Greer urged her M.P. and I urged the one for Barnet, to fight for the release of my seeds. I got a letter in *The New Statesman* and an article in *Time and Tide*, and Mr Lasker telephoned the Canadian High Commissioner in London, but all in vain. Then a second generous gift arrived at the regulation 365 barrier, with the battle of the lucerne seed still raging. An American wild animal dealer sent a very tame black bear to a friend in London. But his wife objected to its 'personal use' as a pet. However, over a hundredweight of bear, sitting up and begging for dockers' sandwiches and posing with Teddy Bear appeal for Fleet Street photographers, soon tore away the red tape, and it ambled away on a chain to a new life in the children's corner of a zoo, closely pursued by a ton of lucerne seed which earned me that £275. That is how the H.D.R.A. began, with a book (my *Russian Comfrey*) a bear, and a ton of lucerne seed. Not a grant from the Government, or a large legacy, but with only just enough cash to make a start.

My first choice for a centre was Coggeshall, because of Henry Doubleday, and Thomas said there was a house for sale in the Tilkey Road. We went down to see it in Puddleduck, but it had been empty for three years, and though it had three acres of land, the asking price was £2,500, and a survey showed cracks in the walls from when a bomb exploded in a nearby field. Then I found Rose Cottage, Stisted, advertised in the local paper at £1,450, with only two bedrooms, but a large garden and orchard. Would this hold my comfrey experimental station?

I went down alone, to find no room in the house or garden for the comfrey and ourselves, so I went back to Braintree and saw Messrs Joscelyns who offered me an order to view, just off the Gestetner, a semi-detached in Convent Lane, No. 20, which had the 26-foot-wide and 175-foot-long back garden of a 1939-built semi, with a Cox, an Allington Pippin, a greengage, a plum, and six rows of raspberries in the back garden. It had three bedrooms, a living room fire that combined both an oven at the side and hot-water heating, and the asking price was £1,750, well inside our limit. Beside it was a vacant plot which could have taken my research station, and at the end of the lane was a triangle of derelict land that belonged to a Mr Hunnable. The agent told me that the building-plot owner was arguing with the planners, but the lady partner phoned Mr Hunnable and got me an appointment to see him at 9 a.m. next day.

When I telephoned her, Mother was strongly in favour of grabbing the house, and of buying curtains, linoleum, and the stair carpet so we could move straight in. My father wanted to move by Christmas and was going to sell Puddleduck at last, as we both were nervous about his driving in the heavy traffic from the gravel pits. In the morning I met Maurice Hunnable.

We spent most of the morning walking round his bird sanctuary beyond the nursery, with a lovely lake that had a breeding pair of herons, where some day he hoped to build a retirement cottage. I talked comfrey to him, and told him what I wanted to do and why. Finally we shook hands on a ten-year lease at £10 a year, to be worked out by our solicitors. Now I know why old Maurice Hunnable gave me that lease on land that Barton the nurseryman had been trying to buy for years. If you are old and have built a business by hard work, enterprise, and ideas, and you meet someone young (43, as I was then, is 'young' to over sixties) and keen, you are reminded of your own youth, and you help him if you can. Though I fought him again and again, with the other people of Convent Lane, over the noise and vibration of his lorries, I still have an affection for old Maurice Hunnable, for leasing me the land on which I built the H.D.R.A. in 30 happy years.

I now needed a solicitor to handle my end of the deal, so I saw the local Lloyds manager, who was as swiftly helpful as the cashier with greying hair who had changed my torn ten shilling note all those years ago. I had no need to start with a constitution. All I had to do was to open a separate account for the H.D.R.A. when I transferred from Barnet. As for buying the house and leasing the land, he recommended Holmes and Hills, next to the White Hart. They knew Maurice Hunnable very well. Mr John Hills, (no relation to us) was amazed at my getting the lease but negotiated toughly on my behalf, both with Hunnable's solicitors and for the house.

Despite his efforts it took till December 14th, 1954, for us to get in to No. 20. The current chauffeur drove us down the day before the van would arrive from Barnet with the furniture. The move was complicated by the fact that Iris and Elizabeth were moving to Glasgow to start the Needlework Development Scheme for Messrs Coates and were sending us the furniture from their house in Chislehurst that would not fit their new flat.

It was still further complicated when my father fell in the White Hart, where we stayed the first night, having had a slight stroke, and was in hospital over Christmas. Iris and Elizabeth arrived, so did their furniture, and we spent Christmas coping. Our next door neighbour, Ron Suckling, who came in and offered help on our first evening, helped me put up my sister's garden shed, helped floor our loft with scrap timber, and sold us a large chicken run for £2 which he erected, so solving our space problem.

By the time my father came out of hospital, to our front room converted to a bedroom because he could now get upstairs for baths only with help, the house was straight and warm, fortunately for January, 1955, was a cold month. I used all my hard-learned stoking skills on the living room fire, designed unsuccessfully to do too much at once, found that what it really liked was 'nutty slack' plus small coke, and we enjoyed generous baths and warm rooms, with fires in my father's room and my writing room. Despite the dust and ashes, with the help of a succession of 'dailies' we managed very well.

I bought for £36 an 8 ft. by 6 ft. shed, with a large Crittall window set especially in the end for my father's workshop, where we fitted up his old lathe, a small circular saw, a work bench and shelves, for though Dad could now do much less, he enjoyed fitting things up, spending some of his first heater royalties and every now and then making something remarkably and ingeniously useful.

Mother took over the garden, with my help. We ousted the fruitless greengage, which had been robbed of its pollinator when a previous owner had tethered a dog to the Victoria plum it needed and the chain had ring barked it just below the stock, so we had only a Mussell stock grown to tree size, which I also helped to remove, roots and all. Geoff came down and helped strip the turf from the surplus lawn and build a long trough above the surface which took all our kitchen wastes between soil layers, decaying slowly with the help of marrows and ridge cucumbers along the top.

Along the fence just beside the kitchen door we trained my favourite Bourbon roses, the deep pink Zephirine Drouhin and the pale pink Kathleen Harrop, both mildew-prone but lovely and long flowering, with herbs below them for my mother's quick culinary dashes from the small kitchen that made such a difference to our meals. As long as she knew where everything was, and it stayed in its place, she could find it without wasteful focusing. On the other side we had Climbing Golden Showers, Danse de feu, and Souvenirs de Claudius Denoyel with its splendid, scented, crimson clusters but the handicap of the most awkward name of all. In the spring I found that some overgrown bushes of *Cytisus monspessulanus* had seeded themselves and I planted the seedlings on both sides, giving us a shortlived but striking hedge.

We had a compost heap at the bottom of the garden into which we put unlimited grass mowings first from Ron Suckling and then from Alan Bates who built a bungalow on the empty plot beside us. With this, and manure at about five-year intervals, plus lime and some wood ashes (we burnt woody wastes) we gradually built a fertile organic garden. After tea at our open days (the first was in 1961) when the crowd had dwindled, I took 30 to 40 members round our garden, which those who came in the 1960s and early 1970s will remember as always bursting with food, flowers, and fertility.

This was very largely from my mother's constant care. She would leave my father, happily painting sailing ships or landscapes in oils on mahogany three-ply offcuts. My father could never manage human figures, but give him a steel, four-mast barque making the most of a light wind, with a bow wave small as a swan's, heeling gently to the wind caressing her acres of canvas, and he would delight in creating beauty, that was true to the shapes of sails at sea that he remembered from his youth, and no one will now see again.

When he died in 1963, Mother said, 'We gave him eight happy years with no one driving him, books and painting to enjoy, and enough happening and to do to interest him without effort.' Mother would never have cut flowers in the house, because she said she would not decorate her rooms with slowly dying people. She enjoyed them growing and living and 'loving' in our garden. I planted the beds round our small front lawn with helianthemums, blazing as they had at Wells, and from the side path to the garage where we had our sheds, a four-foot wide bed of alpines chosen to flower through much of the year, and including my favourites. In place of a front hedge we had *Lavender spicata*, the best for lavender bags among linen. Mother made jams, including 'marrow ginger', my father's favourite, and bottled fruit in quantity, using wartime recipes that were easy on sugar. No. 20 was the last home my mother made, and the last garden we built and enjoyed together was our best.

Competing with our garden for attention was the Trial Ground, which was fenced with larch posts and pig wire, with a strong iron gate fitted on our right-of-way from Hunnables road down to the sanctuary, by a fencing contractor. Then I borrowed Barton's Trusty tractor and hired Pilgrim, the man who drove it. The Trusty had a twin-cylinder J.A.P. engine in front and two long iron handles behind, and Pilgrim wrenched and fought it, hammering, stammering, and stinking, to plough and harrow an 18-foot wide strip beside the garden of the last bungalow, No. 32, and our main beds. Their sizes and positions were determined by the hardness of the soil, because from the right-of-way-gate to the end of our land, level with the gardens in Convent Lane, had been pounded solid by lorries taking the sand and ballast to make runways for East Anglian aerodromes in the war years, from the pit that was now a wide, deep lake. My main path had to be where the going was too tough for the Trusty.

By now I employed two men at weekends — John Tiddy who worked in Crittalls drawing office as a tracer, a small pillar of the local Conservative Party. Wesley was a Prudential Insurance agent, cycling round and collecting small weekly or monthly premiums, cutting the overgrown claws of parrots for

Woodhill, Gerrards Cross Bucks. From a watercolour by my grandmother, Elizabeth Saunders, the home of ten children and four step-daughters.

At 17 I began my apprenticeship with A. Parris & Sons of Bexleyheath. "Mr Fred" the younger Son, then in his 50s.

Myself aged 16 in 1927 as a pupil at Central Park, Dartford. Taken with my first camera, a box Brownie.

"Mr George" his elder brother. They taught me the trade of General Nurseryman from Antirrhinums to Alpines.

My mother, aged about 14.
Photographed by Hill & Saunders
with the wet plate process. She
hated being photographed.

In 1940 I volunteered as an
Air-Gunner in the R.A.F. but failed
on eye-sight. I was invalided out
on D-Day (June 6th 1944).

Whiteleggs rock garden at my first
Chelsea Flower Show in 1933.
One of the last Chelseas of horses,
top hats and bowlers.

My father (left) with my uncle Gordon Saunders in the gateway of Hadley Hurst, where I began in H.D.R.A. with four ex-machinegun belt boxes for files.

My brother Geoffrey in 1943 as an Engineroom Artificer (R.N.). He finished the War as an Engineer Lieutenant.

My sister Iris at the Royal College of Art. She is the taller of the two students.

In 1951 my health broke down from high-gluten cookery; and I had to give up running the research nursery where I first grew comfrey.

This 1971 photograph shows the difference in health and heftiness from twenty years on Cherry's entirely gluten-free diet.

The comfrey plant I grew on my bed-sitter windowsill at Blackheath, where I lived by freelance gardening writing and MSS reading.

Henry Doubleday (1813-1902) introducer of Russian Comfrey, the plant that changed my life. A daguerrotype taken at the 1851 Exhibition.

F. Newman Turner (1913-1964). First President of the H.D.R.A. His practical organic farming books and quarterly "The Farmer" made history.

Mrs Greer in 1953. She marched in the first suffragette procession with a banner "Lady Farmer. Votes for my labourers but not for me?"

Vernon Stephenson, pioneer of the high mineral, high protein Comfrey Diet for thoroughbred horses.

The H.D.R.A. Committee in 1965. Left to right: Malcolm Hickling, Victor Beroux, Mrs Margaret Bowler, Robert Pollard, Mrs Hilda Cherry Hills. Squatting: Lawrence D. Hills. Seated: Mrs Peggy Greer.

A worried foreman staring at a five foot delphinium spire with a four inch wide stem. Photo from "Illustrated" August 3rd 1957.

1957 was the freak plant year. This mutant wild foxglove from near Yeovil, could have been an effect of open-air nuclear tests.

The Bocking Trial Ground in 1980, showing how much we crammed on to under two acres, before we moved to Ryton Gardens.

The H.D.R.A. stand at Chelsea 1987, featuring "Give Up Smoking Bonfires", the leaflet on leafmould and compost making, of which we gave away over 500,000 copies to fold in Rate Demands. Photograph by H.T.V. who film the "Muck and Magic" T.V. Series.

old ladies, drowning surplus kittens or finding homes for them, apart from arriving with an advance cash payment and sound and kindly advice for the bereaved who were inclined to over-spend on funerals.

They forked up as much couch grass as they could and planted the Landrover-load of Webster strain of comfrey from Southery that Mrs Greer brought, the sackfuls of Stephenson strain Vernon fetched down from Little Weighton near Hull, while Newman Turner sent sacks of black and ugly roots of what I called 'Ferne Farm' Survival. These grew behind one of his barns and survived from when this was a famous racing stable between the 1890s and 1930s. Ron Suckling drove me over with forks and spades and we dug some plants from the headlands of the field at Coggeshall that had once been part of Henry Doubleday's smallholding.

George Gibson of Guernsey, who invented the liquid tomato manure made from comfrey leaves and stems rotted in water and used it right through the war, sent us his strain which he had exported to Kenya where John McInnes grew it and secured his record yield. This had been imported from Webster some time between 1900 and 1914, and he dodged the regula-tions by bringing ready-packed parcels over on the Channel Ferry and posting them from Weymouth to Bocking. So we had as full a set as we could of what was being grown as 'comfrey' in Britain, as distinct from what was coming up by rivers, in watery ditches, and by roadsides. From the Gypsy Lore Society I confirmed that when their trading was in horses, clothes pegs, and telling fortunes, gypsies fed a double handful of comfrey root every day for a fortnight to ailing horses. This produced miraculous cures, or at least enough temporary improvement to secure a sale. All the while, customers of Thomas Christy, Sut-tons, and other comfrey sellers were planting the crop the gyp-sies who had always used the scarce wild comfrey, especially for sick horses, even their own, were stealing it, and as horses eating roots by the double handful always drop some, this com-frey grew wherever the caravans had rested.

As my plants grew through the summer, I saw that my first conjecture, that the variation was due to neglect or soil differences, was entirely wrong. Comfrey was not a species (*Symphytum peregrinum*) but a number of mixtures of hybrids resulting from natural self-pollination of the F.1 generation seedlings that gave Henry Doubleday his 100 ton an acre yields, and back-crosses of these with the wild *S. officinale* that John Gerard said 'joyeth in watery ditches'.

Therefore I had my colour vision checked by the local optician who found it normal, then bought an R.H.S. colour chart. This comprised a large number of loose sheets, each printed with oblongs of colours, numbered in sequence from light to dark. It was about the most awkward 'reference work' possible, especially to use on wet and windy days, but it was the only way to identify the variations by the colours of their flowers.

As I slowly sorted these, through 1955 and 1956, I gave them 'Bocking Numbers', and found that each of the four mixtures had a dominant variation. The one in the Webster Strain was Bocking No. 4 which had large, round-ended leaves, thick, solid stems down which the leaves extended in a long triangular fin for about a fifth of the way to the next leaf, and flowers that were Bishop's Violet 34/3. The Stephenson Strain dominant was Bocking No. 14, with pointed leaves, thin stems to which the leaves fitted without a fin, and Imperial Purple 33/3 flowers. The Ferne Farm Survival was dominated by Bocking No. 1, which had large, pointed leaves that folded in from the edges, thick flower stems down which the leaf fins extended almost from one leaf to the next below it, and deep red flowers that were Indian Lake 826/1. The Gibson Strain was very near a Webster but with more pointed-leaved variations near No. 4, differing only in its flower colours.

The plants Ron Suckling and I collected at Coggeshall proved to be identical with Bocking No. 14, but with slightly darker purple flowers. When we were able to afford more analysis, I found that this type of comfrey is higher in potassium than the others and tastes bitter when cooked. Rabbits dislike it, preferring the variations on No. 4, so these are eaten and the least tasty survive.

Sorting the comfrey variations took so long because I had other and more urgent tasks. I had to write the articles and book reports that made it possible for me to work for nothing, keep up the repayments to the Halifax, pay the rates and electricity bills, and keep enough in hand to lend to the H.D.R.A., for the lucerne money was running low.

Among the manuscripts I handled then was *Practical Organic Gardening* by Ben Easy, who edited and wrote the Members' Notes in *Mother Earth*, the quarterly Journal of the Soil Association. It had started in 1946, I joined two years later, and I used to answer knotty questions on organic gardening for him. Relations between our two Associations were always friendly though we were always entirely separate. In no sense is the H.D.R.A., like British Organic Farmers and The Organic Growers Association, a 'split-off' from the Soil Association. My aim was always to avoid competing, extending the frontiers of the organic movement rather than preaching to the converted by poaching members.

When the full results of the 1954 comfrey race were in from Britain and overseas, I wrote the very first H.D.R.A. publication: *Russian Comfrey Report Number One*. This had 38 pages, a plain green paper cover, and was lavishly illustrated with blocks of my photographs from *The Farmer* which cost us nothing.

I sold 1,000 to Bodie Seeds in Canada without the cover and title page, because they thought it safer to call it 'Quaker Comfrey', with the cold war and Senator McCarthy raging in the USA, to avoid the handicap of the name 'Russian', even for a crop that 'chose freedom' in the 1870s. I made a similar sale to the Soil Association, and later bought back 500 when I had sold every one of the original 10,000 except the single copy I still have.

I gave detailed accounts of the competitors in the comfrey race and how they were using comfrey on their farms, visiting many of the British plots. I was driven down to cut and weigh Newman Turner's Ferne Farm plot by Dr T. Bakker, the Dutch Agricultural Attache, whom I knew as a friend of my Uncle Gordon's and because I had written him a small leaflet entitled *English for Catalogue Makers*, based on the correct terms of address on which Col. Grey insisted.

Newman used his comfrey in his 'alternative veterinary medical treatments' described in his *Herdsmanship*, especially for the sterility then common in Jersey cows forced to milk yields beyond their capacity by excessive feeding with concentrates. He used and advised fasting, then comfrey ad lib. His plot won the record British yield in 1955 with 67 tons 16 cwt. an acre, which is still unbeaten.

Another plot I saw was John Wylie's at Dumfries, where he was county engineer and grew it to provide extra compost material for his municipal compost plant described in his book *Fertility from Town Wastes* (Faber and Faber, 1955), one of the manuscripts I had nursed. His work began my interest in composting dustbin refuse and the use of sewage on the land.

Comfrey, however, is very poor material for compost, because it is so low in the hard fibre that provides lasting humus, as I discovered when I made my first comfrey heap. To my amazement, this sank from a four-foot high, dome-topped pile, to about four inches of a tarry substance, with the fibres still recognizable in it. So much of its 12.4 per cent dry matter was protein and carbohydrate that it became such a good imitation of a high-potassium cow manure it deceived the long-bodied, light brown flies (*Scopeuma stercorarium*) that swarm on cow pats. The best ways to use comfrey foliage are, as I discovered, as a high-potash-and-nitrogen liquid manure, as a green manure to tuck in potato trenches, and as a compost heap activator, since it rates higher as a 'vegetable manure' than as a source of humus.

In the autumn of our first year we began to sell comfrey, having placed a very small advertisement in *Amateur Gardening* (circulation a quarter million at the time) which sold all we could spare. The Tiddy brothers used to dig and cut up the plants, replanting the root cuttings in regular rows on cleared ground and bringing the root sections with growing points up to No. 20. Here I packed them on newspapers spread on the floor of my writing room, in dozens, half dozens, fifties, and even hundreds, for we did not have a packing shed until 1957.

I took them down in my saddlebag and in shopping bags slung on my handlebars to the Bocking post office which doubled as a chemist's. This was owned by John Stephens, who excelled in helping old ladies from the guest house, run by the Franciscan Convent that named our Lane, with their pension problems, and making up semi-legal fishing baits. For about 20 years, until they retired, John and his little wife Nellie coped with the ever-rising size and complexity of the H.D.R.A. post, for as we grew in membership we were sending letters and parcels to almost every country in the world. Quite soon he was breaking the regulations on our behalf. He would let me dump my bicycle load of parcels for stamping at his leisure, paying him at the end of each week, to save having a queue stretching right back to the sweet and newspaper shop, where I would refill my bags with empty sweet boxes for the next load of comfrey parcels.

There was a white-painted watermill at Bocking, by the bridge over the river Blackwater just before Convent Lane turned off the A131. This had once been a weaving mill where local tradition had it that the coronation robe for King Edward VI (1547 to 1553) was woven. I used to call at this mill on my bicycle to collect the paper sacks that held some of the ingredients for compounding pig and cattle feeds that the present miller mixed and ground by electric power, now the waterwheel was stilled. As these were made of four thicknesses of good brown paper, I was getting a bargain in packing material when I tipped the very deaf old labourer two shillings for a bundle of about thirty, which I carefully balanced across my handlebars and wheeled cautiously home. When we left Bocking, more than 30 years later, we used to tip his successor a £1 coin, for they were still a bargain.

In that first report I thanked Unilever for the free analysis they did for us, for they were interested in dried comfrey as an addition to calf meal. They would have been glad to add it to their meal, to supply the traditional anti-scour ingredient used by Vernon for his foals and by the older generation of stockmen all over Europe. But, unfortunately, I could not guarantee them a supply of at least 500 tons of dried comfrey a year to make it worth their while to start a production line.

My father designed a solar-heated comfrey drier in the form of a lean-to shed, seven feet wide, four foot six deep, and six feet high in front, made with standard-width corrugated iron, bitumen-painted black, on a framework of two by two-inch timber. The idea was that the sun's heat on the sloping roof, facing south where we had set it at the end of the main path, would draw in the air through an adjustable flap at the bottom of the back and up through six bamboo-cane-bottomed trays full of cut comfrey, and the moisture-laden air would escape over the gap at the top of the close-fitting doors in front.

Unfortunately it failed to work. Though the leaf surfaces of comfrey wilt and dry easily, the thick midribs and stems seal up the water inside themselves — being the gummy proteins that failed to stick stamps for Henry Doubleday — and blocked the pores. John and Wesley Tiddy built the drier, and when it failed they took the trays out and it became our first building, looking like a very well-made two-seater toilet, accommodating our tools, put outside on wet Saturdays so that Wesley, John, and Gordon Tingley could sit in the dry to cut up comfrey.

Gordon Tingley was the husband of Mrs Tingley, my first part-time typist at Bocking who now coped with my increasing mail and, as time went on, he took over keeping the books, which was his job in the local office of British Gas. I remember going up in a mac and gumboots one soaking Saturday to fetch another sack of plants to pack in time to take to the post, and seeing blue smoke pouring out over the front doors. All three men, crammed tight as hibernating toads, with the rain hammering on the roof, were smoking pipes, arguing politics, but cutting up comfrey hard.

My father designed many driers, made by these men or my brother when he came down to stay. We tried a calor gas burner, miniature aeroplane propellers blowing cold air, electric heaters, and chicken brooder lamps. The final drier, which served us for years, was a cabinet of eight drawers with perforated zinc bottoms, one above the other, fitted above one of my father's early heaters. We dried leaves only, leaving them on wire netting to wilt in the sun first and crushing them when dry for comfrey tea. Comfrey is far more difficult to dry than any herb, because of its high protein and thick stems.

In 1956 I began experimenting with composting methods and activators, beginning with Fertosan Manure Maker. The managing director, the late Mr Enoch Cox, was a bacteriologist who had started by selling dried cultures of bacteria to replace those slaughtered by septic tank owners who used detergents, disinfectants and other chemicals. He had an extra powerful bacterial activator he called Myco, but this failed to break down sawdust in the trials we started for him. The firm paid us £50 for our final report, analysis extra, which paid our costs.

Unfortunately, even today, very few organic firms are prepared to pay for any research. They are delighted to supply a bag of what they sell provided you test it at your expense and give them a report which they can use for publicity purposes. In fact, it should be the responsibility of any firm to pay for the work, or do it themselves, in order to establish that what they sell will do the job for which they sell it. After bitter experiences later I learnt to insist that even if a firm paid for tests, they must undertake in writing not to sue, or threaten to sue us, if we found their product was inferior and we said so in our Newsletter. *Which?* can afford to fight manufacturers; the H.D.R.A. could not.

It was in 1956, when the infant H.D.R.A. was growing slowly and informally, without subscriptions, gradually bringing the Trial Ground under cultivation, that an idea came up to me, wagged its tail, dropped a stick on the carpet, and begged to be taken for a run. Authors run this risk. It often leads them to write the book they like best of all, which never sells because it says what they want to say, not what their readers are clamouring to buy and their publishers longing to sell.

The story of the adventures of Captain David Amory Robson (1882) and the steamer *Jesmond* of Newcastle, that sailed into my life in 1952, and the maritime, archaeological, and historical quest that ended when at last my only non-gardening book, *Lands of the Morning* (Regency Press, 1970) was published, is of importance in the journey of my life only because it drew Cherry and me together. I wrote it in the guilty haste in which I always have to write anything that is not practical gardening, taking my title from John Masefield's *April*:

'I have seen the lands of the morning,
Under the white, arched sails of ships.'

I wrote it right through, Faber and Faber rejected it, and it came back battered and hopeless. Then Cherry read it and liked it, translated my archaeological reports on the Canary Islands from the Spanish.

As an experienced publisher's reader, my advice to myself in 1956 would have been to write a book called 'Safe Slug Slaughter' that would sell to at least half the twenty million gardeners in Britain. It would have had to be well illustrated, giving at least nine safe, simple, cheap, and effective, non-cruel or disgusting methods of slug control that would not harm pets, or wildlife, or build up long-term environmental dangers.

I did not know enough to write that book. I still do not know enough and nor does anyone else, but some day perhaps the H.D.R.A. will find an answer to the slug problem, safe not only for gardeners but for the natural balance of which slugs are a part. The trouble is that slugs' courtship habits are so strange and interesting, and they are so beautifully designed to fill their place in the world we share with them, that so far, like Henry Doubleday, we can only 'observe the works of God in humbleness'.

9

The Year the Flowers
Began to Change

EARLY IN 1957 I lunched with a second editor, Mr George
Benson of *The Horticultural Advertiser*, the official journal of the
Horticultural Trades Association, for whom I had written for
the past seven years. This lunch was at the Lyons Corner House
near Charing Cross Station, and it was of far more lasting importance in my life than the lavish one with Tom Hopkinson of
Picture Post.

We talked of possible future articles, including my series of
reports on imaginary nurseries by 'Our Non-Existent Reporter'
which were highly popular. He asked me if I would read
through the reports and odd letters they got in, to see if there
were useful articles in them, and I gladly accepted. Then I told
him about the letters I had seen in *The Field*, especially in the
then current issue, on plant abnormalities, in this case wild
foxgloves with top florets like four-inch-across saucers.

I wrote asking for reports of experiences to both *The Horticultural Advertiser* and *The Field*, hoping to bring in more information on a subject that had always interested me. I had seen
sweetpea stems like wide ribbons, with thick, clustered florets,
and cucumber plants like twisted green planks, and read the
only book on the subject *The Mutation Theory* by Hugo de Vries
(1848–1945), published in 1909. De Vries, a Belgian geneticist,
was the first to notice freak foxgloves like the one reported in
The Field, and from it he had bred the race grown as *Digitalis
monstrosa*. The cause of these abnormalities was unknown. They
did not obey Mendel's law of inheritance, but appeared to have
a level of normal seedlings to which they could be bred. One
was *Celosia cristata*, an annual from the West Indies, grown for
the brightly coloured, flat and distorted stems that made it a
striking bedding plant. For at least 200 years, though seedsmen

120

had thrown away all the 5 per cent of 'freaks' with normal stems, it still produced 95 per cent freaks.

My letter in *The Field* drew a journalist on the minor Sunday paper *Reynolds News*, who gave the orthodox explanation that sudden rain after drought makes roots 'over-eat', producing distorted growth. However, acquired characteristics are not inherited. You can inherit your grandfather's red hair but not his wooden leg, and distortions caused by non-killing doses of selective weedkillers are not passed on in any seed they may set if they recover.

The reporter gave my address, and so did the one on the *Essex Weekly Times* who came to see me. I became snowed under with parcels, mainly of lupin spikes like clenched fists or box-ing-gloved hands, calendulas (pot marigolds) with clusters of distorted flower buds instead of seed heads, and saucer and single Canterbury-bell-floreted wild foxgloves coming second and third. Mrs Greer ran me round the Essex sites in her Land-rover, and we found that gardeners were interested and proud of the freaks they had never seen before, and none had been using the increasingly popular 2, 4–D selective weedkiller for lawns.

Messrs Baker, whose Russell lupins were still new and world famous, had five times as many fasciate spikes on their seed grounds at Codsall as normal. It cost them £4,000 in labour and lost seed. The rise had started in 1956, when they had sent specimens to Kew where tests ruled out a new virus or weed-killers. Only Russell lupins suffered, and one named Russell variety, the blue-and-cream-flowered Josephine, had the most fasciations of all, while Carter's Strain escaped completely.

Blackmore and Langdon's famous mixed delphiniums had only their normal level of fasciation, though the Pacific hybrids they also grew had about 20 per cent more spikes with four-inch-wide stems, and 'Siamese twins' with up to six stems welded together, than normal. (The word 'fasciation' comes from *fasces*, a bundle, from the bundle of rods bound round an axe carried by Roman police.)

Hurst and Sons, the Essex wholesale seedsmen, had grown a quarter-acre strip of their Giant Hyacinth-flowered White Can-dytuft for 20 years with only about a dozen plants with stems flattened into wide fans, on the whole bed. In 1957 these made up more than 10 per cent of the crop leading to barrowload after barrowload being wheeled away for burning. Candytuft are hardy annuals sown in the autumn for a larger seed crop, but plants sown in the spring in the gardens of amateurs escaped, and in every case of fasciation in that fantastic year, the plants affected were already above ground in late March and early April. This applied also to monstrosities, like the wild foxgloves in Essex, Norfolk, and Hampshire.

I felt like the 'I' in a science fiction story, for I could visualize the effects of fallout from American, British, and Soviet H-bomb tests circling the world on the jet stream winds of the stratosphere, at the very best threatening the seed crops of the world, at the worst its babies.

Newman Turner was a fighting Quaker. He splashed the article I did for him with my photographs, and one of a distorted lupin spike, on the cover of the Summer 1957 number of *The Farmer*, altering the title to 'Must man mutate to monster'. I had at last space to fire the facts I had gathered and the implications that I saw, to warn the world. I did not know then that the nuclear powers were going to agree to test their weapons underground, like small boys smoking guiltily in a disused cellar. We shall know if my theory was right or wrong, perhaps, after several Chernobyls or Three Mile Islands in the future, or if open-air testing were to be resumed on a 1956–7 scale.

All plants and trees can take in minerals they lack through their leaves, concentrating these from tiny particles blowing in the atmosphere. This was discovered in France during World War II, when our blockade stopped the French importing copper sulphate to spray their vines. After they used copper nitrate instead, they found this cured not only vine mildew but nitrogen shortage as well, by what is now called 'foliar feeding'. Plants and trees all take in radioactive carbon-14 made by cosmic rays in the atmosphere, and archaeologists can roughly date the past by counting the number of half-lives expended since the carbon dioxide was taken in by the plant or tree.

Suppose a combination of genes carried extra sensitivity to carbon-14, this would account for the fasciations there have always been, like the fasciate wheat ears that happen once in several billion stems, and were exhibited in village pubs as curiosities when harvests were by scythe.

At the University of Stockholm, the biochemistry department grew a plot of a special barley variety chosen for its large number of abnormalities, making it the vegetable equivalent to the special races of mice with naturally high levels of tumours that are bred for cancer research. From 1946 when the experiment began, till 1955, the rate was constant at one in 2,000 ears (0.05%). In 1956 it suddenly rose to one in 1,250 (0.08%), and in 1957 it rose to one in 400 (0.25%). All obvious outside causes such as blown weedkillers could be ruled out, and the 'drought or rain' would have applied to all the other crops grown in the department. The effect is of a sudden 500 per cent increase above a datum line established by nine years counting and recording.

That special barley, *Calendula officinalis*, *Digitalis purpurea* the common foxglove, and Russell lupins are all collections of individuals, each with its inherited qualities carried in genes arranged in chains called 'chromosomes'. If, instead of the normal very-long-odds chance of the extra-sensitivity combination turning up, the radioactive isotope caesium-137 which can be taken up in place of potassium by plants short of this vital food mineral, were concentrated by 'natural' foliar feeding, this would bring in many more individuals with the combination nearly right.

Caesium-137 has a half life of 33 years so it remains dangerous a long time, and its radiations are all mutation-causing gamma rays. Plants that concentrate it, as seaweeds can concentrate radioactive iodine-131 from the polluted sea, have the radiation source right inside them.

My lengthy article in *The Farmer* was quoted in the *Daily Herald*, the *Daily Record* (Glasgow), *The Friend* and a number of provincial dailies and weeklies. It was reprinted in full by *The Statesman*, in the Sunday edition of this Indian equivalent of *The Guardian*. The result was the formation of the Indian Group of the H.D.R.A., the only one so far with 75 per cent of Ph.D.s in its members.

The immediate result was still more letters, many of them enclosing clippings of letters about freak plants, with 'answers to correspondence' explaining them away. Fortunately, a number of the letters, especially from *The Friend*, enclosed donations, and these paid my typing costs. One, enclosing a donation for £10, came from Robert Pollard, a well known solicitor whose firm acted for many famous bodies, offering his services free to produce a constitution if I wanted to form an organization, though in his opinion we should have difficulty in becoming a charity because of the political implications of fallout.

The publicity drew *Illustrated*, the precariously-surviving rival to the now dead *Picture Post*. They wanted a lavishly illustrated article, short, sensational, and fast, so I got permission for them to send a photographer down to Hurst's at Kelvedon, and attacked the problem of cramming the story into 500 words. I took it at last with all my photographs to their office in High Holborn.

It was the only time I have been in the office of a magazine going down fighting with the accountants at its throat, with low wattage bulbs in all the rooms, everything needing a repaint, and the staff smoking, drinking tea, and discussing what they dared put in for expenses and who had a job in view. I was shown the oldest and most battered typewriter in the office to write the captions on. It was a Barlock, and greeted me like an old friend, so I spent an hour and a half getting them right and was in time to use my cheap day return back to Braintree before the rush hour.

Three days later I was fetched out of bed by a telephone call at 11 p.m. It was a very hoarse voice from Odhams Colour printing works at Watford. It was the honorary secretary of the Odham's Allotment Society and he thought that 'those High Holborn blokes' had mixed up my captions. My fellow gardener had, literally at the eleventh hour, saved me from having an article with a huge picture saying a delphinium was a lupin, in *Illustrated* for August 3rd, 1957.

When I got a copy, I found that most of the space was taken up by this more than half-page picture of one of Hurst's foremen, looking extremely worried, staring at a lofty, fasciated, Pacific Strain delphinium. The features editor rang me up and asked me how I liked my article, which had been cut to 396 words so it was hardly recognizable as what I had tried to say. In fury I told him.

'If you had the Ten Commandments exclusive, you'd blue pencil all but the one about Adultery, and do that as a double page colour spread.' There was dead silence then he put the phone down, but he sent me my 50 guineas, and the magazine folded about seven weeks later.

The circulation of *Illustrated* was then still over a million, but the article pulled fewer letters than the one of 2,600 words, with smaller photographs, in the Autumn 1957 issue of *The Farmer*. Both were too late for lupins and foxgloves to stir curious gardeners into writing, but the two articles were edited with two entirely different objects.

Newman Turner was an editor in an earlier tradition, that of

John Wilkes of the *North Briton* who said, 'I have twenty-six soldiers of lead. They shall march and fight under my command and they will bring down the tyrants.' He gave me the space I wanted to say what I wanted to say about the news I had gathered. I was trying to warn the world that nuclear tests could have set nature's alarm bells ringing, and I hoped to find plants or varieties of plants that would be super-sensitive to radioactive isotopes concentrated from fallout. I was unaware, till 1960, that Stockholm University had found this plant.

On September 13th, 1957, the *News Chronicle*, the *Daily Express*, and the *Daily Mail* all carried versions of the Associated Press agency report on the discovery by a Dutch biologist, Dr D. Hillenius, of deformed frogs in a ditch where the Amsterdam Nuclear Research Institute had been dumping radioactive wastes, including iodine-131.

Some had additional legs sprouting from the knee joints, some had legs facing back to front, and a few had from 15 to 20 toes sprouting from the shin bones. The growth changes of tadpoles are controlled by the thyroid gland, and this needs iodine to function. With too little, human beings get goitre, and tadpoles reared experimentally on an iodine free diet never become frogs at all. They live on as unchanged 'Peter Pans' until they die of old age with bodies the size of pullets' eggs and a powerful wriggle stroke round the tank. Only the *Daily Mail* mentioned the iodine, and in all three papers the frogs became 'tiny Loch Ness Monsters'.

Iodine-131 has a half life of only eight days and by the time fallout reaches the ground after circling the world many times, a number of these have been spent, but it only needs tiny traces to trigger trouble in the thyroids of tadpoles. The small amount of iodine in fresh water is concentrated by the algae eaten by tadpoles, especially during their early stages. Cattle consume iodine as they graze over as much as half an acre a day, and may excrete it in their milk. This is why, after the 1957 Windscale disaster, a million gallons of milk were poured into the sea, for all men (and women) can concentrate iodine-131 in the thyroid, and children are more seriously at risk because their thyroids are larger in relation to their body size, than those of adults.

Most of the letters were from gardeners interested in their freak plants; a proportion were from botany teachers who wanted teaching material to pass on to pupils who had brought in freak plants, a few from C.N.D. members, some were from Conservatives who accused me of helping Communism by causing public alarm, but there were none from nuclear physicists, either for or against me.

Fortunately, enough correspondents sent donations, usually with quite brief letters wishing me success, to give me the money to keep answering the letters. I always appealed to them to write to their M.P.s and suggested they read *Fallout* by Dr Antoinette Pirie which gave accurate and detailed information. If it had not been for the science correspondents of the serious press the existence of fallout would have stayed hidden. I like to believe that my contribution did something to build up the pressure on politicians that eventually drove the tests underground in 1963.

Our files had grown out of the fleet of machine-gun belt boxes soon after we got to Bocking, so I bought an ex-army wooden, four-drawer filing cabinet, and the freak plant outbreak made me buy a two-drawer one. They both sat side by side in my back-bedroom office at No. 20, next to a mahogany Victorian 'dumb waiter' that now held my wire baskets of work in progress.

My office and writing room ceased to double as a packing shed. As the postal orders rolled in for the comfrey report, I bought a garden shed, six feet wide and eight feet long. We called it 'The Tingley Shed' because although we had intended to use it for packing and cutting up comfrey, demoting the ex-drier to a toolshed, it became a store for reports and stationery, and a Trial Ground office, where Gordon Tingley kept the books.

A Mrs Alison Foss of Dalry in Dumfriesshire had an 'unexpected windfall' and wished to spend some of this on a worthy cause. Having read my articles in *The Farmer* for some years, she sent us £100 with some fasciate creeping buttercup plants, 'to spend on expanding your work'. I spent £50 of it on a magnificent building, 11 feet wide, 16 feet long, and eight high, with a wooden floor and a not quite flat roof, made of asbestos-cement panels that slotted into each other, part of an ex-London prefab..

It was warm, lofty, light, and dry, but most unfortunately we had sited it near the building line of Convent Lane, to avoid possible planning trouble, because there was a risk that our 50-pound palace would be considered outside the category of a garden shed. It blocked the view from the sitting-room window of our neighbour in the end bungalow, Miss Rosie Neill.

During that autumn the editor of *The Horticultural Advertiser* again intervened. He sent me a clipping from the South African *Farmers' Weekly* about a Rhodesian farmer who had cleared his tobacco eelworm by sowing a pea-tribe green-manure crop, *Crotallaria ochroleuca*, and a report in German from Wageningen, the Dutch equivalent of Beltsville in the U.S.A. or Rothamsted in England. This had a summary in English which told me that the Dutch were growing varieties of *Tagetes erecta*, the African Marigold and *T. patula*, the French Marigold, to destroy several other species of eelworm.

He was hoping for some interesting articles from me. I hoped then, and I hope still, for an organic answer, cheap and simple, to a pest or disease that chemicals cannot control.

I knew that the tomato and cucumber eelworm, then called *Heterodera marioni*, was the same as the tobacco eelworm, which could be controlled in greenhouses by steam sterilization or by crop rotation and keeping the greenhouse temperatures down, as we did at Parris's. What interested me was the idea that the new method could control the related *H. rostochiensis*, the potato eelworm, causing 'potato sickness' in old gardens and allotments, that restricted farmers to growing only one potato crop in nine years on the same field.

So I wrote to Mr Phillips, the Rhodesian farmer, asking him for seed to try in British gardens, and to Mr C. G. Carter, who had replied to my letter in *Peace News* offering to translate scientific German, who turned *Tagetes, Als Feindpflanzen von Pratylenchus*, by M. Costenbrink, K. Kuiper, and J. J. S'Jacob, into readable English.

When I received the translation I decided that it would make our second report, to be sent out for review, and might draw other experimenters, especially research stations. However, because no chemical was involved no pesticide manufacturer would spend money on research to get the process right, and no seedsman would do the work with a green-manure crop that might kill potato eelworm, for fear that other seedsmen would take advantage of his discoveries to sell their own stocks of the same seed.

That report gave me the idea behind the H.D.R.A., of research by members in their own gardens, to test out garden hints, to improve them, and to devise new and effective answers to the problems of gardening without chemicals, by distilling detailed and useful knowledge from scientific papers. This kind of research began in 1946 with a Dutch grower, Van de Berg-Smit, who planted an African marigold, Colorado Sunshine, as a cut-flower crop after daffodils which were suffering from eelworm. The next year he planted more daffodils and had an excellent crop of bloom and bulbs worth replanting. For seven years he followed this rotation with success every time, though he found that other varieties of *Tagetes erecta* were less effective than his original choice. Then he passed over his results to Wageningen, who listened to him.

Three Dutch scientists tried out both African and French marigold varieties and found that *T. patula* Harmony and *T. patula* Sunny, were the best of the latter, while Colorado Sunshine was ahead of all its group, in destroying *Pratylenchus penetrans* and *P. pratensis*, migratory eelworms, none of which are a problem in Britain. In every country where crops are grown too often in the same place these are attacked by nematodes (eelworms), and the species that is worst in any particular crop is known as its 'eelworm'. The Dutch daffodil eelworm is *P. penetrans*. The British species is *Ditylenchus dipsaci*, the stem eelworm, which attacks also oats, onions, tulips, hyacinths, lucerne, clover, and sometimes potatoes, getting right inside the plant where it can be controlled by hot water treatment. The two *Pratylenchus* species also attacked herbaceous plants, roses, and fruit trees, mainly as young stock. In Holland there are nurseries that have been established for over 300 years, and these eelworms have such a wide range of hosts that they are hard to control by rotations.

In order to write *Lands of the Morning* I had read intensively about the ancient civilizations of Central and South America, especially the Chimu of Bolivia and the Chavins of pre-Inca Peru, to whom we owe our potatoes, tomatoes, French and runner beans, and French and African marigolds. The eelworms evolved early in time and they are distributed widely round the world, with members of all the leading races in most countries. I knew that the 32 species of *Tagetes* were 'sacred' flowers to them. It seemed to me likely that people who grew crops that shared eelworms, intensively in irrigated terraces in the Andes, rather than burning the forests and moving on as did the Mayas, might have used 'the Tagetes effect' to control the pests.

I had some very useful advice on eelworms from the late Professor C. H. Duddington, author of *The Friendly Fungi*, about the fungi that live in the roots of trees and trap eelworms. These humus-feeding and symbiotic fungi are the reason nature can grow successive crops of oak trees for 50,000 years in the Weald of Sussex, yet to grow five crops of potatoes in five successive years is asking for eelworm trouble. I had 'nursed' this book, and his later works, for Faber and Faber and was honoured when he dedicated his *Evolution of Plant Design* to me.

As the *T. erecta* and *T. patula* varieties varied in their effectiveness against only three species of eelworm, I thought it likely that the Peruvians were using one of the other species as an anti- *Heterodera* break crop. Only three species were in common cultivation and I thought of the problems of collecting seeds of what could well be weeds in modern South America. My first thought was of Girl Guides, who would probably have patrols named after the wild flower I wanted, and could gather me seed, haversack-fulls, but all would speak Spanish. So would anyone who could tell me how they were used by modern peasants in Peru.

I wrote to *Mother Earth*, the Soil Association quarterly, asking for someone to translate letters in Spanish. That number reached Cherry (then Mrs Hilda Brooke) when she was packing up to go and live in Cape Town to work at the library of Groote Schuur Hospital on the possibility that polio was connected with an imbalance of trace elements. Her fellow-physio friend, Rosalie Evans, suggested that she ought to offer to help, for with her experience as a special examiner in the London censorship during the war she would be ideally suited to making head and tail of the handwriting of Peruvian girl guide mistresses. But she was too busy and put it aside till later.

The Dutch Embassy gladly gave me permission to publish the transcription, but this time I wanted at most 250 copies. Again I looked in *Exchange and Mart*, where all our office equipment came from, and found a duplicating firm, Brocards of Plymouth. For our first cover I designed the H.D.R.A. badge — the Latin Square. This was the very simplest form of replicated plot lay-out which could be done without any extra charge and it appeared on the covers of our Newsletters from No. 2 to No. 99; Number One (1958) was too small to have a cover.

This taught me that however well a report is duplicated, it will never be reviewed by the press, and that folded foolscap will not fit well in a standard envelope. We used folded quarto after this and had all our notepaper and reports printed. The early H.D.R.A. owed a great deal to *Exchange and Mart*, and to Messrs Gill, the secondhand furniture shop in Braintree.

In February, 1958, Mr J. P. C. Phillips of Rhodesia sent a fat, cream, canvas bag of about 7 lb. of *Crotalaria* seed. I wrote a short account of it, with directions to sow it in a Latin Square, four inches apart and eight between rows, ideally trying to get the local horticultural officer to count the potato eelworm cysts before and after. I also suggested that readers sow *Tagetes erecta* Harmony, or buy it as bedding plants.

Then I wrote a letter to *The Daily Telegraph* and on March 3rd, 1958, they printed it, not in the correspondence column but as a news item on the back page. This pulled a hundred letters in the week, and from them I gathered 50 experimenters. Mr A. W. Chowne, a bank manager from Kingsbridge in Devon, who had a quarter acre of kitchen garden infested with potato eelworm, became the very first H.D.R.A. experimenter.

Now I had my organization, but with nothing official that people could join, no subscriptions, and very little money. I saw that I needed to take up Robert Pollard's offer of legal help. I lunched with him in a pub in Victoria Street, near his office, and found him a plump, fast-talking, precise man with a small moustache and a pipe in his mouth most of the time when he was not flourishing it to make a point, or lighting it in a regular ritual with his eyes sparkling through the smoke, and the last match of many thrown away with force and speed. He began as our 'legal eagle', and became our prop and stay, our resort in times of trouble and stress, and my loyal friend through thick and thin.

I had written to him, sending our reports, such as they were, so he already knew roughly what I was doing, but I poured out my story, directed by a first class legal mind towards the relevant points. At the end he aid, 'You will have to be a charity.'

'But we cannot be a charity, we haven't any money.'

'That is just the time to become a charity. When you have half a million, the Charity Commissioner look for supertax evasion and half the cases we get are thrown out.' I began to see how he could afford to be generous to bodies like the H.D.R.A.

'I suppose you get paid just the same if the case fails.'

'Of course.' He sucked hard on the pipe. 'But there should not be any trouble in your case.'

As a charity we would pay no tax, subscriptions could be covenanted to enable us to claim back tax on them, we would not pay rates, or be liable for death duties. But if we failed, the committee would have unlimited liability. In Robert Pollard's opinion, a charity was the best thing to be, and fitted exactly what I wanted to do. Becoming a charity took us from April to October and instead of paying a 50 guinea fee to Counsel for his opinion that our objects were good and charitable, we gave him a dozen comfrey plants, thus making legal history.

Our objects were:

1) The improvement and encouragement of horticulture generally.

2) Research into, and the study of, improved methods of organic farming and gardening.

3) Research into, and the utilization of, Russian comfrey in connection with the foregoing objects.

4) The encouragement of research and experiment in agriculture and horticulture, and the dissemination of knowledge of the results of such research and experiment, among farmers, gardeners, and schools.

5) The advancement of knowledge of, and the fostering of public interest in, the benefits to be derived from the utilization of Russian comfrey and other plants useful in organic husbandry.

Robert Pollard designed our constitution like a boy's first pair of long trousers — to allow for growth. The basis was, I believe, the Constitution of the Royal Horticultural Society, modified to make it a charity. Like the R.H.S., our committee nominated its successors, choosing members who had done useful work for the Association for election by the committee; entirely undemocratic of course, but where members are united behind a common objective, this should not cause problems. We got round the nuclear fallout question by deciding that it did not have to be mentioned in our objects because fasciate lupins, barley, etc. were a part of horticulture and agriculture and any increase caused by nuclear accidents or bombs was not politics but pollution. As long as we studied the effects of this pollution in making crops unsafe for food or feed and their seeds unfit to sow we were working for 'the improvement of horticulture and agriculture generally'.

'The dissemination of knowledge of the results of such research and experiment among farmers, gardeners, and schools' was to make it clear that our job was spreading knowledge of what we found, not teaching the work of others, for we were a research rather than an educational charity.

Even as late as the 1951 edition of the R.H.S. Dictionary, the root-knot eelworm was identified as *Heterodera marioni*, but by 1958 it was realized that they were not one creature but four: *Meliodogyne arenaria; M. hapla; M. lavanica; M. incognita* var. *acrita*. They attack a wide range of tropical and sub-tropical crops including tobacco, maize, soya beans, and bananas. This is why, in Britain, they are a pest only in greenhouses, and Mr Fred controlled his by keeping the temperature low, to slow them down sufficiently for control by crop rotation.

In Britain it would not pay to waste cropping time by growing *Crotalaria* under glass when steam sterilization is much cheaper. As my experimenters had found great trouble in germination of seed, even when they soaked it in water, my father bolted a cocoa tin to a chuck on his lathe and whizzed it round with sand for varied periods to rub off some of the seed coat, till he hit the right abrasion period, and our experimenters were then able to germinate it in their greenhouses.

Unfortunately, our technique failed to make an impression on potato eelworm, which has chemical-proof cysts that can last 10 years in the soil. I speculated there might be scope for raising *Crotalaria* as a pea-tribe half-hardy annual, growing like *Nemesias* (also from Africa) in our summers which are as warm as Rhodesian winters, to bed out in sunny borders that have grown tomatoes too often. So we grew them in 1958, but concentrated on *Tagetes*.

When I wrote an appeal for wild *Tagetes* seed, saying why I wanted it, to *The Christian Science Monitor*, it drew letters from many countries, among them one from the curator of Missouri Botanic Gardens, who had seen Chimu and Chavin drinking vessels from which the mourners drank a very powerful maize brew at funerals. These were painted with scenes narrating the life of the departed, modelled with his face and buried with him.

The farmers had conventionalized paintings of maize cobs, potatoes, tomatoes, and other crops, which the curator had identified. These included some of an umbel-headed *Tagetes*.

As every schoolgirl once learned, daisies belong to the order Compositae (the same order as *Tagetes*) and have white ray florets round the outsides of the closely packed yellow disc florets of their centres. African marigolds resemble very double daisies with extra small centres, but *T. minuta* has only disc florets, spread out into a flat-topped umbel, like cow parsley or a carrot run to seed. It is most unfortunately named 'minuta' from the small size of these yellow star-like florets, because it grows 10 feet high.

It was introduced into Britain in 1826 and into Australia by an amateur gardener named Rogers. There it swiftly became a weed, known as 'stinking Rogers' because of the strong, Dettol-like smell of its foliage. During the 1914–18 war it crossed to South Africa in the hay brought to feed the Australian cavalry horses on the voyage, to spread by its tiny, groundsel-type, blowing seeds as a weed called 'khakibos' by the Afrikaaners, and 'Mexican marigold' when it reached Rhodesia. In Britain it flowers in October, too late to set its fluffy seeds and become yet another hated weed.

A second reader of *The Christian Science Monitor* sent me a large parcel of *T. minuta* seed. He was a Mr Van Elden, of the Botany and New Plants Division of the South African Ministry of Agriculture, who had spent two of his dinner hours gathering it on waste land in Pretoria. He told me it was customary to hang bunches of it in native huts so the smell would repel fleas, and that it was reputed to kill weevils.

Yet another helpful reader was Mr Pelham Wright, director of the British Chamber of Commerce in Mexico City, who also considered that *T. minuta* was the most likely *Tagetes* to be used as a break crop, and got his secretary to collect us the second most likely candidate. This was *T. florida* which grew about two feet high, had larger, star flowers in a more widely spread, flat, flower cluster, and was dried for use as incense in the temples of the Aztec Maize God.

Then, in June, 1958, Newman Turner sent me an advertisement, clipped from *The Times*, for a 'Down to earth gardening correspondent with the ability to make vegetables interesting to readers of a national Sunday newspaper', suggesting that this sounded an ideal job for me. I wrote at once, outlining my experience and sending a selection of my published articles. A month later a reply from *The Observer* asked me to fix an appointment for an interview.

Off I went to Tudor Street to be interviewed by Charles Davy, the assistant editor, after a long journey through dark, polished-woodwork corridors and old-fashioned lifts with polished brass fittings. At the interview I learned that the weekly articles would have to be 515 words long, facing those of Vita Sackville-West of Sissinghurst Castle with whose fourth gardener I had shared lodgings, across the page from the nature article by Richard Fitter, and the large 'art' photograph above him. Three weeks later I was summoned to another interview, this time with David Astor, the editor, whose decision is final. I was interviewed in a large room with an enormous Chippendale dining table, stretched to the maximum number of leaves. It was a Tuesday, the day that starts the week on a Sunday paper, and on it were spread 'galley proofs', column-wide strips of all the features for the next issue.

I had the nerve to tell David Astor that 'articles are like wrist watches — the smaller ones are more expensive,' and got the 10 guineas an article I asked him for. Emboldened by this success I went on to ask for 2/6d (12^1/$_2$p) per reader's letter answered. The elderly man from the accounts department, sitting in on the interview, here volunteered that V. Sackville-West got £2 a week towards her shorthand typist for that purpose, but had not averaged more than eight letters a week for the past 10 years, and suggested I be given the same. But I stuck out for my half crown a letter, and got it.

My first article drew 32 letters, and the figure rarely fell below 30. When one week brought 850 it was insisted that I should send in a copy of my reply in order to have it duplicated for despatch from Tudor Street.

This was in response to my article on broom hedges that began 'There is no hedge that gardeners buy, one half so splendid as the one they sow.' An ornamental broom, grafted on a pencil-thick laburnum seedling and planted a foot apart, grew a quick hedge that made a splendid blaze of colour, but at a prohibitive cost. I bought mixed broom seeds, sowed them in our own garden, and discovered that if they were transplanted at 2 to 3 inches high, they grew very fast and flowered in their second season. The best strain was the 'Monarch', sold by Hurst and Sons, the wholesale seedsmen where I had photographed the fasciate candytuft. They blended their Monarch mixtures as carefully as tea merchants blend teas, including all the brown and yellow, dark red and pink, orange and white, and all the colours of the best grafted *Cytisus* varieties. The hedge would live only about six years but was splendid while it lasted and

colourful seedlings were still coming up from the hedge I grew
from seed for the Trial Ground 25 years later.

That lay far in the future. First, I had to learn to write tightly
enough to pack into 515 words a full account of how to grow a
vegetable or fruit, if it were uncommon like salsify how to cook
it, the best varieties, and how to cope with its pests and diseases
without chemicals. It was not part of my contract to be organic,
but I got away with it.

10

The Road from Silent Spring

I rank *Silent Spring* with *Das Kapital* and *The Origin of Species* among the books that have changed the world. It is still in print in almost every language except Russian and Chinese. Just as Rudolph Steiner and Sir Albert Howard began the compost and fertility aspects of the organic movement, Sir Robert McCarrisson, Weston Price, and Dr Franklin Bicknell added the nutritional and food additives angle that altered the way we think about food, and Lady Eve Balfour, Newman Turner and Friend Sykes pioneered organic farming books, Rachel Carson (1907–1964) awoke the world to the dangers of pollution by pesticides, fungicides and all the chemicals that add up to danger in our bodies and through the food chains of the world.

She had a far greater impact than any of the great men and women of the past because she had genius as well as knowledge and she knew that she was dying of cancer. She also had a first-class publisher who arranged for an abridged version to be serialized taking up the entire serious-article space in three June, 1962, issues of *The New Yorker*. These excerpts were reviewed and comments began to appear in the British press even before Houghton Mifflin published the first edition in October 1962, with pre-publication sales running into five figures. The Washington Correspondent of *The . Observer* (2/9/62) reported that: 'A top American Government scientific committee is looking into fears first raised in a series of *New Yorker* articles, that modern chemical pesticides are poisoning man's environment. The President himself has said that the committee had been formed since the articles first appeared'. When that Committee reported in 1965, its findings confirmed Rachel Carson's facts and vindicated her claims. In 1980 she was posthumously awarded the Presidential Medal for Freedom, the

US equivalent of our Order of Merit and in its obituary *The New York Times* called her 'one of the most influential women of all time'.

The British edition published on February 14th, 1963 by Hamish Hamilton, with a preface by Julian Huxley and a foreword by Lord Shackleton, ran to reprint at the hardcover price of 25 shillings. The British Association of Agricultural Chemical Manufacturers prepared an expensively printed brochure including a section which could be used as a review by the lazy, praising Rachel Carson as a poetic popular writer and implying that she was merely an emotional, wildlife-loving spinster of 55, rather than a qualified biologist with years of experience of what chemicals do to wild and human life. The book, to quote the Association of Agricultural Chemical Manufacturers, was 'highly controversial' it 'gave an unbalanced picture', it was 'one-sided' and its 'conclusions needed confirmation by laboratory research'.

As Gardening Correspondent on *The Observer*, I was sent a copy, as was Vita Sackville-West; Clifford Selly got one as Agricultural Correspondent, John Davy as Science Correspondent, so did the Literary Editor and the Features Editor, with two for the Editor himself. David Astor had, of course, already decided in light of the rave reviews and bitter attacks by the chemical industry, that *Silent Spring* was a major work and deserved a whole half page from the Science Correspondent.

To my suggestion that they should sue the Association of Agricultural Chemical Manufacturers for damages, Hamish Hamilton replied that they could not possibly take legal action because it was impossible to prove they had suffered any financial loss, for the brochure had actually given the book the best publicity it could possibly have had. Significantly never again has any industry attempted to influence reviewers against a book. Public Relations Officers nowadays resort to other weapons.

The Compost and Chemicals Latin square on the Trial Ground ('J' on the maps) was designed to test the effect of a new general fertilizer of the Growmore type, which had aldrin added as a kind of 'mass medication' aimed at destroying soil pests such as wireworm, that may be present, rather like adding aspirin by the ton to London's water supply to cure any headaches within the Metropolitan area. I only had time to use it twice before the makers quietly took it off the market in 1963.

My object was to be able to measure the long term build-up if the fertilizer was used at the maximum recommended dose every year, how much was taken up by potatoes as the aldrin level rose, and how many parts per million of aldrin in a soil prevented the formation of nitrogen fixing bacteria nodules on pea roots, which could easily have been measured by sowing a row of peas on each square.

At the start of the trial I was concerned about the effect of killing ground beetles and their larvae, perhaps our best natural controllers of the underground keeled slugs that eat holes in potatoes, as well as wireworms and black millipedes. Until I read *Silent Spring* I did not know that after four years aldrin turned into dieldrin. Though this is only five times as toxic as DDT, taken by mouth by accident or as a residue in crops, it is forty times as toxic when absorbed through the skin, producing liver damage and convulsions. One worker on the World Health Organisation anti-malarial campaign, spraying dieldrin because the malaria mosquitoes had developed resistance to DDT, suffered convulsions for *four months*, while about half of such workers were affected for shorter periods and many died. These men made no headlines for they were either black or brown. Had we allowed the soils of British gardens and allotments to build up dieldrin to convulsion on contact level, very many people would surely have died before a 'mystery disease' had been tracked down to this 'mass medication' fertilizer. Thanks to Rachel Carson, this did not happen and neither did hundreds, perhaps thousands, of human disasters from other chemicals, such as the chlordane (in worm killers) that lasts up to 15 years in the soil and the lindane used against carrotfly. Bans came into force all over the industralized world, but the manufacturers went on selling their products   forbidden in countries rich enough to worry about wildlife   to the Third World, where users are often unable to read warnings even in the local language and protective clothing is rarely worn owing to poverty and climate.

Silent Spring warned the world of the perils of pesticides but offered no alternative to the chemicals it attacked with such genius. Finding safe and simple answers to pests and diseases that do no harm to the environment takes more than genius — it takes research. The organic movement can only do its best with what it has had the time and money to discover. My task as I saw it was to find those answers.

I began by gathering traditional remedies reaching back through my memory to the hints and ideas I had learnt from the head gardeners of the 1930s, like the shotgun cartridge case trick for earwigs. Then I wrote *Pest Control Without Poisons*, our booklet that sold 120,000 copies at 3 shillings each between 1965 and 1979. Meanwhile, I did my best to use the work of our experimenting members to find those alternatives to pesticides for which Rachel Carson had set all thinking gardeners clamouring.

One of our best experimenters was an architect, Malcolm Hickling, whose work through that summer, with Brian Inglis of the Council for Nature identifying his excellent drawings of the creatures concerned, produced *Biological Pest Control Report No. 1.* He had grown broad beans and had spent the summer counting the blackfly on them, observing how their numbers fluctuated according to predator populations. Here, the highest scorer was not the two-spot ladybird or its tiny black, six-legged, crocodile-like larva, but *Anthocoris nemorum* (so tiny it has no popular name) which, unlike ladybirds, eats red spider and other mites and their eggs. He also observed a small black earwig, *Labia minor*, eating aphids, unlike the large, common species, *Forficularia auriculari*, which damages dahlia and chrysanthemum bloom and ripening peaches.

I hoped that this report, and *No. 2* which followed it, would start a hobby of 'Insect watching', of greater garden value than birdwatching, and Malcolm suggested that by providing better winter hibernation quarters we could help our friends to increase faster than our foes. He invented 'Ladybird nestboxes', short rolls of waterproof building paper to be used by both *Anthocoris* and ladybirds. This work led to our ladybird nest-box campaign that years later got me televized in a programme on the work of the H.D.R.A. with Esther Rantzen gazing down at a ladybird racing round my wrist watch.

The opportunity to buy our Trial Ground came with a legacy of £500 from Lady Seton, founder of the National Gardens Guild, a charity supplying tools and seeds for prisoners' gardening, and editor of its quarterly *The Guild Gardener* whose two guinea cheques for 1,200 word articles had been a welcome part of my income. I hoped this might go a long way towards the freehold, and wrote to Mr Hunnable's solicitors. After a long wait they told me we could have our existing land with 220 feet of frontage on Convent Lane, and the long and highly isosceles triangle behind it, for £2,500.

We had six months in which to raise the money, so we drafted a suitably stately letter to *The Times*, which never printed it neither did those to the 'heavies' who print appeals for money to keep famous paintings in Britain. So I duplicated an appeal with a map of what we were buying on the back and sent it to all 470 members. As I said in No. 9 *Newsletter* 'I had no idea you cared so much and your enthusiastic letters have touched me deeply. I have tried to reply to them all, but you swamped me with over £300 in the first two days and the total is now (2/2/61) £1,150.'

By our sixth committee meeting (27/2/61) the total had reached £1,350, and Newman Turner read out a letter from Dr Sydney Osborn offering to lend us an interest free £1,000 to close the deal, which we accepted with gratitude. Robert then set the wheels turning again. The deeds were 'engrossed' and the transaction completed of buying the first part which we had already leased from M. Hunnable & Son, plus the new portion which belonged to the Clacton Sand and Gravel Co. Ltd., a company in which Maurice Hunnable had a controlling interest.

It was not until March 11th that the land finally became ours and Dr Osborn and I walked over it. In the middle there stood a scrub oak seedling and he commented, 'That's a fine young tree, it could outlast us both'. We left it standing for years calling it 'Dr Osborn's Oak' in memory of the elderly doctor who brought the infant H.D.R.A. into the world, for we had only time to pay him back one instalment of the £1,000 when he died. He had been ill when he wrote to make the offer.

Incredibly, by September 9th the Trial Ground was tidied within an inch of its life for our first Open Day, with every path edged with our new shears, and all 11 newsletters *Comfrey Report No. 1*, *Compost Comfrey and Green Manure*, and our *Report on the Sheen Flame Gun* (a giant blowlamp for killing weeds which we had tested for a £50 fee) displayed on one of the hired trestles set out in front of the shed where we displayed all our machinery. This included a Howard Hako, their smallest model, and a Wolsey Merrytiller, with a belt drive to the front rotors. Benson, our first full time gardener, was there in his best blue suit, demonstrating the Yeoman and the two machines up and 'P' 'Q' and 'R' which were not yet planted. Trying out these cultivators which had been lent for demonstrating purposes was our most popular 'sideshow' among the 96 members and the 8 non-members who paid 2/6d admission.

Everyone passed through the new gate, where the hedge joined the bungalow garden, with its cast metal plaque bearing the name of the Association, and 'all enquiries to No. 20' on it, because people kept wandering in under the impression that our plots were allotments. I had fetched my L.C.C. desk typing table from Blackheath out from retirement as a potting bench and sat by it with Newman Turner who had come across from Letchworth for the occasion welcoming members and distributing Trial Ground Guides.

Perhaps the most important visitor to the Trial Ground arrived on a sunny afternoon early in July. I had been writing regularly to Mrs Hilda Brooke, then living in Cape Town, about comfrey which she grew and gave away and tried on a wide variety of stock, and who was an accredited lecturer for the Soil Association of South Africa. She arrived by the little steam train from Witham to Braintree that connected us with Liverpool Street, and a taxi from the station. I showed her everything from the radioactive wristwatch hands on the candytufts to the new triangle taking shape, and lastly my Crotallaria seed in the prefab packing shed. She told me, years afterwards, that after she had seen me run my hand through those small brown seeds, she recognized that she had fallen in love with me.

I told her about *Lands of the Morning* and she offered to translate the bulky paperback archaeology books in Spanish that could add so much knowledge to the manuscript I had written in guilty haste as a part of me, a poor thing but mine own, my only non-gardening book. She took it back to South Africa, for she was in England for only a short time to have an operation on her ear, which did not after all do her Menière's disease any good. We had tea at No. 20 with my mother, but she never met my father who was in the front room in bed for he could no longer get up the stairs.

Inside this already too fat book there is a love story struggling to get out, but it must struggle in vain until, perhaps, American academics with unlimited funding and no sense of humour will edit and publish 'The Letters of Lawrence Hills' in eight volumes at £500 each thickly sown with footnotes. Therefore the slow progress of Mrs Hilda Brooke to my Cherry 'hung with snow', to quote some rather hackneyed Housman, must go uncharted.

What most struck Cherry, the physiotherapist, was my pitiful thinness, well under eight stone from the malnutrition suffered by all coeliacs unless they are on an entirely gluten-free diet, but though she recognized I was a coeliac it was to be some time before she could alter the diet. The Committee, especially Doris Grant, worried about my overworking, but they all believed in 'Holidayotherapy', that popular panacea, which to me meant harder work to write myself ahead, and still more when I came back to cope with the results of absence. However, finally even mother insisted, and I arranged to accept a very kind invitation from Ernst Baumann, the Swiss organic orange grower, to spend as long as I liked staying with him and his three daughters on his plantations near Valencia in Spain. I had begun writing ahead and contriving to be away for a month, but suddenly I had to cancel all plans. My father's health began to deteriorate fast. Dr Panter got him into St Michael's Hospital, and he died on October 24th 1962, aged 80, slipping away gently with pneumonia before his cancer of the prostate gland brought him real suffering.

It was very sad that he died before our experiment in trapping carrot, onion, and cabbage root flies using the 10 scent oils made from species pollinated by flies in members' gardens. I had the help of Mr J. W. Stephenson, our chemist and postmaster, who diluted the scent baits with ispropyl alcohol, and Martin Austin, a retired Ministry entomologist.

The final report on this experiment, which I called *Perfumes Against Pests*, earned a 28-line review under 'News and Views' in the prestigious scientific journal *Nature* for August 14th, 1965. Father would so have rejoiced in this great honour my work had won. Although we had mainly established that the easiest creatures to catch are fungus gnats (*Sciara* spp) of which there are about 500 species whose tiny, white, thread-like larvae feed on toadstools of every type as well as mushrooms, it did show that dill and fennel oil are the best additives to a sugar bait for cabbage root fly.

Mother and I carried on together. She was now 80, a month older than my father, and I was 51 and greyer than she was. We bought a new stair carpet and reorganized our lives to include more domestic help, for Mother's glaucoma was worse, although she could still see well enough to enjoy the garden she loved, the front blazing with alpines and the back crammed with organic fruit and vegetables. Though we lost my father's pension I sold the widely assorted shares that he delighted to follow through the press City sections.

A member who wished to remain anonymous sent a donation of £200 direct to Newman Turner with the idea that it
should be the basis of a fund to pay me a salary, because I was
working myself to death. This side-tracked the agitation for me
to take the holiday my father's death had prevented and it was
decided to send round an appeal for seven-year convenants to
provide me with enough income to stop writing articles other
than for *The Observer* and to employ more part-time labour. I
got £500 a year from August 1968 the first salary I ever drew
from the H.D.R.A.

The committee still felt I was overworking, but agreed that
there was nothing wrong with me that a good holiday would
not cure.

This time I was to stay with Mr and Mrs Foss at Dalry, near
Castle Douglas in Dumfries-shire. I learnt later that Hugh Foss
had worked in the City, retired, sold his house in Sevenoaks,
and bought a larger, far cheaper one, in Scotland. Here he built
up a new business arranging Highland dances, like a kilted
Victor Sylvester, even 'restoring' those for which only the pipe
music remained. Alison was a roly-poly woman in her sixties
who had often sent us generous donations when they were
extra welcome, and lived in a well worn and happy muddle of
plants, sheep, and dogs, with a river at the bottom of their
garden where the curlews called liquidly through the nights.

Then I got a serious 'attack' and went on that wretched
cream-cracker and milk diet, having unknowingly gone over
the limit for gluten, for I still had no idea what to avoid. I knew
the familiar signs, stocked up with books for my Mother and
myself and went to bed relying on the Sucklings next door, Mrs
McLean, and the Tingleys to keep the shopping going and
kissed my holiday goodbye.

The attack went on and on, with me taking the familiar
kaolin medicine, dictating letters in bed and watching my
hoarded articles drain away down the river of time. I had been
writing more and more freely to Hilda Brooke about her comfrey which she was giving away extensively as part of her work
with the Soil Association of South Africa. She advised me to get
investigated in a good hospital.

In accordance with my custom of sending copies of my books
to the Sisters of the wards I had been in while writing my
Miniature Alpine Gardening, Faber and Faber had posted a
copy of *Down to Earth Fruit and Vegetable Growing* to the

Royal Free Hospital, the last hospital of my R.A.F. career, and had a friendly thank-you letter from the current sister. So I wrote to her telling the story of my health and asking for help, and got a letter back by return telling me that Dr Anthony Dawson, the specialist for her ward, would admit me in three weeks time. So I got up to write *Observer* articles, agreed ahead by telephone, following the year round, inspected the Trial Ground where everything was fearfully overgrown, especially the weeds, but the comfrey most of all, checked the stocks and ordered more of what was running low, and checked that my Trial Ground staff Mr Lock, Terry Johnson, Michael Suckling, and John Keyes (then a schoolboy now a computer expert with three children and a Jaguar) were cramming in everything.

Finally I got away and arrived by taxi from Liverpool Street 19 years older than at the end of my journey from Hillingdon by despatch rider's sidecar, but still hoping for victory over my internal enemy. Very tired and painfully thin, I was ready to relax in a welcoming double ward where 60 men were organized into the traditional parody of family life by a sister in her forties and two strapping tall staff nurses. All I had to do was rest and trust to the skill of Dr Dawson as a medical detective to solve the mystery within, which I would so much rather be without.

I had been in only two days when I got a get well card from Hilda Brooke by airmail, for during my three week wait I had written to tell her that I had taken her advice and got into hospital. She had copied a spirited drawing of a South African otter chasing a fish because I had written of hearing the otters whistling to each other as I did to her at the other end of the world on the empty isle of Ulva when I was in Mull with David and Claudine Mackenzie. (David Mackenzie's book *Goat Husbandry* (Faber & Faber £6.95) the goat-keeper's Bible that I nursed more than 35 years ago, is the only one of my children still in print). In it she sent the first of many verses she wrote for me.

'I'm a very foolish otter
and I don't know what do do
So I'm going out to potter
And then I'm coming to you.

I would like to bring you fishes
But even nice fish might smell
So I only bring best wishes
To speed you to get well.

I'm as simple as a Cottar
Who has no glamour or guile
I'm merely a foolish otter,
But I hope to make you smile.'

I responded also in verse and because we had been corres-
ponding about Beatrice Trum Hunter, the American health and
diet writer, my verse which was nearer an organic McGonagal
than poetry was:

'Here the health food hunters come,
Hunting for the nimble Trum,
The males are blue the females plum,
The young ones sing the old ones hum.'

I rang the changes in the rhyme and she came back with:

'Yes I've often hunted Trums,
Selling wholefood cake and crumbs
From a Health shop in the slums.'

As a result of this versifying I became 'Trum' instead of
Lawrence, and changed Hilda to 'Cherry' in place of her middle
name of Cecilia because of her 'cherry-blossom white' hair. During the five weeks I was in the Royal Free I wrote to her several
times a week, telling her what was going on, what I hoped to
do, and what interested me with time to use words for pleasure,
without haste.

The tubes I now had to swallow were plastic and tasteless,
much less nauseating than those I had downed at Bart's in
1936, and I endured many variations on the theme, particularly one that pumped in a glucose solution at a high level
and pumped it out at a lower one, collecting samples for the
laboratory to test how well each section of my intestine was
working. The final clue, leading to conviction, came from
swallowing a tiny steel capsule on a long tube, X-rayed to
position it accurately on the areas that were not working, and
exhausting the air from it with a plunger pump. This caused
a semi-cylindrical knife in the capsule to remove a tiny slice
of the wall of my intestine. When this was microscopically
examined, it showed my villi lying down poisoned by my
food instead of waving cheerfully as they took in the nutrients like healthy feeding roots, showing I had been suffering
from undiagnosed 'root damage' all my life.

145

In 1950, Dr W. H. Dicke of the University of Utrecht had established that gluten was the cause of the coeliac condition in babies born without the specific enzyme to digest this gummy protein present in wheat, oats, rye and barley, and I had been one of those babies. The traumatic experience inflicted on very young children forced to swallow that tube and capsule can be imagined, and I should always prefer the method used by Dr Alfred Shatin of Melbourne Australia, of putting his cases on a gluten-free diet then diagnosing them as coeliacs if they improved on it, to be used for any child of mine. To be restricted to a diet free from gluten can do no harm to any medical condition, for its only use is to make the sides of the bubbles holding the carbon dioxide from yeast or baking powder that makes bread rise and cakes light. The majority of people in China, India, Indonesia, Africa, and South and Central America, eating maize millet and rice lacking gluten, are never coeliacs. In fact modern hard wheats are bred for higher gluten, enabling bakers to sell more air to the loaf.

There is now no excuse for anyone to suffer the handicap I suffered all my life, for the diet is easy, simple, and no more expensive than any other diet, provided you do not imagine that you have to eat bread cakes and biscuits made from substitute flours. The condition is not an allergy, we are just born with a missing enzyme. Dr Shatin's theory (*Medical Journal of Australia*, **2** ,169 1964) is that humans became big seed eaters with the invention of agriculture, and some modern people, like Australian aborigines, who live without any grain on meat, fish, fruit, vegetables and such extras as witchitty grubs to balance up their vitamins and minerals, have inherited only Stone Age enzymes.

Before she went to South Africa, Cherry had spent three years working single-handed on her allotment on Hampstead Heath only to become one of about 1,100 people turned off their cherished plots for the land to be restored to heath again. Deeply aware how much these 'gardens' had meant to all these people, she and a friend spent two years searching around the London area to find a place where the occupants could have security of tenure to plant their fruit trees, put up huts, and make real gardens like those in Denmark. In 1953, after she found a suitable 10 acre field at Barnet, she founded the Brookdale Garden Community Association with the help of her friend Rosalie Evans and her sister Dorothy and others, while still living in Hampstead and working as a physiotherapist in a Dalston clinic. As members of the Soil Association, she and her friends were gardening organically and their example led to all the other tenants adopting the same methods.

Though the Association had a constitution it had not been officially registered as a charity and as tenant, Cherry merely had a 'gentleman's agreement' with Lord Stafford. So when she heard that the eighty odd tenants to whom she had promised permanence were to be turned out, she came back to England to fight the case. As it would not be heard for some time, she broke the sea voyage at Las Palmas in the Canary Islands, catching a ship to Southampton a fortnight later, which gave her time to visit the museum and other places in search of anything that could be useful to my *Lands of the Morning*.

The Committee were determined that I should have my long delayed holiday as soon as I had got *Pest Control Without Poisons* away for review, and so was Mother. Iris was coming down to stay with her to hold the fort with the help of the Tingleys, Mrs McLean, and Anne Elsey. Somehow I got through the proofs wrote the index and finished *Pest Control Without Poisons*, with a Foreword by John Cripps, editor of *The Countryman*, and a chapter on 'Garden Chemicals and the Law' by Robert Pollard. It would sell at 3 shillings and the Soil Association had already bought 1,000 for £75, which helped with the printing bill of £360 for 10,000.

At last it was all arranged for my first holiday for 10 years, most of these without ends to their weeks, the ticket to stay with Hugh and Alison Foss was bought, and I had arranged to spend the third week staying with Ruth Chester and her family in Hampstead (old friends of Cherry's) and chasing round the British Museum and other archaeological institutions in London. We were also booked to lecture at a vegetarian garden party together. I had all the envelopes for the 200 review copies addressed and stamped, and the letters typed and signed ahead, among them one I wrote to Richard Fitter, *The Observer* nature correspondent, asking him to review it as though it were 'The Mating Habits of British Seagulls — or One good Tern Deserves Another'.

At last the books arrived by road from Plymouth late on Saturday morning. Luckily, Mr Lock was still packing and helped handle the heavy parcels of 200. They were stowed away under the beds in my room, my mother's room and the front room which had been our guest room since my father died, where my sister was to sleep that night. It was then I realised that Latimer Trend had printed extra, 11,600 to use up the paper, an additional £195 at the retail price for our £360. We built them into a stack in the middle of the front room, bonding them like brickwork, piled high without tumbling. They were beautifully packed in corrugated and brown paper which lasted in the packing shed for months, but were a dead weight to carry in through the front door into the downstairs front bedroom from the pile inside the gate.

Iris arrived in time to help Mother and me stuff the review copies into the envelopes with their letters and take them to the post office by taxi, to get them as far as the *Western Morning News* in Plymouth, *The Yorkshire Post* in Leeds, and the Glasgow *Daily Record*, by Monday morning. The three of us talked our heads off, and I had time to show Iris where everything was and what to send with which. A price list and a 'Who we are and what we do' would go out with every *Pest Control Without Poisons* to give each one a chance of making new members.

I got away on the Sunday morning, carrying the new blue suitcase my parents had bought with their hoarded cigarette coupons for my last attempted holiday in Spain. (It was wrecked by Air India 12 years later when I went round the world.) It was a long journey to Dalry, by lines long ago Beechinged, ending in a trip by a pre-war Hillman taxi through pine plantations and villages in the glen bottoms, some sprouting tall 'H' television aerials and others with none, for the small mountains of southern Scotland shut out the TV signals of the day.

Hugh, Alison, and all six dogs were there to welcome me to the first meal of many reminding me of the Mad Hatter's Tea Party. Alison laid her big round dining table at the beginning of the week and we three moved round it, piling the used crockery in the kitchen for the twice-weekly visits of her brawny and incomprehensible (to me) Lowland Lassie who washed and relaid with everything sparking clean. Jeanie 'sorted three leddies' in Dalry, including doing their laundry, and Hugh used to say 'I see we have Old Peg-Leg staying with us again,' when he found himself with a single sock from one of the other 'Good men' (husbands). The dogs also helped and would come racing up the paths when Alison and I were gardening with news of who had called. She would look at her watch and say 'That'll be postie' (postman), 'fishie', 'flesher' (butcher), or 'Johnnie Van', the travelling general store, and she would set off up the garden following a forest of waving tails. Once they arrived in such a state of excitement that I came up with her to find two Jehovah's Witnesses who had lost their way.

The only room in the house kept free from dogs was Hugh's study because when he tried to fit invented Highland dance steps to bagpipe music on his heavy, single-reel tape recorder, the way they leapt, barked and howled became too great a strain on all seven of them. I failed to catch trout in the wide river at the bottom of the garden with the rod once used by their son who was in the R.A.F. and their daughter who ran a pony-trekking business in the Isle of Man, and went for long walks with Alison, each of us with a sheaf of dog leads towing us like Eskimo sledges through the villages.

The whole set-up made a complete and utter change, and in the night I listened to the curlews, the sandpipers, the red-shanks, greenshanks, knots, and wimbrel, learning to tell their cries apart, though I have forgotten their strange music now. Two weeks flew by till away I went in McCrimmon's taxi, a friend of Hugh's, one of the clan that provided the resident pipers for so many Highland chieftains.

At the end of the journey back to Euston, rather less lengthy because I made it on the Monday, Cherry was waiting for me at the barrier, watching for a man with a new blue suitcase. I had seen her only once before for a single afternoon and I was afraid I might miss her. Then — there she was. And a new chapter in my life began.

---11---

Letters Come in Bundles

ON EUSTON STATION, Cherry and I began to turn the pages of a new Chapter, and we are still turning them together. We had been writing the first in our letters through the years and now we had about a week to fill in the unwritten words. I knew from telephoning Mother that Richard Fitter had reviewed *Pest Control Without Poisons*, giving it a generous spread in *The Observer*, *The Times Literary Supplement* had given it three column-inches with our address, and it was selling over 200 copies a day. She and Iris were opening, stuffing envelopes, and sending down taxi loads of parcels, with book shops ordering dozens. I had to get back.

So we crammed the slow and enjoyable journey through weekends of cycling, camping, and youth hostelling into those few flying days that changed a friendship which grew out of shared interests into a love that has lasted. Others remember dances, moonlight, and parties. I still remember the cellars of the British Museum filled with metal shelf racks stacked with mysteries too controversial to exhibit, including the vitrified fort fragments I had sent back from my holiday at Fort William in 1951, Guanche pottery, and obsidian tools.

All too soon we had to part again at Liverpool Street, but engaged, now with only our families to tell. Mother and I asked Cherry down to stay at No. 20, where she slept in the downstairs room. Luckily the great pile of *Pest Control Without Poisons* had dwindled. We took a trip to London to look at sheds, the largest possible size we could put up without planning permission, so we should have somewhere to store books at leaste. We went to Haughley — headquarters of the Soil Association to which we both belonged — and we planted the Sophora trees, which I had sown in my cold frame at No. 20, on the day I first saw Cherry.

Two died, but the largest specimen, which went in at the tip of the triangle bed marked 'M.1' on the Trial Ground Map for

1962, throve and towered through the years. Some couples say, 'listen, they're playing our tune'. It was in Oxford Botanic Gardens, the day before we were married, that I said, 'Look — they're growing our tree'. That tree has now been felled, and so has the one at Bocking (about 18 feet high before we left), bulldozed away and buried under the houses crammed on to the Trial Ground we had shared and enjoyed.

We never saw our Sophora flower, with its wide, creamy bunches of florets spread like hands 10 inches across in September, and the one in Oxford Botanic Garden flowered only after an exceptionally long, hot summer. We have planted another in the garden of our bungalow at Ryton, the largest we could get but, unless I live to 100 and Cherry to 115, we shall not see it flower together.

When I broke the news to Mother (who had seen it coming) she was delighted, for it had been her dread that when she died I would be left alone to wrestle with my health. She counted up her hoard of cigarette coupons and sent off the lot for two pairs of double bed sheets. She also made me promise that I would not 'do a money grizzle' whenever the question of buying anything for the house arose — saving cigarette coupons was the only way she had had of making sure of something we really wanted — and I never have.

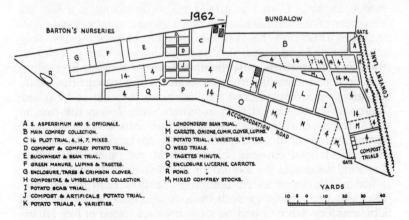

A S. ASPERRIMUM AND S. OFFICINALE.
B MAIN COMFREY COLLECTION.
C 16 PLOT TRIAL, 4, 14, 7, MIXED.
D COMPOST & COMFREY POTATO TRIAL.
E BUCKWHEAT & BEAN TRIAL.
F GREEN MANURE, LUPINS & TAGETES.
G ENCLOSURE, TARES & CRIMSON CLOVER.
H COMPOSITAE & UMBELLIFERAE COLLECTION.
I POTATO SCAB TRIAL.
J COMPOST & ARTIFICALS POTATO TRIAL.
K POTATO TRIALS, 4 VARIETIES.

L LONDONDERRY BEAN TRIAL.
M CARROTS, ONIONS, CUMIN, CLOVER, LUPINS.
N POTATO TRIAL, 4 VARIETIES, 2ND YEAR.
O WEED TRIALS.
P TAGETES MINUTA.
Q ENCLOSURE LUCERNE, CARROTS.
R POND.
M₁ MIXED COMFREY STOCKS.

YARDS

The Trial Ground in 1962, when we had bought the freehold and the back land making 1¾ acres. Note the first replicated plots, the 'machinery shed', which was an asbestos garage.

151

She was going to leave the house to us, even though Cherry and I both wanted her to stay and enjoy the garden she loved and to share our lives. She insisted that a newly-married couple of any age needed privacy. She was 'looking her last on all things lovely', on our alpines blazing in the front garden, the hedges of Zephirine Drouhin, Kathleen Harrop, Climbing Golden Showers, and Danse de Feu glowing on either side, down to the shouting colours of the broom hedge, and the packed vegetable and raspberry rows. She would retire to the Convent Guest House, at the end of Convent Lane, among the Franciscan nuns we knew so well.

As families age they meet mainly for funerals, especially those that are as heavily aunted as we were, so our wedding was an unusual happy event, uniting two groups of people who had never heard of each other, though it was a small introduction that they were all readers of *The Observer*. I told our members in a special 12-page newsletter.

Alas, I could not tell Newman Turner, who had so much wanted to see me married, because he had died early in July when I was in Scotland, and I had to begin the newsletter with sadness. He was only 50 and died suddenly from a heart attack.

Cherry was not South African. Her British father, while articled to an architect and surveyor, was stricken with T.B. before he could qualify. He emigrated to Argentina where he learned cattle ranching from the alfalfa roots upwards, married the daughter of the British Consul in Valparaiso, and fathered five vigorous children who grew up in a life of governesses, gauchos, and galloping horses. A bachelor uncle who was a clergyman in Hull kept them well supplied with English magazines and books, so that reading played as great a part in their lives as riding, enabling Cherry and her sister to pass, in 1910, the External Cambridge Local Examination with Honours. When, in 1911, they were sent home for further education with their eldest brother, then aged 12, in the charge of the liner captain, the clergyman uncle was able to get the girls into Cheltenham Ladies College and the boy into Bedford (Junior) School.

On her father's sudden death early in 1914, the property was sold and her mother came back to a small furnished house in Cheltenham. After a spell as a governess to a family in Lancashire, Cherry joined the Ministry of Pensions as a higher grade clerk, and on promotion to junior administrative assistant was placed in charge of auditing disablement pensions which began her interest in health and helping the helpless. She had hoped to go to medical school. Instead, she left to marry a rubber planter in Ceylon but three years later was granted a nullity decree, and after a few months in Madrid she returned to England where she later qualified at Guy's in physiotherapy, a shorter and cheaper training than medicine.

After a short spell at the Royal National Orthopaedic Hospital she started her own private practice in London. In 1931, longing to be a pioneer and see the Africa of H. M. Stanley, she went to Nairobi, where she built up a busy practice, coping with a great variety of patients, including those trampled by buffaloes, mauled by lions or crocodiles, or thrown by horses. She also found time to play tennis, golf, and above all to ride, mostly on horses lent by grateful patients, and started the idea of the Nairobi Ladies Polo Club, though sternly forbidden to play herself by one of the doctors for whom she worked because of the risk to what he described as her 'valuable hands'.

After three full and happy years she nearly died from malaria and amoebic dysentery — and the treatment then used. She returned to London where, after a long stay in the Hospital for Tropical Diseases, she was forbidden by the consultants to return to Africa and advised to live at sea level because of the damage to her heart and liver. She sold her practice and began slowly to recover, in and out of hospitals, earning money by designing, making, and selling stuffed animals and calendars while compelled to lie flat in bed. Though her career lay in ruins she was determined not to be beaten by ill health. She rented a small flat in Southsea with her mother who came to help her to get back to work, then, when some of her former vigour had slowly returned, called on doctors and was given patients to treat in their own homes. Gradually, her strength increased, her mother returned to Oxford, she took a larger flat, bought a bullnose Morris, and expanded her practice.

On the outbreak of war in 1939 she became an ambulance and First Aid Post driver in Portsmouth A.R.P. near the naval dockyard, a major target, but owing to an injury affecting her balance had to resign in 1941. Fortunately, her time as a student in Madrid having raised her Spanish from its original gaucho level to academic standards, she was accepted as a special examiner in Spanish at the Censorship. It was interesting work with friendly colleagues, constant danger from bombs shared by all Londoners, and varying periods as a patient in the Hospital

for Tropical Diseases. Finally, her balance problem was identified as Menière's disease by the Royal Ear Hospital, and it was
their unsuccessful attempt to cure it by surgery that led to our
first meeting.

We have both, in our pasts, had long struggles with health,
sudden misfortunes snatching sway success and restoring it as
we fought back, an abiding love of literature, and above all the
ability to learn from books and scientific papers. We had both
joined the Soil Association in its early days. Another common
factor is that we have both chosen to live without television,
even before the glaucoma we both developed made it unwise for
us to stare at bright lights. In fact, I have appeared on TV many
more times than I have watched it. We took a long time to find
each other, but we have found each other worth waiting for.

Mother wrote round to tell our relatives and it was agreed
between us that while I was getting married and away for my
week's honeymoon Mother should move into the Convent
Guest House with the help of Anne Elsey, our valued 'daily',
who would leave everything tidy for us to come back to and set
up house together without having to buy anything until we
needed it.

To add to the complications, on September 7th I had to go
into the Royal Free again for yet another 'swallow', so combined this with a shopping expedition to the Army and Navy,
where I bought a new dark suit for £21 (known ever afterwards
as my 'Wedding Garment') and the wedding ring. When I arrived
at the same ward, this time with a fiancée to take my clothes
away in the suitcase and a wedding ring to hand over to Sister
for safe keeping, there was delight all round.

I got out after four days, buying our wedding presents to
each other on the way home, a Remington portable for Cherry
to replace her own small one, for I am strongly in favour of
separate typewriters for married couples, an EXA for me, one of
the first reasonably priced single lens reflex cameras, which we
chose together.

My mother would not come to our wedding because the
glaucoma made her helpless in crowds of people. I left her with
Anne to help with her final packing, take her down to the
Convent, and settle her in. As we parted beside the alpine bed
with the clustered blue trumpets of my sixteen year old *Gentiana lagodechiana*, her final advice to me was: 'never end the day
angry. Make up your quarrels in bed.'

Cherry met me on Oxford station, we lunched at a wholefood restaurant, and spent the afternoon at the Botanic Gardens where I introduced her to some of my oldest friends growing there. I met my new family at a dinner-party laid on at the hotel where most of the guests were staying. We were married next day from the home of her younger sister Betty, whose husband, Professor William Hume-Rothery, had gone completely deaf from cerebro-spinal meningitis as a Prize Cadet at the R.M.A. Woolwich, and could converse only by lip-reading or with his hands. They had married only when he was earning as much as she did as assistant editor of the *Royal Geographical Magazine*. She then attended all his lectures, signalling from the back to keep his voice under control: an outstanding example of how two people who love each other can overcome even the greatest handicaps.

That halcyon period during which we learned to live with each other, both on our honeymoon at Speen and back at Bocking, left three new themes in our lives. First, we bought a really good, price-reduced, Pye stereo record player on the strength of wedding present cheques, at a shop in Newbury that had given up hope of selling it, and a collection of records. We went in repeatedly to hear and choose, discovering Kathleen Ferrier and Kenneth McKellar, and selecting our favourites among Mozart, Bach, Beethoven, Brahms, Handel, and Haydn, also using the other record shop in the town, and got the whole pile packed up and sent by passenger train to Bocking. At last I had someone I could share music with, extending my life to include a pool of peace and enjoyment into which we plunged together whenever we could find the time.

On our country walks together round Speen I began to sing, because I was happy, and from this grew my custom of singing in bed for Cherry's pleasure. Today, singing has become essentially a hearing pursuit, for no one takes their music to social gatherings as did my mother and father. Our voices today have to compete with the finest in the world, for genius happens seldom and when it does we record it, cherish it, and appreciate it. Almost everybody, however, has a voice good enough for a loving audience of one.

My repertoire reached back to Mother's musical evenings at Sutton Coldfield, Worcester, and Dartford, keeping alive in my memory Edwardian ballads that have never been recorded, as well as those I have picked up from records, or from youth hostelling days. My voice is totally untrained and probably gets

155

worse as I grow older. I only let it out in public when I sing 'My love is like a red, red rose' over the telephone to Cherry just before boarding an aircraft or ship for overseas.

Once, but only once, I have sung on B.B.C. radio. This was in 1968 when I was trying to find a silent bird scarer, like a silent dog whistle, and a member who was a director of a hi-fi radio firm rigged me up a gadget that would produce a high pitched whistle at the top of the scale and then go higher and higher beyond our hearing range, though children could hear it further round the dial than we could. We set it up at the bottom end of the Trial Ground surrounded by picnic plates with bread crusts on them, setting a similar ring of plates and bread only at the other end. The sparrows, taking the white card plates for some kind of trap, kept away from both sets for the first two days, then cleared all the crusts. The gadget had made no difference, even when we tried turning it up higher.

When I wrote to *The Field* to appeal for further information on electrical bird, rat, and mouse scarers, it drew the late Jack de Manio of the *Today* programme, in a large black Bentley with a giant tape recorder. I fetched out the gadget, which ran on a battery like a big Oxo cube.

First I explained: 'It seems that we only hear birds singing when they are singing their equivalent to "Down, down, down, down, among the *Deadmen* let him *lie* ". The song the hen likes to hear is, perhaps: "Ah, I have sighed to rest me, Deep in the quiet grave", going up as high as I could in Manrico's aria from *Il Trovatore* which I had once tried to play on the flute.

As I turned the knob up and down, Jack de Manio asked listeners to watch their canary or parrot and write in if there were any effects. Listeners reported hearing the whistle of the first stage but parrots did not even swear and canaries took no notice. Immediately it went out the next morning I had my sister-in-law Betty on the telephone, delighted to hear me, and for the rest of the day members kept ringing me up. This seemed to start my radio and TV period, never a regular programme, always on something unusual, rarely paid, but all good publicity.

The third change to my life due to marriage happened soon after we got back to Bocking, to the clean empty house with the garden glowing. On our first shopping trip into Braintree, we had a cup of tea and a bun for Cherry with a macaroon for me.

This should have been safely made from almond flour but was evidently padded with white flour to save expensive almonds, so the result was an 'attack'.

Rather than stay downstairs alone, Cherry brought up her sewing. (She embroiders, designs, and makes calendars, belts, and toys, and alters and mends with skill and speed, but, unlike my mother, has never knitted since an overdose in World War I of socks for soldiers.) I was starting to read a new library book, *The Cornflake Crusade* by Gerald Carson, a biography of John Harvey Kellogg who changed the breakfast habits of the west by finding how to convert maize enough for a meagre feed for a dozen hens into a giant-sized pack for a family to be sold in the supermarket.

The book began, 'Battle Creek is an up-and-coming town with the finest opera house between Jackson City and Kalamazoo,' which so tickled us both that I began to read it aloud for our mutual pleasure, to learn that the way to get the most out of a first class book was to read it together, and that fast readers, like Cherry and myself, can gain more enjoyment by plodding slowly through any book that is good enough to share evening after evening than by racing through it separately.

When we were still newly-weds with white hair (though mine was grey rather than white, for I was only 53 in 1964) all our weekdays began with opening the post in bed. On slack days, a fat packet held by a stout rubber band would be crammed through the letterbox, but usually the postman's knock brought bundles of letters of all sizes tightly tied with good sisal string that was welcome for tying parcels, sometimes a bundle of bundles as large as a dustbin lid, or even half a mailbag full, which I tipped over Cherry's toes.

For over 20 years we attacked the post with paper-knives, or in my case fingers. Sometimes, when we had as many as 850 a morning, we had to stay in bed busily opening until 10 a.m. after a ten past seven start.

The letter from that era we remember best came in after we had the misfortune to be mentioned in a pamphlet under 'Useful addresses for science teachers'. It read: 'Dear Sirs, I am doing a Project. Please send me full particulars of Everything. Yours sincerely, Hilda Wilkes, Form B (aged 11.)' As it was not possible to cram the Encyclopaedia Britannica into her stamped addressed envelope, we just sent her some of our literature.

The bulk of our fluctuating flood of mail, when letters were classless and cost 2½ old pence to send, came in response to what I christened my 'Jump-ins', letters to national, provincial, and weekly newspapers, linked with a topical item, and my 'Try-ons', on seasonal subjects connected with gardening, offering a free pamphlet for a stamped addressed envelope. These were designed to fold into an envelope with our publication list, a price list, and a 'leaflet that will tell you who we are and what we do' as I said in countless replies to letters of enquiry.

The last of the harvest of our six-day-a-week before-breakfast opening sessions was the envelopes, rammed into the thin white cotton bags, holding the dried comfrey leaves that came from Yugoslavia where they had been dried by peasants. They were sent to us by a wholesale herbalist, to be redried till crisp then packeted by our part-time packers for us to sell as comfrey tea, for we could never have grown enough for the demand.

I used to take these fat bags down to the Franciscan convent at the end of Convent Lane, balanced across my bicycle, to go to various groups of old ladies in the Guest House, or the nuns, to snip off the stamps to sell for various good causes. So I saw my mother every day in her small bedsitting room where she lived under the care of the nuns she had known through many years of meeting them at Mass. Here she gardened when she felt like it, in various beds strictly apportioned between several gardening ladies, continued to read as she still could, for I kept up her supply of library books and cigarettes, and listened to her radio. Every day I told her what was going on, how many letters we had had on the various 'Jump-ins', the donations that had come in, and how the work was going, sharing everything as we had through the years of struggle. Sometimes Cherry came too and they talked poetry, and above all she rejoiced in the change Cherry had achieved in my life-long ill health.

Early in November, 1964, when the three of us settled into our new routine and my weight only just exceeded nine stone but was creeping steadily towards the 11½ which was average for my height and age, *The Daily Telegraph* carried a photograph of two little girls playing among massive piles of dead leaves in Hyde Park. The caption described them as 'Modern Babes in the Wood', and explained that the hundreds of tons of leaves, swept mechanically from the vast area of grass, were awaiting burning. This led me to recall all the leaves I had swept up at Central Park, Dartford, followed by the maturing stacks chopped when mature to add humus to bowling greens and tennis courts, to dig in with bonemeal to feed the magnificent displays of tulips and forget-me-nots, and to spread as a weed-suppressing mulch under the shrub borders. So I wrote to *The Daily Telegraph*, perhaps the longest of all my 'Jump-ins', protesting at the waste of humus, pointing out the excellent example of Toronto as the only city in the Commonwealth to turn its dead leaves into leafmould to sell at a profit, though both Manchester and Cardiff would deliver leaves to ratepayers and allotment societies.

I suggested that gardeners should write to their councils to demand leafmould from the leaves that had been swept up, then wastefully burned at their expense. My letter appeared on the 13th November, 1964, and drew replies from several borough engineers who pointed out that the rental value of inner-city land was far too great to waste under slowly rotting leaves. Toronto had unbuilt areas where leaves could be stacked then left to decay and wait for sale. Authority, knowledge, and experience can always find excellent reasons for doing nothing.

It also brought a letter from Professor F. C. Pybus of the University of Newcastle-upon-Tyne, applauding my letter, and enclosing his paper 'Cancer and atmospheric pollution' (*Medical Proceedings* Vol. 10, June 1964, pp. 232–254 and 268–277). His interest in air pollution and lung cancer had begun when, as a medical student, he first saw the contrast between the soot-blackened lungs of Londoners and those of countrymen. His was the pioneer work that established the link between lung cancer and benzpyrenes. Professor Pybus calculated that the 300,000 tons of garden rubbish burned each year in Britain's bonfires produced 1,000 times more benzpyrenes than the 100,000 tons of tobacco smoked in cigarettes and pipes, because smoke from garden fires holds 70 parts per million compared with 0.2 parts per million for cigarette smoke, i.e. 350 times as much. So every chain-bonfire smoker, even burning only his lawn mowings, is turning his neighbours into 'passive smokers'. To quote the British Medical Association booklet *Clean Air*: 'It is no use playing your part in making the air clean by adapting your grates and using smokeless fuel if you spoil it all by contaminating the air with bonfires'.

Then, on February 27th, 1965, C. Harcourt Roy reviewed the Pybus Report in *The Daily Telegraph* as a big centre-page article which summarized it admirably, aiming at implicating pollution rather than smoking and pleading for the drastic application of the Clean Air Act of 1956. I wrote my 'Jump-in' fast, catching the mid-day post to make sure of next morning delivery in London:

'Sir, Your article "Cancer in the Atmosphere" will be welcomed by all smokers as an excuse, but may I appeal to them to reduce the lung cancer risk to others by giving up smoking bonfires? It is so easy to reach for the matches every weekend and send valuable humus billowing across the gardens in benzpyrene filled smoke. If only gardeners would cut down to one bonfire of rambler-rose prunings and woody garden rubbish on November 5th and another in March for tree and bush rose prunings, their soil health would improve, their potatoes and other crops gain weight and they would save the money they now spend not only on chemical fertilizers but on peat to replace the humus they have burnt. I would gladly send a leaflet on making compost with garden rubbish and leafmould with dead leaves, free for a stamped addressed envelope, to all would-be non-bonfire smokers and those struggling to give up this unhealthy and expensive habit.'

Four hundred letters arrived the next morning and 1,300 by the end of the week, including heart-rending stories from mothers with asthmatic children, bronchitis sufferers, emphysema cases, lung cancer victims, and many others driven indoors by un-neighbourly chain-bonfire smokers. There were also letters from lung specialists, medical officers of health, and hundreds of ordinary smoke sufferers, for roughly 15 per cent of non-smokers are caused active distress by cigarette smoke because of allergies, not necessarily to nicotine tars, benzpyrenes, or the toxic metal cadmium which locks up the nutritionally valuable zinc in our food, but to substances present in all smoke. Hundreds of them wrote offering to pay for pamphlets by the dozen to put through neighbours' letter boxes or to use as ammunition in long-running arguments or letters to local papers. In every suburb and round every allotment site, it seemed, there was a smouldering hatred of bonfire smoke that my letter had fanned into flames.

Perhaps 1 per cent of the letters, mainly on headed paper, came from those whom the scent of burning leaves, with the sharp scent of chrysanthemums, were among the joys of autumn; dozens who wanted to know how to compost privet, yew, or lonicera clippings. Others came from fire officers who wanted me to warn against burning anything other than *garden* rubbish, since all plastics were dangerous, especially PVC which released hydrochloric acid gas strong enough to fetch the leaves off fruit trees, and empty aerosol cans which could explode. Furthermore, burning the cushions and upholstery of modern furniture produced fumes that could kill in about three minutes, and were the reason why all firemen had to wear breathing apparatus.

As the flood continued I learned that not only did Toronto make municipal leafmould, but that Vancouver allowed bonfires for only two weeks in April and two in November, while Calgary, Edmonton, Regina, Saskatoon, and Winnipeg forbade them completely, as did Los Angeles, Sacramento, San Diego, and San Francisco, backed by a $500 fine for what they call 'Backyard Burning'. Ten years later I was to see and smell the smog lying over Los Angeles, which showed me why the USA has far fiercer regulations on air pollution than we have.

Then a member of the Bognor Regis Council had the bright idea of distributing a special edition of our leaflet by folding it into rate demands, which would cost no more postage and only a little extra labour in the Rating Department. The Health Department, under the Medical Officer of Health, was concerned with pollution, and the Highways Department which looked after leaf sweeping came under the borough engineer, so both would be in favour.

Seeing this as an opportunity to tell millions of people how to make compost and leafmould, and also about H.D.R.A., I wrote to *The Daily Telegraph* a third time, on the success of the anti-bonfire campaign, and appealing for donations to launch the rate demand idea. Amazingly, they printed it. It is as rare in Fleet Street for appeal letters to appear, except for those on behalf of theatres, architectural treasures, preventing pictures leaving the country, or disasters, as it is for reporters' dogs to bite advertisers. I also managed to get one in *The Observer*, and together they pulled in £154, mostly in postal orders from bonfire-smoke sufferers.

I had replied to the Bognor Regis councillor, asking him for a copy of the rate demand, and to all the other councils who had written for theirs, and I found that all the demands were much the same size, and a sheet 10 inches long and seven-and-a-half wide would fit them all. So I rewrote my leaflet to fit, adding an outlined 'box' in one corner giving a brief account of the H.D.R.A., (subscription £2 a year), offering free for a stamped addressed envelope a specimen Newsletter and detailed directions for making: (a) a Compost Box, a cheaper 'Bocking Box' of wire netting to line with opened-out cardboard cartons; (b) a wire-netting leafmould-making enclosure; and (c) a trench for composting kitchen wastes in winter.

I publicized this with letters to the many monthlies for borough engineers, medical officers of health and periodicals like *The Muck Shifter and Public Works Digest*, that are eagerly awaited in every town hall. During the five years the campaign raged, we sent out over half a million copies in 5,000s, 10,000s and once even 20,000 when the Minister of Health for Northern Ireland recommended all his local authorities to accept my offer as the only measure against air pollution that cost the ratepayers nothing.

In the end we had to charge councils cost price and postage, which slowed the flood, but every autumn I wrote round to the provincial dailies and weeklies — much as the R.S.P.C.A. does warning people to lock their dogs and cats indoors on Bonfire Night — offering later editions free for stamped addressed envelopes. These pulled in far more members and sales than those that rode with the rate demands because those people who were interested enough to write were gardeners.

I was to think up many more such leaflets that spread the organic message to the unconverted and increased H.D.R.A. membership without spending anything on advertising. Perhaps the most successful was based on the best organic gardening hint I ever found. I wrote to provincial and national newspapers in winter suggesting that bamboo canes should be thrust slantways into rose beds, with a piece of fat hung from the tips. There would be room for only a pair of tits on this, but the birds that were waiting their turns to perch and peck would be hunting in the gnarled bark round the bases of the bushes, 'like patients in the doctor's waiting room, turning over the colour supplements in the hope of finding a *Punch*, finding and eating greenfly eggs, so there would be no need to spray next summer'.

The eight-page folder (stapling costs more and slows stuffing into envelopes of widely assorted sizes) that went with this letter was *In Place of Poisons*, giving simple, organic answers to some common pests and diseases. We printed some 60,000 of these, plus 80,000 *Dig for Survival* on what to sow, when, how, and how soon it would be ready for eating. This we did at the start of the 'Self Sufficiency' movement in 1973 and it was the last of these series before it was killed by increased postal charges.

They really did lift our membership numbers, and provided a new recruiting ground for the H.D.R.A., to replace circularizing my *Observer* fanmail when they gave up having two gardening correspondents after Frances Perry replaced Vita Sackville-West in November 1965. I wrote to *Punch* offering them a gardening column, which accepted me at 15 guineas for 450 words once a fortnight, packing the words still tighter, but less closely tied to the tyranny of inches between rows and ounces a square yard. I enjoyed opening an article, 'Modern onions are mild, but those that sailed with Drake to keep scurvy at bay as long as they lasted were strong enough to send a pirate's parrot squawking into the rigging.'

My first article, on January 26th, 1966, was in the style of Thomas Tusser (1524–1580) whose *A Hundred Goode Pointes of Husbandrie* (1557) was the first concise and practical gardening book, written in verse so it would be remembered by those who could not themselves read. Every January I had written an article in *The Observer* on how long seeds kept alive, and my version in verse was the only one in the seven years I wrote for them that they rejected, but I got away with history in *Punch*. Perhaps my pleasure in getting non-gardening words and ideas into print is merely the yearning of a clown to play Hamlet.

I wrote for *Punch* with pleasure until October 16th, 1968, when they decided to end their experiment of having gardening articles. I then wrote for *The Countryman* published by the same firm, though still a fat green quarterly edited at Burford in Oxfordshire, and writing only every three months, but an allowance of 750 words was a relief as the H.D.R.A. grew and grew.

12

A Time of Beginnings

IN JULY, 1965, I got my first letter in *The Times* on toads as garden pest controllers, pointing out the losses in frogs and toads and suggesting that like the equally useful hedgehogs they could be promoted to the status of 'Honorary Birds'. This drew other letters and finally a 'Fourth Leader' — the accolade for those who win their silly-season spurs. *The Times* letter drew the *Sun* which merely lifted the idea and did not give our address. *The Daily Mail* did two articles about us on July 23rd and 25th, the *Express* spent two hours interviewing me but never used the article, and the B.B.C. spent three hours recording, then used only two minutes of it, which did not even include our name, on the 'Today' programme.

This produced two letters, compared with 50 for *The Times*, and the *Mail* brought a Dr Linzell of Finchley who made a fast trip by Jaguar with his wife, his mother-in-law, and about a hundred very undersized toad tadpoles in a large can. He had been using these in some laboratory experiment, and had fed them liver, which stunted their growth from excess Vitamin B12. Science having been satisfied, he found them a good home in our small pond at the bottom of the Trial Ground, with a gently sloping end, a perfect finishing school for teenage tadpoles, very conscious of their new legs, taking their first trip in a world that makes little effort to understand them.

Reviews of *Hedgehogs and the Gardener* were appearing in *The Observer* where Richard Fitter treated it seriously, gave our name and address, and we sold about 200. *Country Life* and the *Gardeners' Chronicle* also gave it a fair show.

Our best showing was when Cherry and I set off to Norwich at the invitation of Anglia TV, with 'Dunromin', our Mark One Hedgehog House, packed in a suitcase. It was the first time we had seen the ordered chaos of a TV studio, roped with cables, or I had sat on one of the brilliantly lit armchairs with cameras glaring at me. Again and again I assembled 'Dunromin', made by John Tiddy from the plan by Norman Green of Birmingham, our first and most enthusiastic hedgehog watcher. It had a false floor of expanded metal under which we sprinkled a special derris and pyrethrum mixture flea powder to cope with the livestock carried by all hedgehogs, and a wooden 'chimney' to provide fresh air during hibernation. I got a whole five minutes in which to say something useful for hedgehog helpers.

Another beginning was in December, 1965, when Cherry wrote her first article under the heading 'Houswives' help' in No. 24 Newsletter. This was 'Bread without bakers', written during a bakers' strike, including her slightly modified recipe for the Grant loaf (devised by Doris Grant) and was as quick as cake to make for it needs no kneading. Like all her articles which members enjoyed through the years, it was simple, detailed, and practical, without any of the breadmaking mysticism that swells a simple domestic art into an expensive book.

Cherry had the good physiotherapist's one-to-one approach to helping every individual patient. Of all the authors I persuaded to write, the most rewarding was my own wife whose books published in Britain and America have reached far beyond H.D.R.A. The people who have had the most value from us as a charity have been the hundreds through the years who rang up on a weekday morning, even from America and Australia, to talk over an hour about their health.

Cherry charged nothing for her advice, based on recent nutritional work in many countries gathered via photostats of papers selected from *Index Medicus* at Chelmsford Medical Academic Unit at the County Hospital. Her book royalties went into a 'Special Diet Fund' and, with the rest of her work, were part of our 'Giving away department'.

The basic reason for organic gardening is health for soil, plants, and people, and we launched out into five open days a year, with Cherry and our helpful neighbours baking wholemeal bread, including a super malt and raisin loaf which I longed to eat, and scones, for teas on the lawn outside the new cedar room into which we could cram people if it rained. On one occasion, the nuns of the convent at the end of Convent Lane rallied round with extra baking power to our recipes, though Cherry never could convert them to an organic diet for the old people in the guest house.

Gathering the material for Cherry's eight page pamphlet *Basic Food Guide to a Green Old Age*, of which we gave away over

100,000, began during the fertile and vigorous summer of 1966, when she was only 70. Dr James Lambert Mount, founder of the McCarrison Society, the organization of nutrition-conscious doctors, and then the H.D.R.A.'s medical adviser in succession to Dr Osbourne, had long wanted to check whether people lived longer on a wholefood diet, for which there seemed some evidence. We saw an opportunity to do some useful research and together we went after it.

The late Dr Geoffrey Taylor, a professor of medicine, had surveyed the health of old people in 23 homes where everything they ate was known. He found that a number of them were suffering from incipient scurvy, because they lacked vitamin C and the B group, from lack of raw food, institutional cooking, and a cheap, high-refined-carbohydrate diet kept them at a low level of mental and physical activity. During the fortnight after we saw his letter in *Medical News* and invited him down to see us we heard from Mr Osborn, a member aged 96, who was still gardening hard. He was a vegetarian who gave up smoking 50 years earlier and used to distribute copies of Sir Albert Howard's *Soil Health*, the first organic gardening publication, among his fellow allotment holders during the war. We also had a visit from a Mr Wilson, aged 97, a keen comfrey grower who believed in eating a large lettuce every day of his life, who arrived in an elderly Rolls-Royce driven by his chauffeur-gardener, with his youngest daughter, aged 67, who was plump and slow, waddling after her father who darted round the Trial Ground with a spidery speed.

Their diet was a complete contrast to those in the institutions. Both men enjoyed unlimited vitamins C and A, and folic acid, from green vegetables eaten without waiting hours between kitchen and ward, plus the fibre, additional to that in the homebaked, wholemeal bread that supplied vitamins E and the B group. Since neither was a Vegan, eggs, milk, and dairy products, plus fish and poultry in the case of Mr Wilson, provided plenty of vitamin B12, and both men had been eating unsprayed, organically-grown produce for more than 20 years.

Dr Taylor had time to examine about a dozen organic over-85s, and if we had doctor members willing to examine more he agreed to tell them what to check, so a statistically significant number of vegetarian and non vegetarian organic gardeners could be compared with the Control from his investigation (which was funded by Roche, the Swiss manufacturers of vitamin supplements).

There were then 1,118 H.D.R.A. members. The important question was how we compared with the general population in our proportion of active over-eighties. I wrote to *Mother Earth* to extend the search area to the then 4,500 members of the Soil Association, and to *Here's Health*, and *The Observer*. I hoped to make a register of organic over-eighties so Dr Taylor or our doctor members could attract only those mentally alert and interested enough to write a letter and complete a questionnaire, but these were the people we were looking for.

We received some interesting letters from over eighties and nineties, but organizing the examinations proved too expensively difficult. Unlike a giant pharmaceutical company, we could not afford to pay the salary, travel expenses, and hotel accommodation for a doctor to visit them all. Dr Geoffrey Taylor had only 23 stops on his geriatric journey, with at least 20 cases to examine at each, so he was able to gather statistically sound evidence in less than a year of travelling. We did get a doctor to visit Mr Osborn, but he called on his way back from holiday with his wife and small children, arriving unannounced on a day when the great-grandchildren were visiting, which made it a social rather than a medical event.

Cherry, however, set to work on devising what was perhaps the first diet designed to keep the over-eighties out of institutions, healthily active, and enjoying life. It was based on the evidence that old farm workers allowed to keep their cottages as long as they or their widows lived, growing their own vegetables with manure traditionally supplied free from the home farm, keeping chickens, and wiring rabbits to make their pensions go further, lived longer and kept their mental and physical activity longer than town pensioners on high-carbohydrate diets chosen for cheapness.

It was not a vegetarian diet, and did not follow any dietary theory or fashion, because it was written to help as many over-eighties as possible to alter their eating habits. It was, in fact, a good, wholefood diet for any age, and its principles apply to vegetarians as well as the vast majority of people who also eat fish and meat as part of a balanced diet. For over a quarter of century we sent it to every new H.D.R.A. member when they first joined us. It included Cherry's bread recipe, 'Ten Kitchen Commandments' to save vitamins and minerals and, in the later editions, a section on sprouting. When it was finished Cherry sent the manuscript to Dr Taylor who entirely approved of it, making only one suggestion: 'Include at least one pint of fresh milk daily, unless allergic to milk', which was number three in the 'Special reminder' section at the end, the last of which was: 'If reducing at any age, cut out white bread, biscuits, cakes, pudding mixes, sweets, chocolate, sago, tapioca, macaroni, corn-flour, and white rice, rather than potatoes which contain suffi-cient vitamins to break down their starch'.

We launched *The Basic Food Guide* in May, 1967, with letters in *The East Anglian Daily Times*, *The Sunday Sun*, and *The Sunday Mercury*. The one in *The Observer*, with a cartoon by Haro, on July 9th, pulled 3,500 letters, a record for a single appearance. Unlike our hedgehog publicity, this one drew new members, sales, and donations, enabling us to reprint in time for *Woman's Own*, who took about 3,000.

Another seed was sown in that fertile year, which really began at the Attingham Conference and A.G.M. of the Soil Association, where members of this (then) far larger body voiced their demand for 'Silent Springless' food. The Wholefood Shop in Baker Street had been started by Lord Kitchener, our President and Chairman, with Yehudi Menuhin, the violinist, and others in 1960, and was thriving under the devoted management of Miss Lilian Schofield and Miss Mary Langman. There were plenty of healthfood shops, selling the patent medi-cines of the nature cure movement, herbs, and vegetarian groceries, but they had neither the room nor the suppliers to stock perishable fruits and vegetables. There had been an attempt by the Soil Association in the 1950's to start an 'Organic National Mark' and a committee had been appointed, but after five years it had failed to agree.

A member had sent me a clipping from *Liberal News* of an article on factory farming, and my letter on defining free-range eggs and the problems of supplying and distributing wholefood appeared in their February, 1966, issue. It drew over 100 letters asking where people could buy food that was not only free from pesticides, fungicides, and other agricultural chemicals, but produced without growth hormones, antibiotics, or cruelty as defined by Ruth Harrison's *Animal Machines*, published in 1964, with a foreword by Rachel Carson.

In two years it had built up a body, larger than the organic movement, of anti-factory-farm organizations like The Farm and

Food Society and Compassion in World Farming, seeking organically-grown produce because organic farmers do not employ factory-farming methods, and increasing still further the demand that was making it profitable to sell 'half food' as wholefood because there were no standards. Article Two of our Objects was 'Research into and the study of improved methods of organic farming and gardening'. I knew of no aspect of organic farming that needed more improvement than the way in which its produce gets to its clamouring customers. We were entitled to study the subject, get something started, and then turn it over to a separate body, for our job was research.

I wrote an article on the subject, which did not appear until the June, 1966, number of *Health for All*, suggesting that a central body might collect a levy from shops and suppliers to pay for printing and organizing. It would need legal status so it could have a sign which would be a registered trademark that could be taken away in the event of misconduct. This would be a guarantee that the produce was genuinely organically-grown, poison-free food, and met a non-cruelty standard for all animal products. A committee composed of delegates from all the bodies concerned should agree standards and deal with organizational problems and complaints. Its long term value would be out of all proportion to the small beginning that now seemed possible.

The article generated about 50 letters, all from people wanting to buy wholefood and wishing to join such a club. The Soil Association was very interested in the progress of the idea. Health Food Stores Wholesale, the trade association, could not be involved because of 'practical difficulties'. The H.D.R.A., as a charity, could not run such a body that would be of financial benefit to its members. A separate body could be formed but it would need capital and someone to put the drive behind it.

Publicity was easy, but useless without an organization, and this depended on agreement between the conflicting interests concerned. The anti-factory-farmers were concerned with cruelty, not chlorinated hydrocarbons, there were diehard organic gardeners who insisted that sufficient compost cured all pests and diseases, therefore derris, Bordeaux mixture, and everything except ground limestone (calcium carbonate) should be banned, vegans who would rather eat chemically-grown produce than any raised on animal manure or bonemeal, vegetarians shocked at wholefood shops selling sausages made from organic farms' pigs, and Biodynamic people horrified at the suggestion that even properly composted human wastes might have been used on these farms. It was possible for any gathering to stack objections so high that they were a wall against further progress.

The debate raged through the H.D.R.A. Annual General Meeting in March, 1966, which was one of the liveliest in a growing tradition. It was finally decided that the idea was too far from our objects and too time-swallowing to be pursued against so many conflicting principles. Out of the arguments arose another idea.

This was *The Wholefood Finder*, listing with details all the sources of organically-grown and cruelty-free produce. It would include organic farmers and growers willing to supply retailers, those who ran stalls in markets, healthfood shops that stocked more than diet supplements and herbal preparations, amateur gardeners who had room to grow enough to sell surpluses, and co-operatives like those many H.D.R.A. and Soil Association members were starting.

Geoffrey Hull, a member of the Soil Association Council, was our speaker that year, on the implications of research by the big oil companies in growing edible yeasts on crude oil wastes and chemicals to help alleviate Third World food shortages. He suggested that the H.D.R.A. and the Soil Association produce *The Wholefood Finder* together. This I strongly supported because I was all for co-operation between the bodies of the organic movement and I knew that working with only one body was far easier than getting agreement from about sixteen.

Even with only one organization to agree with, it was June, 1968, before *The Wholefood Finder* was finally published. Cherry and I went to Haughley and agreed the four questionnaires (farmers and growers, retailers, hotels and boarding houses, and amateur gardeners) with Douglas Campbell, assistant to the then Soil Association Secretary, Sir Ronald Garvey. We agreed that what was important was to get *The Wholefood Finder* on the bookstalls, without spending months or years arguing whether eggs from laying arks that were dragged to fresh pasture each day counted as free range. If we decided on rigid standards, we had not the money to pay inspectors to enforce them, but the Leicestershire Group of The Soil Association had an enquiry from the John Lewis Partnership who wanted to start selling organic food through their chain of supermarkets, insisting on standards so they could justify the extra price they would have to charge. Increasingly, the inorganic farmer can take advantage of chemical short cuts that save labour, and every year year the gap between organic and inorganic widens, while the demand increases. Both Rachel Carson and Ruth Harrison were stirring the public to demand what was not there — regular supplies of food grown without poison sprays, chemical fertilizers, or cruelty, even at higher prices.

If customers are willing to pay extra for food produced in this way they are entitled to have it, but first the permitted sprays and fertilizers must be decided, and what livestock keeping systems were to be allowed. There are still today several

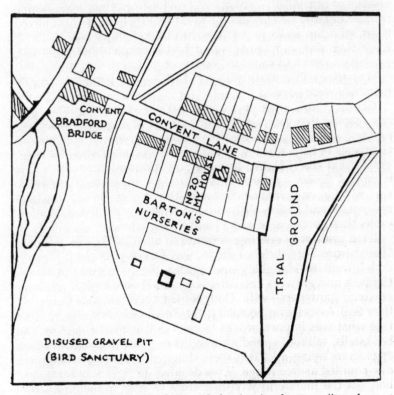

Convent Lane and the Trial Ground showing its shape, an 'isosceles triangle with some angles more equal than others'. We began by assuming that the last bungalow garden was straight, but nothing was.

sets of standards, some designed to allow producers to get away with more chemical short cuts, but then I had to draw lines in what I hoped were the right places.

Typical of the sticking points that had kept the Organic National Mark Committee arguing for five fruitless years was kainite (the name came from the Greek *kainos* meaning 'new' which it was in the 1860s). At Stassfurt in Germany, a sea dried up in the Permian Period. The sodium chloride (common salt) crystallized out first, and potassium and magnesium chlorides last, in a thinner layer on top. This had only to be shovelled off to become one of the earliest potassium chemical fertilizers. It is still used on sugar beet, which was once a wild weed of the seashore and appreciates the residual salt and the magnesium. Other deposits in Europe and Israel had their potassium mixed with the salt, so were separated by dissolving water at 100^0C and cooling them fast. The potassium chloride crystallized first, and was sold separately as 'muriate of potash'.

Continental authorities insist that because kainite is merely dug from the soil it is 'natural' and therefore organic, while the dissolved and cooled pure potassium chloride is not. They also argued that Chilean nitrate of soda is 'organic' for the same reason, and that it is essential to secure 'tillering' (branching of wheat seedlings) early in the year to secure a worthwhile yield. French farmers are especially fierce on this one.

So far as the potato crop is concerned, there is no difference at all. Potassium chloride is responsible for the inferior taste of inorganic potatoes, familiar to every organic gardener when he runs out of his own and buys any grown with chemicals. It makes the tubers take up more water and, as farmers are paid for tonnage rather than taste, is always used by the inorganic. Nitrate of soda, apart from causing complications on heavy clays and increasing the nitrate pollution problem in drainage water, is unnecessary for good grain yields on organic farms.

Organic fertilizers and organic sources of nitrogen from bacterial action are released as the soil warms in spring, but chemical sources can be available at once, so crops always look backward in spring and catch up later, as the spring strengthens and fertile acres rejoice in their strength. On a good mixed organic farm, Newman Turner used to sow his winter wheat early to be able to graze it as early as February with his Jersey herd, which made it tiller just as well as Chilean or synthetic nitrates.

Doug Campbell had listened to all these arguments for five years, and he wanted to get the book printed and published, for we both knew the size of the public demand. There was already a duplicated list of suppliers published by a firm in Devon, but without any attempt at standards. If we went ahead and informed organic farmers and growers, and those who wished to change over and serve the new market, what they could or could not use with a clear conscience, this would tell the public what to expect. There was also a strong anti-Wholefood Finder opinion in the Soil Association arguing that there were so few organic farmers and growers that if we produced a directory it would only increase the demand for food that could not be supplied. The only way to break this 'chicken and egg' situation was to publicize existing suppliers, so they would be able to expand, by getting the booklet on the bookstalls and reviewed in the press.

So I went right ahead, drawing the line where J. I. Rodale drew it, on solubility, because it could be justified in terms of plant physiology, rather than trying to draw one between 'natural' and 'unnatural'. Woodashes are as natural as kainite, for their potash is just as soluble. We had to allow them, and now adularia shale or rock potash provides a potassium source for those who grow gooseberries on sandy soils. Standards stand up until those with commercial axes to grind go looking for loopholes.

I wrote the questionnaire forms and argued fiercely against spending £145 on having them printed because we should not want 5,000 of each, and it would be cheaper to run off 300 of each on the duplicator and use the stencils again if we wanted even 500 more. Michael Allaby, then deputy editor of *Mother Earth*, wrote an article appealing for farmers and growers in the July, 1966, number, and the Soil Association wanted to reprint 50,000 of this for £65 to go in *Health for All*. This would have been wasted because it would merely have brought more demand for *The Wholefood Finder* — the time to spend on advertising is when you have something to sell. *Health for All* gave the idea a big write-up, which cost us nothing and brought in any farmers and wholefood-serving hotels among their readers.

As the agreement was that the H.D.R.A. and the Soil Association should each pay half the costs and have 5,000 copies of the book, and I was to write and prepare the manuscript for printing, I was entitled to make a fuss about excessive spending, and this did enable me to get away with throwing out kainite. I had the help of Simon Harris of the Kent and Mr E. Turner of the Leicestershire Groups of the Soil Association, the Vegetarian Catering Association, the Biodynamic Farm and Garden Association, and the Farm and Food Society. In the end I just wrote the questionnaires and standards. Robert Pollard composed a legal agreement for producers to sign, binding them to observe the agreed standards in consideration of appearing in *The Wholefood Finder*.

I allowed basic slag, even though it was the ground insides of blast furnaces, because it was slowly soluble and an excellent source of lime and phosphorus for high-rainfall hill pastures of Scotland and Wales. Unfortunately, modern methods of smelting make better steel more cheaply but very inferior slag, so it is no longer available. I hid kainite, with nitrate of soda, under a blanket of prohibiting 'all soluble chemical fertilizers' and included nicotine, with derris, pyrethrum, quassia, and ryania, because though it would poison anyone who drank it, when sprayed it was spent in 48 hours and did not build up along the food chains. I wanted it because of the need for an insecticide that would kill a swarm of caterpillars.

By the 18th committee meeting, on January 12th, 1967, I had listed 35 producers, 52 retailers, and 23 hotels and boarding houses. I wrote letters to every farming periodical in Britain, because most organic farmers took the *Farmers' Weekly* or *Farmer and Stockbreeder* as well as *Mother Earth* or *Star and Furrow* the Biodynamic quarterly.

The work dragged on with the entries slowly building up. I finally accumulated 23 amateur gardeners who could have surplus fruit and vegetables for sale, and by the autumn of 1967 had got as far as the final typing. Then I had a letter from four eminent organic farmers referring to a letter from the Soil Association's solicitors. Eventually I discovered that the Soil Association had taken legal advice on Robert Pollard's legal agreement and discovered (surprise! surprise!) that it was legally binding. If they failed to keep to the standards, we could sue them and so could their customers. In the end, after a long argument in the living room at No. 20 Convent Lane, we agreed amicably.

At last we got it out, 84 pages with a plain green paper cover, with 'Why join the Soil Association?' on the back cover, our *Pest Control Without Poisons* and our newest booklet *Fertility Without Fertilisers* (which sold about 40,000 in the first edition) on the inside back, and 'Who we are and what we do' on the inside front, inviting readers to join the H.D.R.A. at £2 a year and ending: 'No Government, Trust or Foundation supports our work among the Cinderellas of Science. Today there are so many expensive Ugly Sisters.'

We sent it round and got it reviewed. It took some time to sell that 10,000 but we bought back 3,000 from the Soil Association and sold them, too. Indeed, it was these booklets that spread the organic message and built up our membership. They were cheap and short but full of practical detail compared with so many books in the organic movement that strove to convince the reader with a flood of quotations from authorities few people had ever read. Ours sold in tens of thousands because I sent them to the gardening correspondents of the provincial daily, evening, Sunday, and local weekly papers, who picked up a good idea for an article and used it in their columns. I also sent them to the religious periodicals.

It was in 1971 before my own *Grow Your Own Fruit and Vegetables* (Faber and Faber) was published, but I was writing over half a million words a year, in Newsletters, H.D.R.A. booklets, pamphlets, and reports, apart from letters, articles, and book reports to earn my living.

In 1966 we were both young and foolish (I was only 55 and Cherry merely 70) and after our crowded spring and eventful summer, I announced at the end of No. 26 Newsletter: 'After the September Open Day my wife and I are taking a holiday in the Canary Islands collecting more material for my book on archaeology. It has been the dream of my life to go there and we are going while we are young enough to enjoy it, for in delay there lies no plenty — as every wise man's father knows.'

13

Lands of the Morning

'I have seen the lands of the morning
Under the white, arched sails of ships'

John Masefield

WE LEFT Cherry's sister, Helen Gainsford, in charge with the updated red exercise book 'How to Run the H.D.R.A.' to guide her, and escaped from Southampton on the big, grey-mauve and white *Pendennis Castle*, out past the Needles with just enough heave on her decks to show she was alive.

We were on deck as Gran Canaria came in sight out of a grey mist on a grey sea, and I took one of the best photographs of my life in the early sunlight, conveying the romance of an unknown island, with cloud shadows gliding over untrodden hills. It made an ideal cover picture for *Lands of the Morning* which was largely the story of that most lost of all lost civilizations — the Guanches of the Canary Islands, ignored by orthodox archaeology because of the taint of the 'Atlantis heresy' that wrecks reputations.

Modern Canarians are a blend of the original, late Cro-Magnon, neolithic, sheep, goat, and barley farmers, who did their duty by their land for perhaps 3,000 years and between 1402 and 1495 went down fighting their Spanish conquerors heroically with stone age weapons against crossbows and armour. Like all Spaniards, they are intensely interested in people, and when Cherry, who had visited the Museo de Canario in Las Palmas when she had stayed there for two weeks on her way to meet me the second time, arrived with an almost equally white-haired husband, Don Jose Naranjo Suarez, the curator, was delighted. So was his secretary, who looked like Carmen as she should be played, not the usual plump prima donna.

He gave me the pick of his photographs for my book, taken over the years beautifully with a plate camera like my father's, and led us round his dusty specimen cases at an excited gallop, pouring out knowledge in his strong Andalusian accent in response to Cherry's Argentine echoes behind classic Madrid Spanish. In Spain, accents indicate region rather than class. Then he dictated a letter of introduction for 'Professor Lorenzo Hills, the famous English archaeologist' asking everyone to assist me in my researches. This was beautifully typed by his secretary in the most flowery and elegant Spanish, and we used it throughout our two week stay as Aladdin used his lamp.

We employed it first at Telde, the second largest town on Gran Canaria, at the end of a long journey by Gua-Gua (Wa-Wa) the local name for the large single seater buses, which I was glad to see were all Leylands of advanced age, for I trusted antique British engineering and learned to trust the Guanche sense of balance.

Naranjo's letter, produced at the town hall, brought us straight to the Mayor of Telde, a town famous for possessing the oldest continually inhabited dwellings in the world — caves, cut out by the Guanches in the soft tufa rock more than 5,000 years ago. He was very anxious that my book should not convey the impression that his ratepayers lived in caves because they were poor. Some caves cost as much as modern surface houses, but were cooler in summer, and their owners were continually agitating for mains electricity, so they could enjoy TV instead of only battery radios and calor gas cookers.

The mayor then summoned a corporal of police, in dirty white breeches, tunic, high black boots, and a peaked cap like a motorcycle traffic policeman but without a motorbike, and placed us in his charge. Juan Suarez — according to the visiting card he produced with a flourish — took us outside, held up his hand, and stopped a bus. We got on and when I attempted to pay, Juan said, 'no matter,' the only English he knew. After about two miles we transferred to a car, which I took to be a taxi, but again 'no matter'.

As we walked up a steep and dusty lane towards the bare hills, with prickly pear cactus and thirsty shrubs among the rocks, he explained why Telde had no police cars or motorcycles. The roads are so steep that wrongdoers would see the arm of the law zigzagging up the hairpin bends far in the distance, giving them time to get away or hide the evidence. They would notice a local car without suspecting that it held a corporal of police on duty bound. He stopped buses, but never took them off their routes because local criminals would spot the diversion at once, and never stopped tourist cars, because strangers would not know the roads. I never learned if this custom was common in the Canaries, or whether the Mayor of Telde was saving money.

It was like being taken round an English village by the local policeman, who knew everyone on terms of semi-official friendliness. Some of the caves had perfectly ordinary front doors with a window beside them set straight in the hillside, but most had narrow ledges with room to sit under shading, often flowering creepers on pergolas, or porches with just room to sit in the sun. Inside they were neat and tidy, with plastic crucifixes on walls where modern emulsion paint thickly covered the stone-age tool marks. Juan had a heavy and powerful metal torch that showed these up beautifully on the roofs of the back rooms used for storage. The tools, ideal for cutting soft rock, had been the picks and mattocks made of obsidian (volcanic glass) bound with hide to suitable shaped branches that I had seen in the museum.

Archaeologically, the 5,000-year-old homes were disappointing after many years of good housewifery in spring cleaning, tidying, and redecorating, at first with whitewash from burnt seashells, on walls easily washed down for a fresh coat. The early Guanches could well have enriched them with vivid cave paintings as their ancestors had in France, for some areas had been rubbed flat and smooth with harder rock, and a few examples remain, but of abstract patterns.

A Mendip limestone cave, used by hunters as a temporary shelter for a long time, full of broken stone tools, bones to show the changing quarry through the ages, and cooking-fire charcoal for carbon-14 dating, would have been far more useful. The Guanches were farmers and the first article I wrote on them appeared in *The Farmer*, entitled 'Fertility farmers for sixty centuries'. They had invented the system of balanced grazing, and skilled herdsmanship, before the Spaniards tore down the forests of *Pinus canariensis*, the now nearly extinct giant pine, the best tree for building large dugout canoes on our side of the Atlantic, and wrecked the climate.

Since farmers believe that the best is cheapest in the end, once they have found something good that works it stays unchanged, wherever the memories of the aged are the only books and the word of the elders is law. In isolation, cultures lock, and those of Tenerife and Gran Canaria, the highest civilizations in the group, stayed locked through the centuries. To the Phoenicians, Greeks, and Romans, these islands, without metals or anything worth plundering, were 'The Fortunate Islands', and the yellow fruits of *Arbutus canariensis*, were the Golden Apples of the Hesperides, to pre-Roman visitors used to crab-apple-sized fruit. The islanders enjoyed a standard of living that struck galley slaves and sailors driven off course in classical times as highly attractive, for these nations of farmers had made themselves rich by keeping their wants few.

Our Aladdin's lamp letter (and Cherry's fluent Spanish, spoken with every muscle of her face) took us to the Jardin Canario, where so many survivors from the green and fertile past are kept alive by regular hosing, and to the Museo Arqueologico at Santa Lucia de Tirajana. This was owned by Don Vicente Sanchez Arana, whose ancestors had taken part in the last stand of the Guanches of Gran Canaria, under Princess Arminda, against General Pedro de Vera on April 26th, 1483. For over five hundred years a ceremony has been held in the great cave of the Fortaleza, holding 2,000 people, to honour that day when the closest descendants of Guanches who fought then recite ancient and modern poems in memory of the heroic past.

Don Vicente inherits their great height, compared with modern Spaniards and our own medieval ancestors. He is six foot two, and had never measured a Gauche mummy taller than six foot four. The 'giant' chieftains who ruled the islands and led their people in the long struggle first against French adventurers under de Bethencourt, and finally Alonso de Lugo who conquered Tenerife in 1495, were no taller than the kind of colonel who is nicknamed 'Old Lofty' in the Brigade of Guards.

They had two outstanding weapons. One was selected round stones, rather larger than cricket balls, bowled overarm with fearful force at the faces of the enemy. The other was their whistling language, a kind of whistled shorthand — there was no written language — used for urgent messages about sheep and goats, as well as for local gossip across deep volcanic valleys. The Spaniards confused this with the song of the wild canaries.

All too soon we were out on the end of the Mole on our last evening at this port where Columbus had called with his three small ships in 1492, when the Guanches were still holding out on Tenerife, watching the *Edinburgh Castle* coming in with all her lights blazing to take us home to Helen. The H.D.R.A. was calling me back again and I had a book to write out of my system.

Had I had words enough and time I might have written a far better book, but at least I finished it somehow, sent it round the publishers who all turned it down, and finally, in 1970, Cherry and I had it published by the Regency Press by paying £640 for them to print 5,000 copies selling at £2 each, now selling as collectors items — giving me a 20 per cent royalty. It was poorly reviewed, with serious publications sending it to archaeological reviewers disgusted by the echo of Atlantis. In the end I sold it to the last copy by keeping it in the H.D.R.A. book list, where it earned the Association a third profit on each, and I got my money back, plus £177 off my income tax towards the expenses of the holiday of a lifetime.

The pile of waiting letters needed four typists taking an hour's dictation at a time and three or four typing back, sometimes with all four coming two evenings a week. By the end of 1966 I had dictated 4,476 letters, not counting those that could be answered by leaflets, 700 more than in 1965, and we numbered 1,221 members. I was no longer doing the books, for after the departure of Gordon Tingley, Logan Lindsay sent us one of his articled pupils, Henry Yearley, young, cheerful, and interested in the extraordinary institution growing at the end of Convent Lane.

Logan Lindsay made quite a proportion of his firm's income by taking pupils, and it was an asset for those tadpole chartered accountants to have worked on a registered charity. We agreed that they would come to us during their last year, working for a small monthly fee while gaining useful experience. It did not work out like this, for Henry became so interested that he stayed with us year after year.

On the Trial Ground we employed one man alternate mornings and afternoons (a postman on shift work), two men at weekends, and two schoolboys on Saturday mornings. They had kept up with the work while we were away, and when we came back in October were digging up comfrey orders and were still awaiting the first hard frost to bring down the foliage of Japanese pumpkins. Pierre Gevaert, of Lima Foods, had shown slides of these at the Soil Association Attingham Conference Cherry and I had attended, and I had bought half a pound of seed for the then large sum of 70 shillings. It was crossed with a local Belgian variety, so varied widely, but always instead of being watery like a marrow, or the pumpkins used by Americans for pies and Hallowe'en Parties, the flesh was firm and deep yellow.

I had spent some of the money that was pouring in on a full analysis from Dr Horace Ward:

	Japanese Pumpkin	American Pumpkin	Marrow
	%	%	%
Oil	0.40	0.40	Trace
Protein	1.80	0.50	0.4
Fibre	1.40	1.90	—
Carbohydrate	8.10	1.40	1.4
Ash	0.90	0.36	0.2
Calcium	0.04	0.03	—
Phosphorus	0.04	0.01	—
Moisture	86.90	97.20	97.8

Pumpkins have always been a favourite food for weaned black babies in South Africa where grey Boer pumpkins are selected to be flat like a squash, so they can be set out on hut roofs to 'cure' in the sun for longer keeping, as in America. Even in England they keep until about February. We tried hanging ours in the attic at No. 20 but as they dried the stems shrank, the strings slipped off, and they fell with a thunderous crash. After this midnight alarm, I collected a small red nylon nets that hold nuts, onions, and other imports from greengrocers, in which to hang our pumpkins from the rafters.

Our best variation, christened 'Monstrous Marmaduke', weighed 23 lb., and though it held about six times as much carbohydrate as the American variety, and three times the protein, it remained greatly inferior to potatoes. I sent the seed out as a Members' Experiment, and they produced an array of recipes for cooking this new vegetable that was a big nutritional improvement on marrows and courgettes. The best was a veganic lemon curd made without eggs, devised by Dr W. A. Blythe, of Bristol University, who is still our Scientific Adviser. We eliminated 'Useless Eustace', which had small, cucumber-like foliage and only male flowers, and concentrated on

Marmaduke and 'Prolific Penelope', in the hope of developing a line that could produce six or eight 3 to 6 lb. pumpkins rather than single monsters too large for anything but weight-guessing competitions.

Its real value lay in countries where babies cannot digest cows' milk. The Boer pumpkin, the commonest kind in Africa, holds 0.3 per cent of calcium, without any oxalic acid to lock it up as it does in spinach, and is far better for building bone structure than expensive European infant foods.

Always I thought of comfrey as food for a hungry world, as Henry Doubleday did, but every ton of the 12 tons of dry matter in the 100 ton an acre crops common in Africa needs 500 tons of water. Pumpkins can snatch water quickly when it rains, build their proteins, carbohydrates, and nutritionally useful oils, and gather their calcium fast, to store through long months of drought.

So I wrote to the editors of *The South African Farmers' Weekly*, *The Cape Times*, *The Johannesburg Sunday Times*, *The Rhodesian Herald*, *The Fiji Times*, *The East African Standard*, *The Mauritius Advance*, *The Jamaica Gleaner*, and *The Seychelles Times*, offering small packets of seed for trial, free for an international reply coupon. This gathered a total of 357 experimenters and spread the genes for high dry matter, five times as much vitamin A, and twice the calcium, through the pumpkin populations of Third World countries. We had 241 people in South Africa, 34 in Kenya, 32 in Rhodesia, 8 in Fiji, 8 in Jamaica, 7 in Mauritius, 2 in Seychelles, 3 in Swaziland, 3 in Tanzania, 1 in Angola, 1 in Louren o Marques, 1 in Madagascar, 1 in Malawi, and 1 in Zambia, bringing stamps that delighted the small sons whose mothers were working for us part-time.

Among the replies were 20 from research stations, 12 from schools, from Makerere College in Uganda, many missionaries, and field officers of the American Peace Corps, Oxfam, and the Save the Children Fund. The whole 'Operation Cinderella', as we called it, cost us about £75 in postage and labour for typing and packeting, and got our Japanese strain compared with local varieties in a large number of countries with suitable climates and populations.

There was so much interest in South Africa, especially from Cherry's friends there in the Soil Association, that we had the idea of a lecture tour that would gain recruits for both bodies and perhaps lead to a South African Group of the H.D.R.A.

Cherry's circle fixed up the dates, we arranged far ahead for Mrs McLean to take over the custody of the Red Exercise Book, and bought our tickets. I would lecture on the pumpkins, on comfrey, and organic gardening. Though composting is international, the great need overseas was (and still is) to get experimenters working on improved methods of farming and gardening without chemicals, to suit local conditions and local pests and diseases. My hope was not merely to preach to the converted, but to start people experimenting.

In the autumn of 1966, while I was still catching up and keeping pace, my mother caught pneumonia in the Convent garden and was admitted to Black Notley Hospital. When she came out she required more looking after than our Franciscan Convent could provide, so they arranged for her to go to another Convent at Danbury, beyond Chelmsford, run by a Spanish Order, where Cherry was soon fast friends with the Mother Superior. Iris and I managed weekly visits by train and bus, and all through that spring I watched the shrubs in the suburban gardens blossoming in sequence, as I kept her supplied with books, cigarettes, and news of what we were doing. From there she went into the County Hospital for an operation for the cataract which stopped her reading through the slit of vision she had left in her only eye. There she caught an infection from one of the then new antibiotic-proof 'bugs' and lost even the little vision she had. She died on May 12th, 1967, aged 85. All I am, have been and will be I owe to her.

In addition to 'Operation Cinderella', the publication of my *Down to Earth Gardening*, one of the first books on ornamental gardening for organic gardeners, in August, and the launching of *The Basic Food Guide* through the letter with the Haro cartoon in *The Observer*, we had seven open days on Saturdays, plus weekday visits by 16 Essex rural science teachers and 24 members of the Frinton-on-Sea Horticultural Society. The 'Give Up Smoking Bonfires' campaign was gathering speed and I was still trying to get *The Wholefood Finder* through its final stages, with hang-ups from waiting for Soil Association Council decisions. It was one of our busiest summers and I had to think ahead to ensure the H.D.R.A. could run for six weeks without me, for this time Helen was not available, and even at this slackest time of the year, by sailing on November 10th by the *Edinburgh Castle,* getting home on January 1st by the *Pendennis Castle*, there would be a fearful pile when I got back. My leading typist then was Mrs Willcock and I wrote out a number of stock letters which she could vary to fit a large number of situations, supplementing them with our duplicated advice sheets. Mr Lock and Michael Suckling would get the parcels away, Mr Yearley would collect the money from Mrs McLean, leave pay envelopes for everyone, pay John Stephens at the post office, and put the money in the bank. Fortunately we had only one 'pet' which we took with us — several billions of *Lactobacillus bulgaricus*, which we called 'yogs', otherwise 'kefir grains' which converted milk to do-it-yourself yoghourt.

Cherry had been given them by a grateful patient, had nursed them all through the war, and they would now be embarking on their fifth journey to Africa and back. In Newsletter No. 23 (September 1965) she had written an account of how exactly to look after them, and we used to send out small bottles of the washed grains, which looked a little like tiny cauliflower curds, free to members by post. By the time we went to South Africa we had despatched about 150 of these awkward little parcels to members, as part of the family service that was part of the H.D.R.A. in its early days. After about 10 years, the growth of the Association made us pass on the 'Milk With The Mostest' as Cherry called it in her article, to a Mrs Hegarty of Dundee. Today, cultures of various strains of *Lactobacillus* can be bought, and their sale is strictly controlled by E.E.C. regulations.

Once more we took the boat train from Victoria, with six fat suitcases full of clothes, literature, books, pumpkin seeds, slides for lectures, and Cherry's portable typewriter, down to the seas again to the lofty echoing sheds, the long queue, and the salt smell and a seagull crying. At best, an air journey provides only a relief map unrolling below, a roar of air conditioning, and a cramped seat with longer queues in airports identical in every country. We had 12 days each way of a real rest, and a holiday for the yogs, too, with a pint of just warm milk from our cabin steward for them every evening. Our cabin was one of the very cheapest double ones, far down below the water line, with everything creaking and groaning as in Kipling's short story *The Ship that Found Herself*.

We paused at Las Palmas just long enough to buy a camel leather document case that I have still, to sit listening to the wild canaries in the Parque Catalina, and to enjoy a slow Spanish meal at The Three Waterwheels, our favourite bar restaurant, with wine at fourpence a glass. Then south, down the long sea road of blue and bluer seas with its traditional milestones.

There was the Captain's cocktail party and the announcement on the loudspeakers that: 'Flying fish are in sight from the First Class Promenade Deck'. As tourist class passengers, we could walk right round the ship only before 8.30 in the morning and the first class quarters, towards the bows, got the flying fish, because the ship's bow wave, spreading out on either side, started the shoals leaping. But Cherry and I were always up early and saw plenty, and also porpoises, as we enjoyed the beauty of the wide, clean sea.

There was 'crossing the line' with much tactful horseplay, for the *Edinburgh Castle* was full of elderly hotel keepers and seaside landladies enjoying being waited on and catered for after a successful season, and the Fancy Dress Dance, for which many passengers had brought elaborate hired costumes. Cherry wore a long black evening dress to dinner which was 'cut on the cross'. We went as 'Exchange is no robbery'; she wore my cream linen tropical suit (bought at the Oxfam shop in Braintree) in which she looked like Harpo Marx, and I wore her dress which stretched to fit me, with her handbag and my own shoes, so I was nearer Charlie's Aunt in modern dress. We won fourth prize — a £1 voucher to spend at the ship's shop.

The final event was the only rough weather of the voyage, when we met the cape rollers where the Agulhas current from the Antarctic meets the warm Atlantic, and we tossed and creaked through a noisy night before Table Mountain rose out of the sea, clothed in the white cloud known as the 'Tablecloth', with Cape Town spread below it.

Francis Watermeyer, President of the South African Soil Association, and Eleanor his wife, with whom we were staying, and Cherry's great friend Norah Rowlands who arranged the lecture tour, were on the quay to meet us, and with the help of a surprising number of porters our luggage was loaded into the elderly American cars which it was the delight of Francis and his sons to restore with loving care. At their rambling bungalow in Bergvliet, a suburb of Cape Town, they had laid on a reception party, where I met the editor of *The Cape Times*.

Like every lecture tour ever planned, my first one tried to fit in far too many lectures in view of the distances involved. My first was at Stellenbosch University, a kind of South African

Cambridge but with streets lined with jacaranda trees, glorious with purple-blue blossom that my colour slide film simply murdered. Next day we drove more miles through country that could have been Surrey except for the startling brilliance of the flowering trees, to address the Hottentot Holland and Hout Bay Horticultural Society. There were about 70 of them in a lovely garden that could have been Cheam, owned by Fred Leathers, a member of ours, who grew comfrey and made compost, putting empty tins in his heap which trapped just enough air inside them for good decay under African conditions. His problem was that his compost broke down too fast and too far, while if it got too dry the white ants ate it.

From there we went on to speak to the fruit growers at Elgin, high up in the mountains where the climate changes and suddenly all the gardens are full of English flowers. Here I saw the only hoopoe (*Upupa epops*, a lovely name), I have seen in my life, walking on a lawn in the grey of the morning, hunting worms as casually as a blackbird. This is where South African apples are grown and we went over an organic fruit farm, or rather one as organic as regulations would allow. The trees are heavily mulched with compost made from maize and slaughterhouse wastes, but they must all be sprayed with every possible pesticide because no export apple may show the slightest blemish.

Cherry caught the full force of blown spray, and when we woke in the morning in Hermanus, a lovely little seaside town like Frinton, she lost her voice entirely, and that evening she was to speak on 'Food fences against cancer' based on one of her 'Housewives' Help' sections in the Newsletter. A major problem of laryngitis is that everyone whispers back. I called a doctor, the only person who spoke in a normal voice to her for the whole week she had to stay there. We needed the doctor, who was expensive, because, being covered by insurance, we could recover the hotel bill, and we dreaded possible South African non-NHS hospital fees. Luckily, staying in bed in silence and feeding on yoghourt made by our faithful yogs, working overtime under the care of the maid, cured her of the pesticide effect.

I stocked her up with library books, with the help of the Hon. Secretary of the Hermanus Ladies' Literary and Botanical Society who had sponsored our lectures. She undertook to collect all the books from the hotel and to pay for any that were missing, and I selected about 20 non-fiction to last her and allow for duds. Her lecture went down well, from her notes and in my voice, and after my own one of the ladies produced the most extraordinary plant of fat hen (*Chenopodium album*) I have ever seen. Its growing points were deep maroon-purple. In Britain, we see a pale maroon-pink on these weed seedlings on phosphorus-poor soil, but this specimen was the result of an almost total lack of this important plant food. It seemed that the North African phosphate-rock suppliers refused to sell this raw material for superphosphate to South Africa as a protest against apartheid. It was only extensive green manuring with the bitter, blue, annual lupin that saved South Africa from disaster, for this species has special fungi in its roots that make phosphates available from stores deep in the soil. The other source is poultry manure, and the deeplitter system, with open, wire-netting sides on Dr Fairchild's idea from Rhodesia, recycles the phosphate in wood and poultry food.

In the morning I left Cherry for the longest time since our wedding, and drove off with Norah over Frenchoek Pass through the mountains to Cape Town, in her little green 'tree-toad' Morris Minor, on a journey that started like Wiltshire with maize, then wheat, and finished high and grim with wild helichrysums blowing in bitterly cold winds across the top. We returned in time for me to give Cherry's talk as well as my own at the Electricity Theatre in Cape Town, where we found that the plug on the slide projector provided would not fit the sockets in the hall. We kept about 500 people waiting while Soil Association members hunted for an electrician who slept over his shop to wake up and sell them one that fitted. Since then, however much the committee or my hosts want me to answer their personal gardening questions because there is 'plenty of time', I insist on getting to the hall early enough to run my slides through the projector on a trial trip.

I gave three more lectures and visited a big organic farm owned by Mrs Parker, growing cattle, fruit, wine, and grain. Her great problem was the Argentine ant, one of the curses of South Africa because it moves its aphids on to the vines. I put her on to our remedy of equal parts borax and icing sugar, which was cheap, safe, and simple, but I never learnt how she got on with it.

My last lecture before I was due to collect Cherry, after a whole week in which she could only whisper to me over the telephone, was at the Open Day and 'Braivleis' of the Bootsma's organic market garden at Phillipi on Cape Flats which is probably the best in South Africa. The soil is poor, white sand, like parts of Surrey, low in minerals, especially manganese, with a fierce appetite for humus. The Bootsma family market all their crops, mainly courgettes, curly kale (which they can pick almost all the year round), French Beans, globe artichokes, lettuce, melons, pumpkins, and sweetcorn in Cape Town, bringing back all the vegetable wastes from the market. These they compost with straw, nightsoil, and slaughterhouse wastes, making so much that they even have some to sell. They were up at 5 a.m. on market days to meet their customers and sell their produce at premium prices — on quality and appearance, not because it is organic. The master's foot is the best dung, as the old proverb goes, but today it is his best compost heap.

Brai in Afrikaans means 'burn', and a *braivleis* is a 'burn party', the South African version of a barbecue, reaching back to the days when meat was free for the shooting, with wood burnt to glowing embers in trenches crossed by small steel ladders, on which large lumps of meat are roasted. Eleanor roasted me about a week's ration for half a street in wartime Britain, which I ate with salad while the others had wholemeal bread. You bring your own meat to braivleis and the butchers simply love it.

Another great friend of Cherry's, Barbara Newton, a downright person who never took 'um' (short for umbrage), collected me from the Bootsmas after I had given my talk in the darkened great barn, and took me back over the mountains in another lion-hearted Morris Minor and down the dark and twisted road to Hermanus and my waiting Cherry.

We got back to Barbara's flat in time for lunch, for which she cooked an excellent fish called a kingklip, apologizing because it was the wrong season for snoek, which is delicious fresh, though tinned it was one of the housewives' horrors of the war. We three decided that the afternoon was our only chance to drive right round the tip of Africa and this we did. I bought Agfa colour slide film in Kenilworth, the suburb where Barbara lived, and it brought out the blues of the sea and sky beautifully, on that day of mountains, heroic views, sun, and gliding shadows.

The Watermeyers got us away, early next day, to Jan Smuts Airport to catch a Vickers Viscount to Port Elizabeth. Either the fumes, or the effect of the changing pressure in her ears, upset

Cherry's Menière's disease and we were glad to come down at last to meet John Humphries and Mr and Mrs Neil Boss, the organic farming members we had flown to meet. John Humphries farmed earlier in Rhodesia, but was beaten by 10 years' drought. One year, two years, three years without rain, you can manage, at four years you start borrowing from the bank, at seven years you are convinced it cannot go on any longer, and at 10 years you give up.

John Humphries then began shooting game to send to the copper mines in what is now Zambia, for meat to feed the African mine workers. He shot enough to pay off all his debts and start again with a civil engineering contracting business and a small farm outside Port Elizabeth. He had a charming young wife and a little boy of three. In five years he aimed to convert his 300 acres of dry bush land, not virgin veldt but land exhausted by greedy farming without even chemical fertilizer, by his policy of 'one *dam* thing after another: pushing up earthen dams across the mouths of the dry valleys that become torrents, tearing the land away, when it rains, and planting opuntia (prickly pear cactus) hedges, not the ordinary spiny species but the spineless variety bred by Luther Burbank, so in case of drought he could cut his hedges to keep his stock going on the water stored inside them.

I lectured that evening at the local farmers' club and next morning Neil Boss collected us to go round the several square miles of his estate, including acres and acres of oranges, all heavily straw-mulched to hold in the moisture, but all under government regulations had to be sprayed to kill the Mediterranean fruit fly (*Ceratitis capitata*) which produces one generation every 30 days, the curse of all countries where fruit is ripe all year round, so Cherry could eat none. The main enterprise was a huge dairy herd, with magnificent milking parlours and complete, modern, recording methods for every cow, all run by a black farm manager, a mission-trained Christian, with an agricultural college degree, speaking perfect English. I took a lovely slide of his five-year-old son as their youngest 'farmworker' wheeling a relatively huge wheelbarrow at the side of Neil Boss, 80 years older and about six foot three. Except for the very modern machinery, the whole set-up reminded me of one of the great estates I had seen in the 1930s, in their pre-1914 glory, with blacksmith's shops, dairies, piggeries, entirely self-contained. The 'stately home' in the middle was whitewashed

189

Dutch Colonial, the fashion in Holland 300 years ago, with magnificent gardens where every bed and many individual shrubs had ridges of soil drawn round them to hold the water. The furniture was all 'stinkwood', made on the estate from home-grown timber.

Our next stop was Durban, where Kay and Arthur Howes met us and drove us to Amanzimtoti, or 'Toti', a very pleasant seaside place of which Arthur had been mayor for many years, with splendid swimming pool, complete with a small and shallow version for children, filled by the tides of far cleaner seas than we have in Europe. He was chief engineer with the South African subsidiary of ICI and could have had unlimited chemicals as free 'perks' but ran a 20-acre organic fruit holding without using any. Earlier he had won a prize at the local show for 19 different tropical fruits ripe at once, from their garden where pests are baffled by intercropping with everything grown in a glorious mixture.

Near the equator, with the equal day lengths and night falling suddenly at about 6 p.m., there is none of our 'leaving gardens rough dug for winter'. Everything keeps on growing without a slack season, and French beans can be picked almost right round the year. They are sown in shady places under the fruit because the main problem is the scorching sun, and shade is treasured. They grow bananas, paw-paws, guavas which are enormously rich in vitamin C, guavadillas, and granadillas, as well as the beans, and sweet corn for cobs and compost material. Deep-litter poultry manure and compost supply the fertility, and the main value of the intercropping, rather than crop rotation system, lies in keeping the ground always covered so there is no loss of plant foods in heavy rains. The basic staff were Joseph and Lucy, a Zulu couple, who spent most of their time picking the produce of what was more an enriched jungle than a market garden of neat rows and powerful machinery.

The aim was to maintain a constant supply of fruit and vegetables for sale in the morning market, run by an organization that could well be copied in other countries, the Woman's Exchange, to which Kay belonged, was in the municipal car park where there was a large L-shaped shed of corrugated iron (painted white to absorb less sun heat), open along the front, normally used to protect parked motorcyles from the sun and tropical rain. From 6 a.m. to 8 a.m. it had trestle tables along the front, where local smallholders or ordinary housewives displayed fruit, vegetables, cut flowers, poultry, eggs, and dairy produce for sale to hotel buyers, campers, caravanners, self-catering flat tenants, and other housewives. A charge of $2\frac{1}{2}$ per cent on the takings to the Exchange paid for the labour of putting up, taking down, and storing trestles. Prices were lower than in the local shops, wholesaler's and retailer's profits being cut out, with transport costs minimal.

Kay drove us up to the cottage at Hineville in the high plateau of the Drakensburg which they had offered us for our honeymoon, their second home in the cool which Cheizi, the Zulu gardener, looked after, growing Cherry's original Bocking 14 comfrey plants for sale. Here the days were the right length for year round yield and yet cool enough for pigs to thrive. I saw Leslie Brophy's herd of Landraces showing me again the great value of comfrey as an 'infant food'. When sows have larger litters than there are teats for the weakest, then by feeding plenty of mineral-rich comfrey foliage to the sow, the stronger piglets start eating in from about four days old, giving the smallest a chance to feed.

From Hineville, Kay drove us right across the Zulu Reserve, and on that journey Cherry bought the only oranges safe for her from two Zulu girls offering nets of them by the roadside, all showing the fruit-fly bites that were proof they had not been sprayed. We stayed in Pietermaritzburg that night and then on to the Valley of a Thousand Hills, home of the Valley Trust run by two South Africans of genius, one white and the other black.

Dr Halley Stott, a member of the H.D.R.A., trained at Edinburgh and in 1951 gave up a very lucrative practice in Durban to serve the medical needs of the reserve, to find that almost every health problem arose from the Zulus' abandonment of their native diet for one based on white sugar, white flour, and sifted maize meal. One of his first enterprises was a co-operative mill where Zulus could grind their own maize to wholemeal, gaining a 317 per cent increase in thiamin (vitamin B1), 300 per cent more riboflavin, 100 per cent more niacin, 40 per cent extra fat, 31 per cent more iron, 25 per cent more calcium, and 19 per cent more phosphorus, than if they had sold the grain then bought back the same weight of maize flour. In 1956, he was joined by Mr Robert Mazibuko, son of a Zulu chief, with a missionary-agricultural-college training and the genius that can adapt and invent as well as the leadership and skill to graft new methods on to rigid customs.

One of the many examples of his persuasive skill was the overcoming of the Zulu prejudice against fish, from the belief that it would turn the courage of their warriors to water. There is a Chinese proverb 'if you give a man a fish you feed him for a day, but teach him to fish and you feed him for many days'. If, like Dr Stott and Mr Mazibuko you teach him to build small earth dams to hold back the rains in ponds large enough for tilapia (delicious herbivorous fish resembling a chunky golden herring) you add protein rich in tryptophan, the amino acid lacking in a maize-based diet. Though there is no refrigerator cheap enough to keep fish fresh for the hundreds of millions of people who live far from the sea in the tropics, harvesting the valleys between the Thousand Hills has given the Zulus of the Transkei fish fresher than any available to Londoners.

The clinic is paid for by the South African Government but the unique agricultural experiment round it is financed by the subscriptions of members of the Valley Trust and donations from individuals and bodies like Oxfam. The Zulus come to be treated, often bringing their relations, and they see and learn the methods of improved agriculture invented by Mazibuko.

From the clinic at Botha's Hill we looked across the valley at what could almost have been rice terraces in Java. These are a series of Mazibuko trenches, known as 'fertility trenches' in South Africa where it is not officially recognized that a Zulu could invent something more important to dry Africa than the Indore compost heap or the New Zealand box. The faces of the terraces were gay with lucerne flowers, for the Valley of a Thousand Hills has no stone to build retaining walls, and the deep, strong, root web of this perennial crop, cut regularly for cattle fodder, holds the soil firmly provided the safe angle of slope is not exceeded. It sounds unlikely but it works, because lucerne is rich in vitamins C and A, and Mazibuko and his wife (an S.R.N. at the clinic) have publicized it until it became a popular Zulu vegetable.

Behind each root-held terrace 'step' lies a trench cut down into the hillside with hoes like spades set at right angles on hoe shafts, designed for bare feet. These trenches are about six feet wide and four deep, filled first with a sprinkling of topsoil on the bottom, then a foot-thick layer of cut crass, millet, and maize stems, and all domestic wastes, especially feathers and chicken bones, even worn-out clothing. On this is piled about a foot of soil, then another layer of compost material, and so on until the trench is filled.

On the final soil layer, heaped high enough to allow for sinkage, sunn hemp (*Crotallia juncea*) is sown. This legume sends its long roots down through the layers where its powerful nodule bacteria release quantities of nitrogen as the foliage is cut for cattle feed. This provides the activator for the underground compost heaps and when the rains come, instead of tearing the soil away in gullies, or at best growing a single crop, the water soaks into the trenchfuls of organic matter, step by step down the hillside, where it stays soaked into the sponge of humus for year round production. Maize, millet, carrots, pumpkins, and many native vegetables follow to crop right through the dry season.

An experiment designed and recorded by the University of Natal on 36 replicated plots had established that the system ranks far ahead of chemical fertilizers used without this source of compost, and though these fertilizers, when used in addition, increased yields by 10 per cent, using nothing bought or imported remained the most important advantage of the system.

In the years since 1967, when we made Robert Mazibuko an honorary member of the H.D.R.A., he has retired from the Valley Trust, which still carries on its excellent work, and founded the African Tree Centre which grows trees given free to Africans for firewood and erosion control. On June 26th, 1987, the Rotary Club of Pietermaritzburg gave him a Community Service Award, with the following citation:

'For outstanding service to the community both through the exemplary performance of his self-imposed duties and also through the unselfish application of his special skills to the needs of society, particularly on the occasion of the Unemployment Relief Fund Project in 1986 and also the establishment of the African Tree Centre.

'For more than one year sixty previously unemployed people were usefully employed under the direction of Robert Mazibuko in constructing conservation structures and planting riverside trees in the Edendale area with the commendable goal of containing soil erosion. Furthermore, Robert Mazibuko has recognized the necessity for malnutrition and undernourishment to be redressed by training people to be self-sufficient in vegetable production, using the methods of organic cultivation. In this field he has achieved international recognition while the

FIGHTING LIKE THE FLOWERS

Rotary Club of Pietermaritzburg has given due recognition to and paid tribute to Robert Mazibuko for his unique contribution to community service.'

No organic gardener of any colour in any country has had such a tribute from the orthodox or deserved it so well.

I did some Christmas shopping in Durban where West Street was decorated like Oxford Street, with Father Christmases sweltering in tropical heat, then took off on the first leg of the long journey home, with the high spot of the trip coming in over the mountains, with the lights of Cape Town spread below.

14

Fertility, Pollution,
and Oranges

CONVENT LANE welcomed us home to thick snow, also to cut shoots of *Daphne mezureum* packed with buds to open and fill No. 20 with fragrance, and seven weeks of letters Mrs Willcock had been unable to answer from stock — all the awkward and interesting ones. Among these were many from borough engineers, appreciating *The Fertility Finder* which had been well reviewed by *The Muck Shifter and Public Works Digest, Municipal Engineering and Sanitary Record*, and other glossy periodicals in this important field.

It is important because fertility is not only the ability of our land to grow good crops but to keep on producing food for man and beast as long as the rain falls, the sun shines, and the vital cycles of life keep turning in the biosphere. There are a nitrogen cycle, a carbon cycle, a sulphur cycle depending partly on *Thiobacillus thioxidans* that brings back the sulphur concentrated by our onions and our cabbages into circulation, and others.

Among my waiting letters was one from Mr Arthur Wright, Clerk to the Upper Tame Main Drainage Authority, responsible for the sewage disposal and water supply of Greater Birmingham, who could proudly boast that every gallon of the hard-working River Tame was drunk 14 times before it thankfully reached the sea. On behalf of his Authority he wanted the H.D.R.A. to take part in a five-year research programme on the value of dried sewage sludges for gardeners and sports grounds. I reported at length, bearing mind that the U.T.M.D.A. would do all the analysis at their Birmingham laboratories, and asked the incredible sum of £230 a year which covered my costs and made it possible to do this work for the benefit of organic gardeners and farmers everywhere. I should have asked three times as much, for even then this was a bargain.

195

My object was not to make a profit towards other experiments, but to help close the 'broken cycles' of phosphorus, potassium, and trace elements, especially zinc, flowing away as effluent down polluted rivers to the sea, or dumped there expensively by special ships, or discharged down long pipes below low-tide levels. Once, carts returning from Covent Garden had spread an ever-widening ring of fertile market gardens around London with the manure from an all horse-drawn city. Now, the wasted humus and plant foods from much of Britain was growing an even wider ring of seaweed beds about 10 miles beyond low-water mark that gales broke up and tossed up on the beaches, causing expensive problems for seaside resorts.

In 1955, I had 'nursed' *Fertility from Town Wastes* by J. C. Wylie for Faber and Faber, and later his *The Wastes of Civilisation*, published in 1959, a popular work which should have become the 'Silent Spring' of sewage and municipal compost, but this aspect of the organic movement has never captured the imagination of either public or politicians because it is hard for either to think far enough ahead.

Sir Albert Howard at Indore was composting high-cellulose wastes, spreading thick, tall, sunn hemp, millet, maize stems, and even some bamboos in the road outside the research station, where the slow crushing by the large wooden wheels of the bullock cart traffic was just as effective a pulverizer as those at a modern municipal compost plant. His activators were human wastes, as mine would have been in the R.A.F. had I been able to follow his advice, not cow manure, the only fuel for cooking in most of India, and his heaps reached the 180–200° F that destroys tapeworm eggs, as well as the waterborne diseases cholera, typhoid, and dysentery, just as effectively as the modern sewage treatment plants serving Greater Birmingham. The use of human wastes is not an essential part of the Indore composting system — it was merely Sir Albert's way round the problem of fertility in a country which uses its manure as fuel, wasting the nitrogen and potential humus in the atmosphere and reducing the potassium to a highly soluble salt that washes away rapidly in tropical rains.

On behalf of his Authority, Arthur Wright invited Cherry and me to Birmingham to stay at the best hotel, dine with Dr Jenkins, his chief chemist, and both their wives, and to see their laboratories and massive treatment plant. This was the first time we had met the majors, colonels, and brigadiers of the army of dedicated men who spend their lives saving our cities from burying themselves in their dustbin refuse and drowning their streets in sewage. What was surprising and interesting about this unknown but essential world was the enthusiasm of those who ran it. Their pride in such feats as getting their B.O.D. (biological oxygen demand) to 20 milligrams per litre, ensuring that the effluent leaving the works was safe for fish, was shared by their men who kept the grass mown, the flower beds blazing, the brass knobs on the mighty pumps shining, and insisted that the dark grey powder they loaded on lorries in brown paper sacks blazoned with the arms of their city was vastly better than the product from their rivals.

Our sewage days were agreeable interludes in our lives until the late 1970s introduced the municipal composting of dustbin refuse. They gave Cherry the unique distinction of having been conducted round more acres of grey concrete tanks, frothing with air blown in by electric motors as big as drums to power the watery composting process that makes our sewage safe, than any other woman over 70 in the world. She saw the slow-turning Dano composters and the cheap, fast, and simple Tollemache pulverizers that could smash a dozen old TV sets thrown away by a local shop in seconds, throwing out the metal chassis by centrifugal force, and followed me up the steep iron ladders taking notes while I photographed and asked questions that drew enthusiastic answers.

My long-term aim was to find a permanent answer to the question the inorganic always ask — 'How are you going to feed a hungry world without the extra yield from chemical fertilizers?' The easy debating answer is to ask the further question: 'How are you going to go on feeding a world population that doubles every 27 years even with chemical fertilizers?' Real and lasting answers are far more difficult, especially when it is not the hungry world that has the power but the greedy world industries that double and redouble the pollutants they add to the sewage we pour into the seas.

Men who can read on their dials the effects of fitting bathrooms into terraced houses as a district moves 'up market' do not think only of doubling food demand as population multiplies. Doubling the world population more than doubles the need for sewage treatment plants because so many countries are developing from the original system of pigs and dogs eating everything, to baths every Saturday night. In the opinion of many a sewage works manager, Britain should forget about space and microchips to concentrate on research to find low-water-demanding methods of sewage disposal. In the age of Sir Edwin Chadwick (1800-1890) we pioneered modern sewage treatment and we could again lead the world from pollution to lasting fertility.

I used to begin my lectures on municipal composting and sewage, major concerns of that period of the organic movement, with a slide showing Cherry on the Trial Ground between two Benedictine nuns. They were Sister Candida, the tallest woman I have ever known, 6 ft. 2 in her habit and wimple, and the late Sister Laurentia Dombrowski, about five feet high and round as an apple. They had come to see the comfrey which they grew and used in Germany, and at their feet was a mound of greener grass, rather crowded by thriving yarrow (*Achillea millefolium*). As I explained, this was a rabbit's private toilet patch, designed to protect them against the spread of parasite eggs, an instinct shared by humans however safe our sewage disposal methods; and this instinct is exploited by the chemical industry, in propaganda against competition from this low-cost organic fertilizer.

My second slide was always of the four huge pipes bringing 57 million gallons of sewage a day from half a million people and the industries that employ many of them, into the Maple Cross works at Rickmansworth. Richard Woods, the manager, pioneered a different system, spreading, free, 150,000 gallons a day of concentrated liquid sludge on farms within a 45-mile radius, in tankers holding up to 3,000 gallons each, spread direct by rear-mounted sprinklers, or stored in excavated ponds through the winter before spreading in the spring when farmers all wanted it together. Mainly it went on pastures, grazed hard after an interval to keep the grasses, stimulated by the 6.8 per cent nitrogen, from swamping the clover pushed ahead by 4.7 per cent phosphorus. It also went thickly on to straw, chewed up behind the combines — instead of burnt as it is today — then ploughed under, and was used in the Scottish lowlands to grow crop after crop of grass silage for overwintering hill cattle and sheep.

This was at East Kilbride, 12 miles from Glasgow, where Tom Russell was getting Scottish farmers to pay nearly £5 an acre for 6,000 gallons spread by irrigation guns like giant lawn sprinklers.

Though this system was good, especially when farmers learned the rotations, timing, and frequency that suited their land, it was not a complete answer to the problem of the broken cycles. Only the concentrated 150,000 gallons of the 37 million a day pouring into Maple Cross went back to the land. The other 36,850,000 went down to the sea, though purified and repurified after use and repollution again and again on the way. The chemical fertilizer industry calculations, designed to discredit sludge, always ignore the dissolved plant foods wasted in the effluent, and the increasing flood of 'nasties' they add themselves. Later, on lecture tours in Australia and the USA, I was to see better systems, returning both effluent and sludge to the land, raising the sinking water-tables for thirsty cities. Fresh water is also a wasted asset and, as I had emphasized in those lectures, the challenge of the seventies was not space but sewage — space can wait.

The object of our work for the U.T.M.D.A. was to gather new knowledge to help gardeners get better value from the dried sludges on sale, and on how toxic metals were absorbed by the different crops. I invented an activator, which was 75 per cent U.T.M.D.A sludge and 25 per cent seaweed meal, based on the fact that seaweed is rich in alginates used for culturing bacteria in hospitals, while the sludge provided the nitrogen and phosphorus for their rapid increase. This was the fastest heap-heater I have ever known, but I could get no firm to take it up.

An experiment to see the effect of 7 lb. a square yard dressing every year for four years gave the surprise result of growing a splendid crop of lucerne, for the zinc, then regarded as a 'nasty', is essential for this crop (known as 'alfalfa' in many countries), and British soil can lack this important trace element, especially on inorganic farms where superphosphate which locks up zinc is used in quantity.

Through the years, I feel I gave the U.T.M.D.A. value for money, and did my best to help them, and the other sludge and municipal-compost-selling authorities, to sell more to the gardening public. Its main handicap was lack of marketing ability on the part of the chemists and engineers concerned.

During that summer, in which we published *The Wholefood Finder* at last in June, 1968, I was gathering material for *The Good Taste Guide to Fruit and Vegetable Varieties*, H.D.R.A. edition. It had begun with two half-page articles in *The Observer* in which I had condensed the results of an appeal to readers to send in lists of their favourites for flavour. I had appealed through the Newsletter to our members, 1,332 at the time, and fetched in many more from our higher proportion of keen gardeners, interested in flavour, because they were organic. The results were democratic rather than statistically accurate. It reflected what those who troubled to write (probably the keenest) liked best out of the varieties they had tried, and we reprinted the 24-page Bro-cards-duplicated leaflet, which we sent out first in January, 1969, again and again, with a new, enlarged edition split into the 'Vegetable Finder' and the 'Fruit Finder' in 1978. This is now the *The Good Fruit Guide*, covering over 1,000 bush and tree fruit varieties, their pollinators, their seasons, and their suppliers which I worked out with the help of Harry Baker, the famous fruit foreman of Wisley.

A letter in *The Sunday Telegraph* drew a mass of hedgehog enthusiasts, so, also in January, 1969, I enlarged *Hedgehogs and the Gardener* to *Operation Tiggywinkle*. It had a cover picture of a cat and a hedgehog sitting side by side on friendly terms, and illustrations included Norman Green's Mark II model hibernation box and a wire-netting saucer cover to stop cats stealing the hedgehog's milk. Dozens of letters reported a lack of slugs since their gardens had resident hedgehogs, and several people had observed theirs eating aphids off the lower branches of roses. Hedgehogs had become a kind of 'poor man's peacock', to be watched and enjoyed as we enjoy our local pair of robins pecking up the pest pupae as we dig.

I recall a bedridden old lady from Bristol who telephoned that she had found a reason for the hedgehog circling, reported in a letter in *The Times*. Her large lady hedgehog (they have been 'sows' and 'boars' ever since Shakespeare's 'Thrice and once the hedgepig whined') was sitting under a rose bush making the noise like a rusty saw, their equivalent to the lowing of a bulling heifer, and the owner of the elderly and aristocratic voice on the telephone told me she was watching through her bedroom window with a powerful torch. Six male hedgehogs appeared in the torchlight one after another and began converging on the sow, until there was a spiney mix up, which ended in the sow trotting off into the darkness with the smallest boar who had been getting the worst of the battle. She had observed the solitary males trotting in a circle on two occasions and considered it was their way of locating a distant female by taking 'bearings' from opposite sides of the circle, perhaps choosing between several attractive voices in the night. The calling might continue for two or three nights when swains were scarce.

It was *Operation Tiggywinkle* that brought my first full-scale TV show, to film our hedgehog houses. Hedgehogs like to hibernate 'with the windows open', ideally in hollow trees, and our Mark I models had wooden chimneys, each with a neat little roof to keep out the rain and snow and draw a current of air through them. John Tiddy made them with great care.

They wanted a live hedgehog to film but I do not believe in keeping wild animals in captivity, so they hired a stuffed one, balled up for hibernation, for £10 a day. Though it only took ten men (and their dog) to mow a meadow, I found it takes 13 people to make a full TV crew. This includes not only the interviewer or 'anchor man' and the producer, but a man with a giant furry sausage that is the microphone, the cameraman, the assistant cameraman, two electricians with lights and cables, a man with a wooden gadget to clap in front of the camera for each 'take', and plenty of brisk young girls in tight jeans with clipboards writing a record of everything.

First you speak your agreed line, not from a script because only professional actors can do this without sounding wooden, and you stumble and spoil it (Scene 1 Take 1). Then you do it perfectly and an aeroplane goes overhead (Scene 1 Take 2). Then the interviewer himself fluffs his line (Scene 1 Take 3) and so all through the day with breaks for coffee organized by the girls in jeans. By the end of the day I was stiff from crouching over the hedgehog houses and demonstrating the expanded-metal false floor under which we spread a derris and pyrethrum powder mixture to kill the ticks and fleas that hedgehogs harbour. It taught me that TV can be hard work.

At that time there was a spate of of war books on Operation This or That, so I started 'Operation Eggbound' that summer. When Cherry was still living in South Africa she had asked the right questions at the highest medical level that had led to samples of mother's milk being taken in maternity wards and tested for D.D.T. and other organochlorine compounds which build up in body fat through our whole lives. If we take in

D.D.T. with our mother's milk, when we lose weight, from an illness or with age, this is released in our bloodstreams with far more serious consequences than for our grandparents who had a pesticide-free start. Professor Goran Lefroth, of the Swedish National Institute for Public Health, repeated the South African experiment and discovered an average of 0.117 parts per million of D.D.T. in mother's milk, 70 per cent above their maximum safety level, and on January 1st, 1970, Sweden became the first country to ban the organochlorines.

Since eggs are also rich in fat, and a major food for toddlers and adults, the public had been advised in large advertisements by the Egg Marketing Board to 'Go To Work on an Egg'. I wrote to this Government-financed body, telling them that the R.S.P.B. had established that D.D.T. was present in all wild birds' eggs, but the H.D.R.A. was more concerned about toddlers, who were worth many sparrows, and demanding to know what they were doing about it. This drew an interested letter from their Dr Thorogood, part of whose job was to test random samples of eggs from packing stations for organochlorine compounds. He welcomed my offer of samples from organic farmers for analysis to help his research to find how the compounds got into eggs, so if the level, which was stable, shot up suddenly they would know what to ban.

I wrote an article in *SPAN* (Soil-Plant-Animal-maN, the new Soil Association monthly tabloid) and another in our Newsletter, which drew nearly 100 samples, sent direct to Dr Thorogood, who finally reported that even free-range eggs had a trace of organochlorines because these compounds blew on the wind and came down in the rain to the worms chickens ate and the grass they grazed. The main source was fishmeal, and commercial compound foods, eggs from organic farmers who fed their own grain or made up their own foods containing the least.

The average organochlorine level of the sea at that date was less than one part per thousand million, but phytoplankton, the tiny floating plants which absorb more carbon dioxide and emit more oxygen than all the forests of the world, concentrate these compounds in the top two metres of every ocean, as they now also concentrate all the worse chemicals with which we now pollute the seas. There is D.D.T. even in the fat of Antarctic penguins that ate the small fish that ate the smaller fish, that ate the zooplankton that ate the phytoplankton that concentrated the organochlorines, in the 'House-that-Jack-built' effect we neglect at our peril.

Because we had allowed ourselves a holiday in South Africa, our member Monsignor David Greenstock, principal of the Collegio de Ingleses at Valladolid in Spain, founded soon after the Reformation for training English Catholic priests, invited us to spend a holiday there. In 1970, he had to go to Rome for a ceremony at the Vatican, where seven of his earlier Old Boys were canonized, making him the first English headmaster to have saints, as well as the usual sprinkling of sinners, on the school Honours Board.

David had trained as a biologist before he became a priest and was interested in biological pest control, so we were bringing him a stock of *Anthocoris nemorum* to see if it could control the red spider mite of oranges and lemons as well as it did *Panonychus ulmi*, the apple red spider of English orchards. This is one of the many 'man-made pests' which formerly grazed lichens and algae on fruit-tree trunks, and acted as a standby food for *Anthocoris*, just as saucers of milk feed cats as biological mouse controllers. In the 1920s, tar-oil winter washes had become popular, cleaning all the trunks bare and destroying many pests and eggs, but unfortunately *Anthocoris* also.

As these hibernate only in hard weather, spending most of the winter scuttling in and out of bark crevices eating red spider eggs, the winter washing caught them before they could migrate in spring to feast on lettuce-root aphids overwintering on poplars or willows and the willow-carrot aphids, before either can do any harm in gardens. Our hope was that, given milder winters, they would stay in the orange groves where red spider mites are active all the year on the evergreen leaves.

Martin Austin, our consultant entomologist, had collected for us several hundred *Anthocoris* in five test tubes, which he had kept in his well-turned-down fridge, so they would assume it was time for their late winter nap before their spring holiday on poplars and willows. Whatever happened we must not let the customs men open the tubes, because 'when they wake up they'll be hungry, they'll dart out desperate for aphids and red spiders, and they'll starve'.

When we arrived at Bilbao on the *Patricia*, the ferry from Southampton, Cherry chatted up the customs man so skilfully in Spanish that he suddenly remembered the impatient queue and hurriedly scrawled white chalk on our suitcases and let us through without opening anything.

We arrived late at the Casa de Campo by train, and I still recall watching through the carriage windows the flames of burning maize stalks in long streaks of fire across the flat fields, while Cherry blossomed in conversation with the other passengers. David Greenstock, plump, genial, and wearing long khaki shorts like an Empire Builder, welcomed us, allotting me a narrow bedroom, of the size for visiting parish priests, and Cherry a magnificent one, with a remarkable bathroom containing a shower above a porcelain bath made only to sit in, usually reserved for bishops and cardinals.

She was only the second woman in history to stay at the Collegio, the first being the wife of the French ambassador who had been motoring with her husband during the Spanish Civil War and got caught between the two sides, so the Principal had taken the couple in until a safe conduct could be arranged. David had exploited the precedent.

The Collegio had its own organic farm and market garden supplying all its needs, except wine which came from a neighbouring estate, even wheat ground in its own watermill and olive oil from its own trees. After their first year, the students grew the food for their evening meal and cooked it themselves. They formed 'supper clubs' for camp-fire cookery by the river, and in the winter (Spain can be cold and wet) in their rooms, which they had to keep clean and tidy. Since Catholic priests will never have wives, learning to cook well, do all their own housework, and sew on their own buttons, is part of the training.

When new students arrived, David insisted that they turned out their pockets and luggage, for aspirins, laxatives, and the many drugs taken today were to be discarded. If they were genuinely ill the Collegio doctor was always available. Otherwise, good food and plenty of it was the best medicine, and when I lectured to about 20 early arrivals for the next term I told them I was glad to learn that England's Catholic priests were organically grown, entirely without chemicals.

On our first morning we took our *Anthocoris* tubes to the orange grove and David distributed the black and brown bugs, which are only a sixth of an inch long (4mm), among the trees with red spiders, and as far as I know they lived happily ever after. They have no English popular name but may well earn themselves a Spanish one. David was working with the Spanish Ministry of Agriculture and wrote pamphlets for peasant farmers.

He was also working on garlic as an insecticide and a medicine, though when he began the hunt through reference works and papers on what is not so much a bulb as a way of life, he was certain of only one fact. The peasants of Valladolid are still convinced that wearing a necklace of garlic cloves repels vampires and there has not been a genuine vampire in the district for 900 years.

We spent a happy, restful, but stimulating week with our Monsignor, which led to a lasting friendship built through the years of letters typed with pale Spanish ribbons almost as poor as their paper. Then we set off by train for Alfaz del Pi, a village near Benidorm, where Helen Gainsford had bought a bungalow for her retirement, on my longest-ever rail journey across the empty country of towns and cities lost in sun-baked plains where history is dried like a fruit. We travelled by 'Talgo', expresses regarded with even more pride by Spaniards than that we Britons had for our 'Flying Scotsman'. They were fast and comfortable, with private-enterprise take-away buffet cars where paellas were served with enthusiasm and good cheap wine.

Helen's bungalow was one of thousands built fast for foreigners, mainly Swedes and Germans escaping their long cold winters, with a dry garden which she had designed carefully, like the many gardens in her life, with everything ridged round with soil to pond hoarded water for thirsty plants. It was like South Africa, with more peasant poverty but no racial tension — just eloquent, friendly, and cheerful Spaniards, enjoying life as a gift from God.

From Helen's bungalow we hired a taxi to take us the long journey Jativa, a small town 35 miles south-south-west of Valencia, famous historically as the home of the Borgia family, but today for probably the finest organic orange orchard in the world. It was established by our member Ernest Baumann who had invited me to take a much needed holiday from Bocking in the early days, prevented by the illness and death of my father. Now I was in Spain I wrote and found that Ernest was dead, but the estate was still being run by his daughters. In Spain, daughters are taken into partnership in family businesses instead of only sons as in Britain, and the firm had always been

205

Ernesto Baumann and Daughters, and had now become 'The Daughters of Ernesto Baumann', who would be delighted to see us both.

We stayed with Mr Muller, the manager, a Swiss like the Baumann family, in his house among the factory-like complex of endless-belt sorting machines making the traditional three-compartment orange boxes out of poplar wood, machines that wrapped oranges, and machines that packed them, at the centre of the estate. The average crop from 15,000 trees (orange yields are not measured per acre or hectare but by number, for Spanish groves can be on rocky or awkward land) was 450 tons of perfect oranges and 450 of equally perfect grapefruit.

Mr Muller, like John Hapgood who grew organic coxes in Essex, had the habit of whisking a powerful lens from his pocket and offering it to his visitors, that they might share the pleasure of seeing some tiny creature, friend or foe, that plays a part in the balanced ecology of his orchard. The orange woolly aphis is completely controlled by *Novis cardinalis* and *Cryptolamus monstrosus*, developed by the Orange Research Station at Valencia, and David Greenstock has discovered that *Aphelinus mali*, which controls our woolly aphis on apples, will tackle the orange scale insect as well. If and when the *Anthocoris* we had brought from Bocking proved itself useful, it would go to that research station for testing and distribution.

The worst pest of oranges in countries where there is fruit ripe all the year round, is the Mediterranean fruit fly (*Ceratitis capitata*), with one generation every 30 days. Because the skins of citrus fruit is full of oils they concentrate organochlorine compounds, while the high rate of increase allows the pest to develop resistant varieties to every new chemical sprayed on it within months rather than years. The Baumann Daughters never used even the pesticides such as derris, pyrethrum, or nicotine, that do not produce resistant varieties, only Mr Muller's invention of the Casa Del Mas Fruit Fly Trap.

This is made of glass by a manufacturer of cheap wine bottles and looks like a giant, old-fashioned school inkwell, about six inches across and four tall. They are hung on the sunny side of each tree. Men go round all 15,000 trees refilling the traps as the liquid bait evaporates from knapsack sprayers, filled with a mixture of vinegar and water and fitted with hooked tubes. They poke the tube through the bottom hole of the trap, squirting in just enough to replace evaporation. A cork in the top can be removed and the trap emptied completely if it becomes jammed with flies.

The drawback was the high labour cost, but the extra price for blemish-free organic oranges, and the saving in labour from fewer girls on the endless belts picking out fly-damaged fruit, paid for the trapping. The modern control method is to sterilize male fruit flies by exposing them to gamma rays but this is still costly, and there is nothing inorganic about employing more labour than your neighbours if you are selling the organic perfection your customers will pay for.

A few months after our return to Bocking we had a letter from David Greenstock. He was in great distress because in the summer of 1968 there had been student unrest, especially in France, and it had crossed the Pyrenees and reached his Collegio. Behaving like an English headmaster many years ago, he had come down on the offenders like a ton of theological bricks and expelled the ringleaders. now he had been summoned to England to justify himself to Authority, and feared he would have to take early retirement and live on his pension. Could he come to us at Bocking to work for us, unpaid, to develop our biological pest control aspect, carrying out experiments to make life easier for friends like ladybirds and hoverflies?

For this we should need a whole pre-fab, not just a portion of one like our packing shed, which would be fitted together by the specialist builders who were taking them down all over London to be replaced by tower blocks. It would cost £195, about £250 erected and decorated, with another £250 for the concrete base, and the asbestos cement panels could be slotted together to make one room 32 feet by 11 for insect cages and perhaps lectures on one side of a central wall, plus another 16 feet by 11 facing south down the Trial Ground as a study for our Monsignor, and a third the same size, for books and storage.

Fortunately, we could afford to pay for this out of an utterly unexpected windfall. Jack Pye and his wife Mary, who had just lifted the Soil Association out of its financial difficulties with a generous gift of £350,000, had come to see us and we took them round and showed them everything. When I took him up into the roof space of No. 20, as a man who made a fortune out of post-war speculative building he was amazed at the thickness and strength of the joists and beams of a £650 'semi' built in 1938. It carried him back to his youth to see such craftsmanship.

Before he left he wrote a cheque for £1,000 to buy anything I badly needed for the H.D.R.A.

At the next committee meeting it was agreed I should spend £500 on the new building and Steve Statham, an architect member, offered to draw plans and handle the planning application for something far too large for us to describe as a 'garden shed'. As an 'agricultural building', or 'horticultural research laboratory', it should last at least 20 years, and because it was not legally a 'dwelling' no planning permission was required, but the council had to be satisfied that it was both sightly and safe.

The council, in the shape of earnest young men who insisted on concrete thick enough to support a three-storey building, delayed us for only about a month and added £50 to the costs, and we looked forward to having our Monsignor safely installed, complete with ladybirds and ground beetles, ready for an opening ceremony to be attended by Jack and Mary Pye. One Saturday, when Keable the bricklayer living in the Lane, Michael Suckling, Alan Bates, Ron Suckling, Cherry, and I were keeping pace with the mixer lorries from Hunnable's ready-mixed concrete works, the Hunt rode along the 'accommodation road' shown on the Trial Ground maps. They raised their top hats and gave us a surprisingly musical tootle on the horn as they clattered and jingled their way through the bird sanctuary where Cherry would often smell fox on our snatched walks round the lake.

Then we heard from David Greenstock. The Assembled Ecclesiastical Authorities had highly approved of his rather old-fashioned methods dealing with student unrest, they would have done the same themselves! They also made him a 'Protonotary Apostolic', in lay terms a Bishop without a See, entitling him to say Mass wherever he happened to be, so were he to come to us on final retirement he could say it among his insects where, like Henry Doubleday, he would continue to 'observe the works of God in Humbleness'.

So, instead of the 'Pye Horticultural Research Laboratory', and all that could have become, we had a building christened 'The Pye House' into which we grew through the years, making it possible for us to expand from 1,500 members to 5,000 by the time we moved to Ryton in 1985. The storage room we subdivided into the students' kitchen and common-room, which they festooned with posters, crammed up to 10 people into for meals, and in which they played guitars and pop on a hi-fi record player that was more hi than fi.

David's stillborn 'study' became the general office where up to four part-time young married women worked like beavers with files, typewriters, racks full of leaflets, stationery cupboards, account books, and a clamouring telephone that at last took some of the answering off me. The might-have-been insect room changed through the years and finally blossomed into an 11 foot square packing room where Mrs Rose Whybrow and her helpers, through the 21 years she was our prop and stay, packed more and more parcels, with less and less string and more and more polythene as the years went by. The other 20 foot section became our shop, crammed with racking and display space, and crowded with customers on open days or when we had parties of visitors.

The party I remember best was of 33 French organic farmers, members of 'Nature et Progrès', the French equivalent of the Soil Association, led by Suzanne Triolet, their charming young secretary who had stayed with us during her earlier visit to arrange a tour of the British organic movement. She brought her mother, M. le Curé in a very odd kind of clerical collar, and M. l'Agronome, a dapper little man in riding breeches from the local version of A.D.A.S., who spoke some English. As interpreters we had Cherry speaking good French and Spanish, a Swiss member with French and German, and a local schoolmistress.

I took the party round, pausing for translations, with Cherry and Charles Naeglei, the Swiss member, answering questions direct. It was all much slower, but it seemed appreciated except by one small, quiet man who seemed utterly bewildered. As they were trooping into the Pye House, Cherry approached him in her best French, and he replied, 'I can't understand a word, I'm only the coach driver'. We had a battery of electric kettles laid on and plenty of teapots, with Cherry's organic wholemeal bread, home-made scones and strawberry jam, and large dishes of Windermere lettuces. These are the Webb's Wonderful, non-bolting type, but with thicker midribs. As a large one weighs about a pound they are too big for a couple of dozen to pack in a standard lettuce crate, making it useless commercially though an ideal amateur variety. The French farmers had never seen anything like them, and several of them spread a huge leaf of this unknown vegetable with strawberry jam. Obviously the correct way to end the extraordinary meal eaten by the English in order not to spoil their appetites for dinner!

The party stayed until 7 p.m., trooping all round the garden of No. 20 like a swarm of excited bilingual bees, before they piled into the coach for the hotel at Haughley where they were staying before seeing the Soil Association. Later we would get German, Dutch and Danish parties, and countless students of all nationalities who arrived on the Harwich ferries and hitchhiked down to see us, with just our name as quoted in some periodical, and heavy rucksacks, expecting us to feed them and put them up for the night. Often they slept on the floor of the Pye House, and when we had students I just took any stray visitors down, introduced them, and let them sort themselves out. Youth was discovering organic gardening and demanding to learn more about it.

All these new development were possible because of the sudden and startling generosity of Jack and Mary Pye. That £1,000, just then when we needed it, gave the expanding H.D.R.A. the space to spread, like repotting a growing tree into a new green tub.

15

The Crowded Years

MY MOTHER used to say: 'Between 60 and 70 are the best years of your life, between 70 and 80 the going gets tougher, between 80 and 90 it *is* tough'. In 1969 I was 58, balding, with greying hair, and learning that nothing is harder work than success, or more enjoyable. Thanks to Cherry inventing a wholefood version of the prescribed gluten-free diet for coeliacs, my body was no longer 'driving with the brakes on' but fit to drive flat out through the crowded years that lay ahead. I, too, had given Cherry something. I had persuaded her to write books and leaflets instead of limiting herself to lectures which can reach only a relatively few people, and she began her *Living Dangerously* in 1969, which was a kind of domestic 'Silent Spring' on pollution in the home. Although her first publishers (Tom Stacey) went bankrupt, the first edition appeared in 1973. Later editions were published by Roberts Publishers Ltd.

We were both working hard on books through that fast and fruitful summer, for I had started *Grow Your Own Fruit and Vegetables* which Faber and Faber published in the spring of 1971. In the 16 years it stayed in print it went through six editions, perhaps because it was the first organic gardening book not to attempt to convert the chemical user by quotations from authorities and even newspapers. I assumed that, like our members and my fanmail writers, that people wanted to read about how to garden without chemical fertilizers and sprays. The serious press reviewed me well, which spread the organic message far beyond the readers of the few organic or health food periodicals.

It was just when I was at the stage of fighting for pieces of time large enough to get this book to 'come alive' as all books should that an old and keen member sent us another £1,000, this time for medical research on comfrey. We had no room, time, or money to carry out experiments on poultry- or pig-feeding with comfrey, but every Newsletter contained a comfrey section, very largely reporting experiences of its healing powers sent in by members. It became clear that it is not possible to write about this most popular of all folk remedies without drawing dozens of letters, some about elderly relatives who used it for wounds, skin troubles, insect bites, but mostly direct personal experiences from people who had used it successfully for everything from nappy-rash to arthritis, the last in the greatest quantity.

Our comfrey ointment, tablets, and the oil which had the great merit of not staining clothing, brought in still more people who used it often for conditions of which I had never even heard. We had now acquired another medical adviser, a Dr Mulken, who was a consultant to the London Nature Cure Clinic, and in his opinion any serious medical research on any aspect of comfrey would cost at least £100,000. Any attempt at investigating the anti-cancer effect that cropped up through the years would need nearly £250,000 and would involve experiments with the special strain of white mice that have a genetic liability to cancer tumours, which would shock all our members. So we spent the money on supplying comfrey tablets, ointment, and oil free to doctor members to try on psoriasis and other awkward skin conditions, to the Nature Cure Clinic, and to a Leprosy Clinic in India, where it had no effect on the leprosy but was most helpful in healing the burns, grazes, and other injuries that lepers endure because of their insensitivity to pain on the surface of afflicted limbs. However, though we gave away a great quantity of material we got back very little in the way of useful reports.

Early in February, 1970, I had a telephone call out of the blue from a rapid, almost breathless voice, inviting me to lunch with him at Rules to discuss starting a new environmental magazine. I knew of Rules as a famous restaurant, far too expensive for me, but I had never heard of Edward Goldsmith who wanted me to meet him there the next day. It sounded exciting and with the rapidly rising interest in the environment, it looked like a chance to sell some useful and perhaps well paid articles, so off I went with Cherry's shared excitement to speed me on my way.

Teddy was short, plump, bearded, and brilliant. We had the longest lunch of my life, during which I became an associate editor, finishing with liqueurs (my first) which gained us more time for talking at breakneck speed while the waiters breathed down our necks with impatience to clear our table.

I threw off ideas and so did Teddy, as *The Ecologist* expanded between us. It was to be a monthly, serious, well illustrated, and vivid, with articles large enough to develop important subjects such as pollution, the protection of primitive peoples, population and all its implications in terms of exhausted resources, and would be anti-nuclear and, above all, concerned with the world as a whole. We agreed that I was to do a 1,000–1,500 word article every month, under my old *Observer* title 'Down to Earth', on some aspect of his theme relating to horticulture, agriculture, or the countryside, for a fee of 15 guineas a thousand words, plus book reviews and shorter or longer items if I had an idea that fitted.

Teddy wanted to find writers who knew what they were talking about on subjects that fitted the themes of the magazine, and periodicals that would give him publicity. I suggested a small, light brochure with an order form for subscribers, to circulate with the organic-movement publications, of which the H.D.R.A. Newsletter went to 1,700 members, if he would put mine in his first issue, and hoped the Soil Association with 4,000, would do the same. I recommended writing to John Hillaby at *New Scientist*, John Davy, science correspondent of *The Observer*, and Michael Allaby of the Soil Association, and later heard from Michael that Teddy had rung him up and invited him to an even longer and more expensive lunch at the Ritz.

The first issue at 4 shillings (20p) came out in July, 1970, and though I told Cherry when I got home that I thought it might last a year, it is still flourishing with a quarterly circulation of about 8,000, mainly to university libraries, especially in the USA. It enjoys international respect as both lively and tough enough to criticise the World Bank, and the folly of the giant dams in Third World countries that make thousands homeless, silt up swiftly, and take much of the land they irrigate to pay the interest on the vast sums they cost. Once again I found an editor with the courage to march his 26 soldiers of lead into action for causes I cared about.

I got my first article, subheaded 'The menace of the milk bottles', from my brother Geoff, an environmental 'mole' on my behalf inside ICI. Their sales department was endeavouring to promote the idea of PVC milk bottles, which would mean about 20 per cent more on fewer vans because of reduced weight, with no returned empties, no washing, and sales of about 3,000 million bottles a week. The research staff, with whom Geoff worked, were firmly against it, and a tough article in the first issue of a newly-launched magazine which would go out to all national newspapers and periodicals would be an ideal way of stopping what any chemist who knew his polyvinylchloride could see as a menace.

There was no way that the leak could be traced back to my brother and his colleagues, for a graphic foretaste of the pollution burning hundreds of thousands of tons of PVC milk bottles a year would cause had already appeared in a local paper. A small metal-recovery firm in North London had a furnace in which they burned condemned cotton and rubber insulated wire in order to sell the copper. They burned their first PVC-insulated batch late one early autumn afternoon when smoke lay in low layers beneath a temperature inversion. It made people's eyes smart, fetched leaves off roses, and scorched bedding-plant leaves like early frost.

When PVC burns it releases hydrochloric acid gas, exactly like the old Leblanc process for making caustic soda from common salt, which has been illegal in Britain since 1860. The gas destroys vegetation, attacks metals, brickwork, building stone, and mortar, and readily dissolves in water, to become still more poisonous in dew-drops on leaves, on our tear-moistened eyes and, because all living beings are damp inside, it is deadly to breathe.

The day my first article appeared I was rung up by the B.B.C. 'Today' programme at 8 p.m., just as I was finishing my evening meal, wanting me to come for an interview to go out next morning. I protested that though I could get to Broadcasting House in time I should miss the last train back from Liverpool Street. They offered to send me all the way home by taxi, so off I went and arrived home just before midnight after a journey that cost the B.B.C. much more than my 10 guinea fee. During that first year I was interviewed four times as 'Lawrence D. Hills of The Ecologist' perhaps because I was willing to dash up to London at a moment's notice when they were stuck for a fill-up, and they thought I was worth the taxi fare.

These articles gave me perhaps the best platform I have ever had. I settled down to 1,200 words on a single page and always, as in my first article, concentrated on something practical that could be done about a problem. During the months in which copies of The Ecologist went right round the press many of my columns were noticed, mainly because I was unusual, concise, and quotable, though the longer articles giving environmental authorities space to deal with serious subjects seriously, with plenty of photographs and references, received their share of attention.

It is easy to underestimate the value of Teddy Goldsmith as a pioneer of the environmental movement, because his genius really lay in finding others to use the platform he provided. He brought in the young and intelligent who cared fiercely about what they were writing.

By October, 1970, we had acquired our first scientific adviser, Dennis Long Ph.D., of the Michaelis Nutritional Foundation, who was doing analyses for us and working on a project to develop a slug killer from extracts of *Phytolacca americana*, an American Forest weed related to *P. decandra*, an Abyssinian species that was a possible poison for the bilharzia-carrying water snails. He was also exploring the dangers of herbicide residues in straw, and of non-stick frying pans.

His greatest value to us arose from the Japanese work in 1968 showing that the root of *Symphytum officinale*, common comfrey, contained pyrrolizidine alkaloids of the type found in ragwort (*Senecio squalidus*) which had caused liver damage in experimental rats. Dennis's brother was concerned in the work on these alkaloids at the University of Exeter, and the Medical Research Council laboratory at Carshalton was also involved. Here Dennis could represent us. The quantity present was very small but the risk was of these adding up to danger. At our committee meeting on October 29th, 1970, it was agreed that there was not enough evidence to justify sending round a warning before the M.R.C. advised it, because if it turned out to be a false alarm it would be hard to call it back, but that we should spend freely from the research fund for travelling and analysis.

As I said to the committee at the time: 'Because of the centuries for which comfrey has been fed to stock and used medicinally, it is likely that the alkaloid is not in the leaf or is present in a harmless form. I have worked for 22 years on comfrey but if Comfrey Report No. 6 had to be a warning to all users that it had a cancer risk like a food additive, I shall have to write it and put it round the world.'

I recalled Phil Phillips feeding his hundred tons an acre off his 25-acre field to batch after batch of bullocks with never a beast condemned for a diseased liver, Tom the boar and his hefty harem guzzling comfrey for 14 years, and Vernon Stephenson's stallions siring winners on generous comfrey rations. Above all there had been generation after generation of North Country women keeping arthritis at bay by drinking 'knitbone tea' and using the healing leaves for injuries. Surely, if there were a genuine danger to any stock or human being there would be *some* record of *something* suffering, especially from the 1880–1890 period when it was fed in such quantities to horses?

At the committee meeting held before the A.G.M. in 1971, Dr Long was able to announce that the M.R.C. had found that comfrey tea held 0.028 per cent of the alkaloids and his own tests had shown 0.020 per cent. Assuming that men had the same sensitivity to alkaloids as experimental rats, anyone weighing 160 lb. would need to drink 102,000 cups of comfrey tea one after the other to produce toxic symptoms. If the same amount was necessary to induce chronic toxicity, then, at five cups a day, this would take 56 years. Arthritics average it for 20–30 years, no one had yet achieved 56. Today, our vigorous vegetarian member over 80, Miss Aughton, who eats her own comfrey as spinach about three times a week in summer and dries it for tea to drink through the winter, is unlikely to live until she is 113, but she might. If she misses her comfrey for as long as three weeks on holiday the arthritis is back, and she feels safer taking it than orthodox anti-arthritic drugs.

The Japanese work brought comfrey into *Poisonous Plants in Britain* (H.M.S.O. 1984), with the verdict: 'The carcinogenic response followed continuous high dosing over long periods and it is unlikely that human consumption of comfrey in much smaller amounts could cause liver damage, and no examples of poisoning by the plant have been reported'.

At the same committee meeting the question arose of reprinting *The Wholefood Finder* because our stock had fallen to 200, and the Soil Association had 500 left of the original 10,000. A new edition, adding new suppliers, would have to be completely reset, which would mean an expenditure of £320 for us £680 for them if we split it 40-60 as before, for another 10,000, and neither we nor they could afford to lock up the money. Rather let it run out of print I wrote to the British edition of *Prevention*, suggesting that they should take it on.

I learned that they were not only interested, but that Robert Rodale, the son of Jerome Irvine Rodale, founder of the American

Organic Gardening and Farming which he had built to a circulation of more than a million a month, was starting a British edition and wanted me to write for it. We met in the lounge of the Northumberland Hotel, Jerry Goldstein of the Rodale Organization, Keith Etson, manager of the British operation, and I. Again I talked flat out to get the organic movement a popular publication on sale to the general public from newsagents and railway bookstalls, not just by post from relatively small societies.

Newman Turner's *The Gardener* had died from advertisement starvation, the only high-profit commodities consumed by the organic movement being vitamin and mineral supplements, vegetarian foods, and herbal and homeopathic preparations — there is no advertising revenue in not using chemical fertilizers and poison sprays. His health publication *Fitness* had made a profit which was swallowed by the loss on *The Gardener*, and *Prevention* had a quarter million more circulation than *Organic Gardening and Farming* in America. The British version advertised selected American healthfood products which were imported in bulk then sent out from Berkhamstead. This could subsidize *Organic Gardening* by sharing advertisement gathering, clerical, and other costs although this would otherwise have to pay its way.

Jerome Rodale lost money for the first 15 years on his publications, meeting the losses from the profits of his highly efficient firm of electrical engineers, for this was his profession. He fathered the organic movement in America, by spreading the teachings of Sir Albert Howard, and died of a heart attack in a broadcasting studio where he was giving a talk on organic gardening — the phrase he had himself invented. Both his major publications were making money, but his third, *Compost Science*, was still losing it, while earning a world-wide reputation. This was the only publication in the world devoted to municipal composting, large, well produced, scientifically serious with tables and references — entirely unlike the two popular monthlies — full of articles and advertisements for machinery for reducing dustbin refuse, with or without sewage sludge, to compost for use on the land.

Indeed, he shared my own vision of fertility running to waste from a throw-away civilization. I was asked to become associate editor of this journal, which put my name 'on the masthead', on the contents page with other authorities on the subject, entitling me to make suggestions and express opinions to the editor, though not to any payment. Like my associate editorship of *The Ecologist*, this was an honour, in a field where honours are few.

The Rodales, father and son, had not only built *Organic Gardening and Farming* to the largest organic circulation in the world, they had more readers than any inorganic gardening publication either, and the widest circulation of any horticultural magazine. They had even grown their own advertisers.

Jerome Rodale had created a market among organic gardeners for compost heap activators, compost choppers, and small garden machinery of all kinds, organic fertilizers, ground minerals, worm capsules for those who wanted more and better earthworms, deep-frozen ladybirds — and a host of organic commodities that England had no idea existed.

The question was whether, in an England where the orthodox weekly *Amateur Gardening* was leading the gardening periodicals with a circulation or 250,000, a new, organic gardening monthly, in a popular style, could gather not only new readers but advertisers fast enough to become established before the Rodales had spent all they could afford on the enterprise. Two years later the answer was clearly No. The Rodales, like Newman Turner, were ahead of their time for England.

The editor of the new publication was John Bond, whose duties included searching back numbers of the American magazine to see if he could find usable organic articles among the jungle of Japanese beetles, cinch bugs, gophers, ground turtles, and other all-American pests that filled its pages. My task was to offer advice, suggest ideas for features, use my knowledge of the British organic movement, and write articles.

In addition I kept the H.D.R.A. going, taking publicity as it happened and striving to keep a little ahead of the game in case something sudden struck. During this period I changed the Newsletter over to a system of typing, then known as photoprinting, which gave the advantages of proofs to correct, with quicker delivery from a firm in Colchester instead of parcels hung up in the post on their way from Plymouth, and smaller but clearer type which packed more words on to a page and saved postage.

In No. 45 Newsletter, Cherry's 'Housewives' Help' was devoted to a special regime for arthritis sufferers which drew so many requests that it became 'Preventing and aiding Arthritis', one of the best-sellers among the reprints of these articles through the years. Through the good offices of the county librarian, she had become an honorary member of the Medical Academic Unit at the County Hospital in Chelmsford which gave her access to the *Index Medicus*, the monthly publication listing under authors and subjects scientific papers even remotely relevant to health, published throughout the world. She read Spanish and French easily, Italian with a dictionary, and we gathered a fleet of helpful members translating German, Russian, Scandinavian, Dutch, and even Japanese. So she could dredge information from a very wide area, requesting photostats of anything of value for study and 'distillation' as she had in the library of the Medical School at Cape Town University.

Early in November, 1971, Robert Rodale wrote to me, enclosing an article entitled 'Goodbye to the flush toilet', on the Lindstrom lavatory, invented in Sweden as a kind of one-family municipal compost plant, using the energy in kitchen wastes to dry out and decay human wastes into a black powder suitable for direct garden use. He asked my opinion and I gave it, in the minimum number of words, for I was racing to finish a Newsletter in time to get it to our new printer to have it back for posting to over 2,000 members well before Christmas.

'This sounds to me like the answer the Chinese have sought for 40 centuries. I will believe it when I see and smell it. I can fly to Sweden for £100.' Back came his cable with a draft for £100 and the message: 'Fly to Sweden. Find Lindstrom'.

On the 21st November, 1971, *The Observer* published a report about a doctor who had made a special study of the fingerprints of coeliacs, finding that few had any. This had aroused the interest of the police who were concerned that there should be some 25,000 people who could commit crimes without leaving a trace. A note from the medical correspondent explained that coeliacs were such poor physical specimens that they were incapable of active crime.

This was too good an opportunity for a 'jump-in' to waste so I sent off the following letter to the editor:–

'As one of the 25,000 coeliac disease sufferers referred to in your "missing finger-prints" news story (21/11/71) may I point out that oats, barley and rye, not only wheat, contain the gluten that produces the effect. Maize, rice and millet alone are safe. I have kept fighting fit for seven years by sticking to a diet which excludes the nutritionally inferior and unnecessary gluten-free flour supplied for our special use.

Details of the cheaper and simpler diet that I use will gladly be sent on receipt of a S.A.E.'

This was posted on the Sunday the item appeared (Sunday collections then), Rodale's cable arrived on the Monday, and I had my no longer pristine passport. I left directions to the staff, Cherry to write the leaflet that took this unique opportunity to help thousands of unknown coeliacs, out of her unique experiments, knowledge, and experience with me — the proof of the diet is in the husband.

Before I left Heathrow I began a custom followed on every trip out of England, of singing 'My love is like a red, red rose', Robert Burn's perfect love song, over the telephone. Unfortunately airports no longer have red, red telephone booths.

Since 1941 I had flown only in a Dakota and four Viscounts. Now for the first time I felt the enormous power of a four-engined jet opening up down the runway, lifting us strongly and smoothly into the sky, compared with the 'Wimpeys' of 150 squadron. I managed to select a coeliac's lunch out of the plastic-encased meal by asking for extra helpings of what I could eat, far easier than explaining, while gazing down at the monotonous carpet of untrodden snow, the upper surface of the clouds that for most travellers has replaced the dragon-green, serpent-haunted, blue-and-white- flower foaming sea.

We came suddenly out of the clouds to a country of thick, real snow, black pine woods, and blacker roads cleared with the efficiency of countries where the chains go on the tyres in October and stay there till spring. Lower and lower to piles of logs in the clearings and houses with strangely steep roofs to shoot off the snow, then down with a bump, a thud, and a rumble. There was only one likely person among the waiting 'meeters' at rlande Airport, so I marched up to the tall, black- bearded man with a magnificent briefcase and said, 'Dr Lindstrom, I presume'. He beamed at me through the beard and said, 'Yess, that iss my name. Clearly he had never heard of Stanley or Livingstone.

His Saab waited outside, with the first cassette record player I had ever heard, on which he gave me a snatch of Bach as he hurled the car along with chains jangling past huge blocks of 5 to 8-storey flats in solid stone, rather like Glasgow, flying by in the headlights that lit up many large fibre glass bins stamped 'SAND' in large letters. 'But that is in English,' I protested. 'You will find many of the words are the same, from the Vickings who invaded your country'. I learned that Swedish often looked like English spelt wrongly with dots in unexpected places, and that he was driving fast to get sooner to Tyrsoe, on the shores of the Baltic, where he lived with his parents. I was to stay at a guest bungalow and in the morning I was to see the directors of Electrolux, which made many things beside vacuum cleaners, because they had a lavatory, too, and also a device for dealing with bath and washing water, and had changed a plan to fit me in. He was sorry he could not entertain me himself because his father, Rickart Lindstrom, was reading his poetry to a great meeting that evening.

I found myself alone in a very warm, two-bedroom bungalow with a fridge packed with unusual food and bottles of lager. Dr Lindstrom had left me with full directions and a map on how to get back to Stockholm by the Swedish equivalent to a tube train and find the offices of Electrolux in the morning. After discovering how to turn the central heating down and selecting what I could eat from the generous supply, it was very comfortable. I was glad I had bought at Heathrow two of the fat paperbacks sold on all airports because air travel involves long waiting. Books that last are the best buys.

I set off next morning after 'Kornflaks', eggs, and excellent bacon, through suburban streets without privet or lonicera hedges because the snow would break them. Fine, dry snow was falling steadily from a dark grey sky and sifting safely through the clipped twigs of *Caragana arborescens*, the Siberian pea tree, with yellow flowers in May, their safest hedge.

The Electrolux contribution to conservation was the Sanivac, replacing the 11 gallons of water a day we use for flushing lavatories with air in small-bore pipes. This took the 'black water', as it is called, direct to the sewage works, while the 'grey water', from baths, washing up, laundry and all the other uses that consume our daily 12 gallons, apart from gardens and car-washing, had separate pipes and treatment.

In Sweden (and Denmark) water was metered and charged at a rate that covered the cost of sewage disposal. Refuse collection was charged by the number of standard dustbins emptied, ensuring that every ratepayer knew exactly what he paid for. Any invention that saves water reduces costs, but not necessarily pollution. Thousands of Swedish families owned houses, spread along the rocky and lovely coast of the almost tideless Baltic, which averaged about five miles of blasting and rock drilling to connect them with a sewage works. This was charged

221

at cost by the local authority, and to avoid this they paid for a shorter journey for all wastes, straight down to the Baltic, entirely untreated. Almost as many owned yachts, and these also discharged their wastes direct into the water.

The authorities enforced the use of Sanivacs on the big Baltic ferries, discharging when they came to land, but pollution by ratepayers cannot be banned because this shared sea, like a wide and beautiful lake, is polluted by yachts of all the nations round it, including more from Sweden than any other country. 'Every boat means a vote', to quote a saying that looks almost the same in Swedish, and Sweden is a democratic country of free enterprise determined to be fair even to its wealthiest citizens.

The Lindstrom's house, like some Cherry and I had seen on our lecture tour in the Lake District the previous summer, was built with the living rooms in the upper storey, with large windows looking far across and along the cliffless coast with the woods coming down to the mirrors of the sea where the gay little yachts drew their wakes as they glided by on wings of nylon and polyester. Under the house was a sauna bath, the vegetable store next to it for warmth, the wood store, the garage, and the Clivus Multrum, which is the Swedish name of Rickart Lindstrom's invention.

In 1939 he had named it for the 'declivity' or slope which is the ingeniously simple key to the process. Over a thousand had been installed in Norway and Sweden since 1964 when their father-and-son firm developed the idea. They had built a business, at first making fibreglass hulls for dinghies, and they had made the mould to turn out the compost containers in quantity, about 10 feet long, three feet wide, and fitting into five feet height. The builder was instructed to allow space at the side to get to the inspection window, and in front for the removal of roughly 1 cwt. a year of high-potash compost, from a family of three adults.

A chimney came from the top of the container, going up beside the three other chimneys — for cooking, central heating and sauna, and livingroom fire — through the peak of the roof which kept it warm. Two other openings led up from it, one to the lavatory pedestal and the other to an opening in the stainless steel kitchen unit, covered by a lid. This held a stainless steel bowl pivoted across it, in which waste, like potato peelings, tea leaves, and everything that usually goes in the compost bucket under the sink (in the families of organic gardeners), is dumped and tilted over to fall down to the compost chamber below. Because of the suck of the chimney there is a down-draught which prevents any smell reaching the kitchen, and Rickart Lindstrom was so keen that I should see this that to my horror he placed the bowl of his lighted pipe inside his mouth and blew white smoke down the stem for me to observe it being sucked down by the air current.

He repeated this parlour trick in the lavatory where the draught was even more powerful, and Dr Lindstrom (who alone spoke good English, his parents having been born too early to be educated in this language) explained that the trick was such a useful sales point that his father had taught himself the breath control that was the secret of circus fire-drinking acts. Down beside the sauna room he scooped up the compost that was accumulating in the last compartment which was 18.32 per cent moisture (I had it analysed afterwards) and black, showing that it was far more completely broken down than dried sewage sludge, with only half the organic matter left but 1.04 per cent potassium instead of only a trace.

When a Clivus is started, the owner must go right inside it and spread a 4 to 5-inch layer of peat on the bottom, followed by two inches of good garden soil, and another two inches of lawn mowings or other green compost material. Then the ordinary use of the lavatory and the dumping of kitchen wastes via the tilting bowl could continue indefinitely, with the removal of the finished fertilizer the only attention required. The peat soaks up the urine, and its ammonia filters through the soil and layers of garden rubbish, building up a vast population of denitrifying bacteria, especially *Nitrosomas europaeus*, and species specializing in the breakdown of organic matter in the soil. The bacteria selected by the conditions in the Clivus are not those that would devour compost material fast, shooting a good garden heap up to a temperature of 180° F. during its first fortnight. There are soil bacteria present everywhere, recycling the bodily wastes of wildlife, that can have their ecological balance upset by temperatures above 90°F., so the sliding ventilator on the front needed adjustment to keep down the heat.

The Swedish Ministry of Health fully approved of the Clivus because it killed pathogenic bacteria, not by heat as in a municipal compost plant, or by the competition of the methane-producing bacteria in a sewage digester, but by keeping them for as

223

long as a year under highly unfavourable conditions. Other treatments can fail to kill the cysts and eggs of the beef tapeworm, *Taenia saginata*, common on the continent where undercooked or raw meat is eaten, but the Clivus destroys these and all human internal parasites. The energy in our bodily wastes produces methane enough to run the pumps and a bit more on a sewage treatment plant, but the Clivus uses this and the power from the sunlight that fell on the plants that grew our kitchen wastes, slowly and efficiently, to evaporate the water in the urine and wastes as water vapour up the chimney with the gaseous nitrogen and carbon dioxide from decay. In Sweden the warmth from the other chimneys keeps the vapour from freezing, but in warmer winters this is unnecessary. If the compost container itself freezes solid in an empty holiday home in winter, when it thaws in the spring the bacteria will carry on composting.

Just why did the Clivus Company not become larger than Electrolux, and the Lindstroms become millionaires, out of this excellent invention? The Lindstroms showed me the piles of letters, all containing envelopes self-addressed and mainly stamped with US stamps, that were still arriving every day from the first Rodale article to a million people. Dr Lindstrom had produced a very well illustrated pack to send to them all, with drawings so good that a great many enquirers started making brick or concrete versions and variations that failed to work. I imported three from Clivus with a vast amount of trouble and cost, one to instal at Bocking, one for Teddy Goldsmith and one for the Centre for Alternative Technology at Machynlleth in North Wales, and we finally got them installed.

Apart from the cost of delivery, there was the builder's problem of fitting one in to an existing house. Teddy Goldsmith got his into his fine old farmhouse in Cornwall, but the difficulty was getting enough kitchen wastes down it to provide sufficient energy, and the baled straw they tried as an alternative fuel failed to slide smoothly down the 'declivity' of the slow road to compost. Eventually, about 1974, we got the Bocking one built into something that looked like the stokehole of a nursery, with a double lavatory above it, the second compartment holding the 'Bio-loo' (another waterless toilet). Both were brick built, with hand-washing facilities, electric lighting, and an extractor fan on top of the Clivus chimney. They were handicapped by the excess urine on open days and the fact that the stokehole flooded in winter. They served us well for some 12 years — 'we' being four students at a time in a couple of caravans at the bottom of the Trial Ground and eventually six girls in the office.

At about £1,200, the Clivus was cheaper than installing a small septic tank. Its real value in my life was as part of the best book I never wrote — *Feed the Soil*, a paperback on municipal compost and sewage sludge. The Clivus would have been part of a chapter in a book that could have changed the world for ever to one of cleaner seas and rivers and more fertile land.

——— 16 ———

Over the Hills and Far Away

BY THE TIME I returned to Bocking, at the end of the week in which my letter had appeared in *The Observer*, there had been 250 requests for the diet and Cherry had already replied to 10 doctors, four dieticians, and a biochemist. Within a week she had written the first edition of the leaflet of which we gave away about 50,000 during the next 10 years.

Early that Sunday afternoon, after a phone conversation, Dr Jean Monro came over with her husband and their two coeliac small sons, listless and pale on the orthodox allegedly gluten-free and refined-carbohydrate diets advised by all dieticians and the Coeliac Society but totally rejected by Cherry. Dr Monro retired with Cherry to her writing room. When they emerged some hours later it had been agreed that Cherry should enlarge her leaflet into a book, and Dr Monro would write a foreword if she approved. This they duly did. Before the end of 1972, the H.D.R.A. had published the book.

Since both schizophrenia and M.S. (multiple sclerosis) needed different supplements to the diets, we had separate six-page folders printed for each, paid for by the donations and the £150 Cherry earned by writing 12 cookery articles for *Organic Gardening*.

Much later, when the letters had reached a total of 36,000, Jean Monro devised a questionnaire which we sent to 1,000 M.S. cases, and had the replies (about 400) analysed by a medical statistician Jean found. Forty per cent of those who stayed on the diet improved greatly, 30 per cent slightly, and 30 per cent experienced no change.

I drove this campaign through the years with 'jump-in' and 'try-on' letters in local dailies and weeklies, and especially religious periodicals and those for social workers. This enterprise allowed Cherry to use her knowledge, skill, ability, and energy (she was only 76 when this opportunity offered) to help thousands of unknown people.

In that crowded spring of 1972, with the Gluten-Free Campaign building up, I had to prepare for a 16-day trip to the USA, where I was to speak at the National Conference on Organic Farming and Municipal Composting, to be held at the San Francisco Hilton, and at the University of California at Santa Cruz, where I should be staying part of the time. My trip would include visits to compost and sewage plants for material for my proposed book.

Before that I had to arrange a stand at Chelsea for the British *Organic Gardening*, returning from America in time to attend it, and get the spring Newsletter written. Unlike nursery exhibits, which are free, gardening periodicals count as 'sundries' and pay heavily.

I had managed to book the smallest and worst-located stand in Sundries Avenue, where *Popular Gardening*, *Amateur Gardening*, *The Smallholder*, and *Garden News* all had large and heavily staffed displays. Still, it was cheap and custom was quite good at my twenty-fifth Chelsea.

First months, then weeks, and then days remained for my Great Adventure, made possible by the generosity of the Rodales. Then at last I was on the coach from Victoria towards a still longer queue for a still larger aircraft, a Boeing 747 that looked as long as a lecture hall and as filled with faces when at last I got inside it. Flight is an interlude, a blend of hospital ward, with stewardesses as nurses, and a very long and uncomfortable coach journey through the night, striving to sleep through the remorseless roar of the air-conditioning.

I was awake as we flew over Greenland, and a stewardess (who had been a nurse) brought me a cup of cocoa — the malted milk she first offered could have been lethal for me as a coeliac. It was clear moonlight, no clouds, but nothing to see, 'just black rocks and snow,' she whispered in the dim, ward-like light. People began stirring early because their bodies had gained or lost time, and tooth-cleaning and shaving make hours seem more real. Tea arrived, then breakfast with small packets of cornflakes, pale milk, and cool but overcooked bacon and eggs. I asked for extra cornflakes and got them because I could have no toast, and stewardesses are always helpful, especially to the elderly. If you are a coeliac, never ask for a special diet — it only results in tinned tongue and salad.

When we came out of the clouds there was a grey sea breaking on the beaches of Manhattan Island. I missed the Statue of Liberty as I watched the skyscrapers, and the cars growing larger on the streets, as we slid into Kennedy Airport. Down with a rumble like thunder and I was in America, where my first American told me I was Welcome and invited me to Have a Nice Day.

I had a two hour wait for the small, twin-engined commuter aircraft to take me to Allentown, in Pennsylvania, the nearest airport to Emmaus — headquarters of the Rodale Organization, which I was to visit first.

Jerry Goldstein was waiting at Allentown Airport. He ran me in a big new station waggon to the motel where I was to stay.

It was a great pleasure, after lunch in the wholefood restaurant run by the Rodales in Emmaus, to see that the organic movement had something as large, efficient, and solvent as the offices of *Organic Gardening and Farming*, *Prevention*, and *Compost Science*, and their five-acre demonstration garden and shop site, the only one of its kind in America.

Next day, Jim Foot, the farm manager, drove me into the middle of the Pennsylvania corn belt to a farm that has grown maize without a break for 30 years. They sow in late May, 20 rows at once, with a complete fertilizer, and inject anhydrous nitrogen at intervals through the summer, which produces the most nitrate run-off of any fertilizer. Weeds are controlled with 2,4–D and Atrozin. They harvest in November and plough in the 'straw' which is the only humus the land ever gets, then leave it bare until May, with the rain washing away plant foods and top soil. On this system two men can manage 2,500 acres. The high capital investment in machinery, repairs, spares, and chemicals makes relatively high corn prices essential; in 1972 they were making only 15 dollars an acre profit.

This farm, and many like it, act as the 'controls', or chemical contrasts, to the Rodale organic farm of 306 acres in its first year, formerly managed by a German mixed farmer who had let it run down, especially after the blowing soil filled all his drainage ditches. It was being reclaimed under lucerne, oats, leys, and a beef cattle herd to build up the land. Jim Foot, an agricultural college graduate, was working with a young

Mennonite farmer to find out how the Mennonite system of organic farming could be modernized and improved.

The Mennonites were Protestant pacifists from Holland, Germany, and Switzerland, one of the first communities to sail to America hoping to support themselves on the land, while worshipping God in their own way. They had 'chosen freedom' in 1663. Like the better known Amish who were followers of Jakob Ammann, leader of a split in the religion in 1693 who arrived in Pennsylvania in 1720, they still wear 17th and 18th century costume, and refuse to use chemicals on the land, or own cars, tractors, radio, or TV and contract out, as it were, from modern American society. Mennonite and Amish farmers still drive to market behind their own horses in smart 'buggies' — light, four-wheeled carts with canvas hoods. They pay cash for everything they buy, never borrow, mind their own business, and farm their own land the way God intended, as they insist, although Jim Foot's colleague would use a tractor to help out, or take a lift in a car in an emergency connected with his livestock.

The day after my trip to the Rodale farm, Jerry drove me to Rutgers University in New Brunswick, where he had 'majored in English and European Literature'. Our main objective was to meet Professor Drinkwater of Agricultural Engineering. He was working on what he called 'The ultimate disposal unit', a large Fordson tractor with a trailer holding several tons of manure or concentrated sludge, which a giant screw, driven from the power takeoff, forced into the very deep furrow it ploughed. This was already in use, disposing of manure at the rate of 200 tons an acre.

Then Maury (short for Maurice), editor of *Compost Science*, took me to Altoona to see a municipal compost plant, where paper and polythene were removed by controlled air-blasts, bottles tipped off the endless belt, and tins whisked out by electromagnets.

My last long trip with Maury was to Penn State, the University of Pennsylvania, which is one of the largest in the world with 30,000 undergraduates and staff and 20,000 people running the shops and services. We went to the Institute of Land and Water Resources to see Professor William Sopper whose research on his invention of the 'living filter system' was of fundamental importance in the field of sewage treatment. The people of Penn State produce three million gallons a day, 60 gallons each compared with the British 32, for frequent showers add up to more than all the bath nights of Britain. They have a neat little treatment plant and no toxic metal problem — because of lack of industry and the fact that the storm water off the streets goes straight into the river with the lead dust from the petrol. Here the problem is not pollution but the 60-foot fall in the water-table since 1960, due to deforestation and the demands of industry in neighbouring Philadelphia.

The effluent and sludge go together down a four-mile pipeline to an experimental area of farm and forest where they are spread by spray irrigators at a rate equivalent to two inches of rain every month. Every 10,000 people require 130 acres to absorb what Professor Sopper calls their 'waste water', and in 10 years the experiment raised the water-table by 14 feet. The waste water leaves the pipeline with 10 milligrams a litre of phosphorus, a level that once filled the river with algae, killing the fish by eutrophication, but as it soaks through the filter provided by the living soil the level falls to 0.04 mg; the nitrate level falls to 0.5 mg., far below the US permitted limit of 3.0 mg. per litre, and foot-depth samples show one lonely coliform bacteria per litre (the American maximum for safe swimming is 2,000).

The worked-out farm taken over by Professor Sopper had grown mostly 'poverty grass' (*Dathonia spicata*), but now the maize yields were 116 bushels an acre compared with 107 from complete artificials plus the same irrigation with well water. Lucerne hay produced 5.42 tons an acre, compared with 2.27 for the chemical and well-water control, because zinc is the essential trace element for lucerne, wasted in the effluent in orthodox sewage treatment. Furthermore, waste water provides a balanced, dilute, liquid, organic fertilizer with 18.6 parts per million of potash which, like zinc, comes from urine and is present as only a trace in even the best British tanker sludges. Professor Sopper's system returns all the vital trace elements to the land, without the toxic heavy metals added by industry.

In winter, the portable aluminium pipes and sprinklers are removed from the farm and transferred to the forestry areas where the leaf humus prevents the soil freezing in the hardest winters. Though the spray can freeze, with fantastic iceberg effects, these thaw and trickle away. However, the system does not suit conifers because, although Penn State has no industry, every housewife uses detergents which contain boron and even a mere 1.1 lb. per acre of this trace element, essential in tiny traces to vegetable crops especially brassicas, begins producing toxicity symptoms in red pine (*Pinus resinosa*), the most sensitive species.

The trees that do best on waste-water irrigation are oaks (showing an 83 per cent increase in girth in five years compared with a control plantation), and black walnut (*Juglans nigra*), an American species with thick-shelled, poor-quality nuts but excellent timber, growing 80 to 120 feet high and used for furniture and gun stocks, which put on 65 per cent more girth than the controls with plain well water. Halving the time to maturity for either timber would be a very profitable investment, trial fellings showing no difference in the quality of the wood.

The most rewarding development in terms of pollution control and water and wildlife conservation would be 6,500-acre farm and forest sites, each taking waste water from 500,000 people, sited on green-belt areas round cities. These would be half under alder, ash, beech, oak, and walnut, with the other half organic farms growing barley, wheat, kales, and pasture for dairy and beef cattle, or milking and mutton sheep. These fresh woods and pastures new would be as enjoyable for ramblers and wildlife as those of Penn State, for the Pennsylvania Conservation Societies have monitored the effect of monthly waste-water irrigations and find there is an increase in all species, from deer to woodchucks and porcupines, from the extra wildlife food that is grown.

Trees will take waste-water irrigation right round the year and the land is not waterlogged as is so often the case with plantings of cricket bat willow (*Salix alba caerulea*) at some British sewage treatment plants, where too little land is given too much sewage. Dr Wiktor Dragun, of the Institute of Agriculture near Warsaw, is growing poplar (*Populus robusta*) for paper-making, matchsticks, matchboxes, and for making non-returnable crates for horticultural produce. He uses the same two inches a month as Professor Sopper, but distributed by flood irrigation after merely primary treatment, ignoring any toxic metal risk, for timber is never eaten and even lead does no harm in matchsticks.

Toxic metals, such as lead and cadmium, are problems where land may be built on and become part of people's gardens, but under timber trees and on grazing land the danger is a distant one. The work of the Grassland Research Station at Hurley (Oxfordshire) has shown that 95 per cent of the 2 per cent of the lead in the soil taken up by grass is returned in manure, and most of the 5 per cent retained is stored in the bones which we do not eat. This is why there have been no poisoning cases among stock or among the human consumers of meat and milk after more than a century of cattle grazing on sewage farms. The first 80 years of this period, however, were before industry began polluting sewage with man-made molecules whose effects we learn about only when they build up to danger.

We humans absorb only 15 per cent of the lead in our food but 70 per cent of the vastly greater quantity we breathe. It is now likely that lead in petrol will be banned in Britain, as in so many other countries, to remove the risk of brain damage to our children. Cadmium, the other really nasty toxic metal, which can kill fish in concentrations of only a hundredth of a part per million (0.01 p.p.m.) and can be built up to danger levels by shellfish and certain bacteria, could be extracted easily before it gets into sewage.

Zinc smelters, pigment makers, and electroplaters could install an electronic process which removes the dangerous metals to sell at a profit. However, as long as it remains easy for conservationists to blame farm slurry and silage effluent for pollution, or to trade on the instinct of the public to ignore sewage disposal as 'horrid', it seems unlikely that the industries permanently polluting our soil and our seas will be forced by government action to employ known extraction processes, or finance research to find answers to the new problems they pour into our environment.

Jerry picked me up at the motel in the morning and drove me to Allentown Airport, with a bunch of air tickets and directions. I would have to pay for my own accommodation in Chicago, because my expenses so far had been covered by my potential book and *Organic Gardening and Farming*, though when I got to California they would be part of the cost of the Conference. I was on my own, bound for the largest sewage works in the world, serving 10 million people.

My first stop was Cleveland, Ohio, on Lake Erie, like a great sea with no land in sight across it even from the aircraft, where I had a two-hour wait for a tiny plane that had just time for the air hostess to tip a full cup of coffee over my trousers in a sudden lurch and to mop me with paper towels through a barrage of hints on taking out coffee stains, before landing me at Peoria, Illinois. Here the loudspeaker was calling for 'Doctor Lawrence Hills of England', and I learned that Dr Halberson, my host, would be 45 minutes late. One of the larger and louder helpful ladies on the plane came dashing back from a drugstore flourishing a bottle of dry cleaning fluid smelling fiendishly inorganic, and I filled in time cleaning my trousers in the gents.

Dr Halderson, Frank Kudra's deputy, had about 300 students to take round the disposal site in coaches, and over the Chicago plant in helicopters that afternoon. An enthusiastic college had sent an extra coachload. Would I mind riding in the extra coach and telling the students about how the treatment compared with England? They would just love my English accent.

Chicago poured $1^1/_2$ billion gallons of effluent a day into Lake Michigan, while the solid fraction plus 95 per cent water, about 22,500 tons daily, was delivered by motorized barges down the lake and along a canal, with some making the 190-mile journey in railroad tank cars. It was stored in lagoons to 'cure' for 30 days before being sprayed on 7,000 acres of land devastated by opencast mining, as part of a reclamation project.

After this hasty briefing, he pushed me on board the 60-seater coach, introducing me as 'Doctor Hills, the British expert on sewage treatment,' then dashed off to see about his hired helicopters, whose pilots were worried about a weather forecast of a low cloud base. Dr Halderson was evidently not Having a Nice Day.

I sounded British at least, even through the loudhailer, to my coachload of environmental studies students, and I was helped by the fact that American sewage is the same as British — only there is much more of it. I got a fine slide photograph of about 20 of them standing in the scoop of one of the mining grabs which had extracted a 15-foot thick seam of high-quality coal, leaving the 7,000 acres of 70-foot-deep pit full of assorted rock as dead as a lunar landscape. This was being reclaimed as an integrated development plan for woodlands, farms, and small communities, by the University of Illinois, compacting and crushing the levelled upper layer of the rock, spreading a foot of top soil from other similar pits, and soaking this with the sludge — which was about as thick as tar and smelt like old socks. The project had started in 1967, and the areas reclaimed first were growing splendid crops of lucerne for hay and grazing great herds of beef cattle behind miles of electric fencing.

The coach tour ended with lunch in a church hall with trestle tables, folding chairs, hamburgers, hot dogs, 'icecream', and Coca-Cola. I was anticipating eating icecream till I froze, when yet another large, blue-rinsed lady produced tinned tongue and salad — 'Do you have this in England? I'm sure you'll like it'. Jerry's secretary who had arranged the trip had told them about my gluten-free diet with the usual result.

After lunch, Dr Halberson arrived and announced that the cloud base was too low to see anything of the sewage works from the helicopters, so he had cancelled them. So all the students piled back into their coaches, and I was offered transport back to Peoria Airport by a character who introduced himself as; 'Big Jim, I'm a Roustabout,' who had my luggage in another huge station waggon.

The United Airlines 727 for San Jose in California, which I caught next morning, lifted me off, with the surge of power I still enjoyed, into the clearest sky I have ever flown in. Very few Chicago suburban houses had cultivated gardens. Just mown grass, perhaps a tree, with swimming pools like blue-green sucked sweets, and no vegetables anywhere. Up and up steadily and straight to 38,000 feet for the long haul half-way across America, just a few clouds far below sliding their shadows over the farmland, darkened with ploughing for maize and soya-beans.

The air hostesses produced maps (advertising United Airlines) and one told me she had once taken quite a good photograph by focusing at infinity and holding the lens right against the window. I used a whole film and got just one slide good enough for lectures. I should have hired a survey plane with a special camera and kept it waiting for a clear day. Instead, like a man with a borrowed box Brownie and the Loch Ness Monster staring him in the face, I just took shot after shot and hoped for the best.

The roads the Romans drove through our forests, dead straight for marching legions, losing themselves in villages and towns and lining up again later, show on every flight across England. American history shows from the air only in the corn belt of the Middle West, the country of perpetual maize, when the vast fields are bare before the crop hides the equally straight surveyors' roads covering the great unrolling map below with a grid of square miles. These were 'sections' and could be registered to become the freehold property of the men who developed them as farms. The smallest potential farm that a young man going West with his family in a covered waggon could take free for the pioneering, was a quarter section of 160 acres.

Below the grid of 640-acre squares, like medieval ridge-and-furrow cultivations or the lines of newly-murdered hedges that show from the air on the 30-acre fields of modern English inorganic farms, there are black, almost charred areas, like clouds of flat smoke — the ruins of the fertility slaughtered by the pioneers.

Through thousands of years the vast herds of buffalo roamed, and the deer and the antelope played, building up one of the world's deepest fertility stores, as deep as the Argentine pampas or the black earth of the Ukraine, by grazing what was in effect a giant Newman-Turner-type herbal-ley pasture. The deep roots of legumes and 'weeds' went down below the grasses, drawing up the minerals and water in drought, which had been cycled and recycled through the centuries in a stable ecosystem, wolves and Indians culling the herds by killing the weaker beasts.

Nature, like all good farmers, builds up a reserve of the lasting parts of humus, hemicelluloses, and lignins which are black, and some so hard for bacteria to break down that they are furniture rather than food in the soil. Their dark ruins will last a few years more before the yellow and light brown subsoil shows where the ploughs are now scraping the bottom of the fertility barrel for crops that only chemicals can grow.

I was met at San Jose airport by a short, red-bearded Scot, John Macpherson, whom I always thought of as 'The Smallie' — the Scottish equivalent to Robin Goodfellow — an expert on redwood trees. He was my guide through the rest of the longest and most rewarding day of my life. I met him at 12.30 a.m. as arranged, but my body insisted that it was nearly tea time, at 3.30 p.m., for I had raced the sun across America and gained three hours of afternoon.

The redwood (*Sequoia sempervirens*), growing up to 340 feet high and 25 feet through the trunk, is the largest living land creature in the world. Though the giant kelp is reputed to float its relatively slender stems 600 feet up from the deep-sea rocks off Tristan da Cunha, spreading its branches through the top 10 metres and stilling the stormy South Atlantic enough to give boatmen of that loneliest island the only shelter they have, its weight is waterborne, and, as the Smallie said, 'It's in a different ball game'.

He drove me to the trees he loved in his battered Volkswagen, mile after mile of tracks with Californian poppies (*Eschscholzia californica*) blazing orange beside them, blue and white *Lupinus hartwegii*, the annual lupin, in drifts like bluebells, yellow and white poached egg plant (*Limnanthes douglasii*), whose nectar and pollen are the favourite food of the hoverflies that eat aphids, and once a whole rocky hillside covered with *Ceanothus dentatus* with its blue ball flowers, like a thousand Surrey gardens together.

Sequoias are designed to last — *Sempervirens* means 'everliving and growing' — and their tough, corky bark is a foot thick, proof against kicking, rubbing by grizzly bears, and even forest fires, so there seems no reason why they should ever die. The closely related species *S. wellingtonia*, which can grow over 30 feet in diameter with massive buttresses near the ground, has died at the age of 4,000 years calculated by ring counting. One of the oldest in Britain, where it was introduced in 1846, is over 150 feet tall, but is reckoned only a 'boy-chap' as they say in Somerset, where it grows near Butleigh. A huge section in the South Kensington Museum has 'Great Pyramid built' inscribed on the relevant ring, while the Butleigh specimen, if ever it is felled, could have 'First Somerset branch of the National Union of Agricultural Workers formed' near the centre.

The problem worrying the Smallie was that redwood roots are not designed to be trodden over by the shod feet of 10 million visitors a year. There is no risk that the flow of visitors will dwindle, for thousands of visitors, especially the elderly, walk among their favourite trees every week because of the peace they find there.

Sequoias grow only on the Pacific slopes of the Sierra Mountains where the mists roll in from the sea, because every pound of the hundreds of tons of dry matter these giant trees contain takes 500 pounds of water to fix. Saving the surviving Sequoias was the first victory for the forbears of the modern Sierra Club. I owe the H.D.R.A. 'leave the drink' idea to them.

The Smallie safely delivered me to the reception office of the University, dwarfed, like the automobiles in the car park, by the 150 to 300-foot Redwoods that towered round it. I was issued with a large key to one of a batch of double-bed-fitted bed-sitting rooms reserved for parents, and a student to take me round. I would eat in the students' dining room, larger than most town halls, with cafeteria service, and although students had to eat in timed sittings for breakfast, I need not bother. My base would be the Organic Gardening Department, under Alan Chadwick. I was told by Frank and Beth, his two assistants who took me round the four-acre site where about eight students were working, that he was bio-dynamic, English, and away lecturing but would be back in the morning. Beth fetched me a cup of coffee and two Hershey bars — famous, but inadequate for someone who had had only a quick salad-and-tongue lunch four hours earlier.

Finally, I found myself changed into my other suit (the inorganic cleaner had not been all that good) and careering down a very steep hill with the trees opening out to show evening sunlight on a glittering sea — my first sight of the Pacific. We enjoyed a vast meal of a kind of Portuguese paella in a fish restaurant built out over the sea on piles, with the incoming tide sucking and splashing below us. When at last we got back to the University, the students' dining room was lit up and an informal concert was in full swing. So my longest day ended with hearing about five hundred students singing *Where have all the flowers gone?* and meaning it.

My student guide called me in time for the last breakfast sitting — a meal far too low in protein and high in processed carbohydrates for growing youth, featuring a vast assortment of breakfast cereals in individual packets — and a feature of college life I had never met before. Students with something they wanted to publicize — meetings, outings, societies, sleeping bags or other property to sell, or even opinions to express — could stand up on the long heavy benches and speak for not more than five minutes. If they went on too long, or wandered from the point there were shouts of 'Sit Down', instantly obeyed. It was good training in concise speaking and confidence and I may well have heard a future President speaking in public for the first time.

When I got to the Organic Garden, Chadwick had just arrived and it was amazing how pleasant it was to hear an English voice after ten days of assorted American. He was tall, in his fifties, and dead tired for he had come back from his lecture by night flight and failed to sleep on the plane. Now all he wanted was sleep, for America is so large you can get jet lag between garden clubs. Then the head of a procession of worthy American matrons, with a sprinkling of white-haired husbands, appeared at the top of the path. 'Good God — The Los Angeles Garden Club. I'd forgotten all about them. You take them, Hills, I'm off to bed.' So once again I was introduced by Beth as 'Doctor Hills, the English organic expert', stepping in because Mr Chadwick's plane had been delayed, and my tour the previous evening served me well. Beth and Frank answering the more bio-dynamic questions.

I spent the next day and a half with Alan Chadwick and his students — to whom I became 'Larry the Limey' — on their organic 'truck garden', where Alan was developing his invention of raised-bed gardening, using quantities of bullock manure from feedlots, delivered free. He was running one of the few residential organic gardening colleges, perhaps the only one, where students worked for keep only, paying no fees. Later he moved his college community to Round Valley, in northern California, and thanks to a way with trusts and foundations he managed to train large numbers of organic gardeners for nothing. They worked hard, though not so hard as those like Jerry Goldstein who worked as waiters to pay board and tuition fees at Rutgers.

I was booked at the San Francisco Hilton as a speaker. For the final stage of my trip I was driven in by Beth, with four other students, across the Golden Gate Bridge. They were all attending the Conference, driving in and out each day, and my room could act as a base. I left a bearded young senior lecturer in physics in the foyer, arguing furiously with the manager that as he had arrived on the most efficient transportation known to man, instead of a stinking, fossil-fuel wasting automobile, he was entitled to park his bicycle in his room if they refused to let him put it in the car park.

We had hardly reached my room when the manager arrived, with three hefty house detectives and a policeman, under the impression that I had been followed in by a gang of hippies off the street who intended to rob me. Then the senior lecturer wheeled in his bicycle to continue the argument in which we all joined. Again and again in America I felt as though I were acting in an old film. This time it was pure Marx Brothers.

The Waste Recycling Conference, one of the three in progress, was packed with county engineers (American States are divided into counties) and council members and their wives, all potential customers for municipal compost equipment, plus a sprinkling of students and organic farmers and authorities such as Ruth Stout and Wendell Berry. It opened with a Famous Figure, who had typed himself a script four spaces between each line and read from it steadily whisking each one over with a flourish as he finished. Then there was a less monotonous speaker presenting non-standard slides, which showed all the totals on his tables off the screen. Even when a larger screen was fetched, wasting scarce time, this was still a waste of a good lecture.

This was the first time I had ever spoken at a really big conference and through the next 10 years I was to observe again and again how men with great knowledge can waste their wisdom. The worst habit of all is continually turning your back on the audience to write figures on a blackboard with chalk that keeps breaking, then turning, chortling with amusement at the elegance of the calculation. Some of the speakers were excellent and Frank Kudra was brilliant. He ended, 'I jest kant afford to think big — I gotta think kolossal'.

I got a better press than I deserved because I spoke third, after two dull speakers. I had brought a full set of organic gardening slides, in case I was required to speak at the Organic Farming Conference and during the remaining evenings of the Conference. My room again resembled the Marx Brothers' cabin, for Dr Bargelya Rateaver, an extension lecturer in organic gardening, had hired a projector and asked me to lecture to batches of her students. I think we got in as many as 30 at a time, piled up over the twin beds. All were filled with an enthusiastic thirst for knowledge that was a delight though by the end of the week I was so exhausted that I even slept for part of the 13-hour flight from San Francisco to Heathrow.

The Circles Stay Broken

AS ALWAYS, I came back to Bocking and found that everything had grown and even in the 16 days I had been away it seemed to me that 'Our Tree', the *Sophora japonica*, looked larger. There is a tide in affairs of trees that sweeps them on to tower, and ours, now eight years old, had its roots well down and was gathering speed until it was growing like the H.D.R.A. We now had 2,756 members, about 700 of them overseas. Mrs Adams worked five mornings a week in the office room of the Pye House, filing, copy-typing standard letters, and coping with the post, and we were co-operating with Essex University.

In the expanding summer of 1972, Mrs Bigg, a member from Jersey, gave us a donation of £500, and we spent it on what we called 'The Bigg Building' both to honour her and because it was a really big architect's site hut, found through an advertisement in the ever useful *Exchange and Mart*. With the help of neighbours and a bricklayer, we got it up and painted for £390, and spent the balance on steel filing cabinets for the office and ex-N.A.A.F.I. folding chairs. This gave us storage room, a place to work on wet days, to spread things out to dry, and above all a place for teas on open days. Year after year the Burco electric boilers bubbled, the home-made trestles, with reject hardboard doors on top that served as tables, were set up with the ex-cookhouse benches for the members and visitors who poured in after I had taken each party round. We had to restrict numbers then to up to 300 people on Saturday afternoons only, because we could use Hunnables lorry park that day alone and on any other day we would have jammed Convent Lane. As I had made all the paths too narrow, so we had to have 'pausing places' where I could gather perhaps 50 people round me to talk and answer questions, it took about an hour and a quarter to get round the whole acre and three-quarters.

The students took baths at No. 20, our house, where our Mrs West did their washing, and we contrived adequate but primitive sanitation that served till we could afford to install a Clivus. Cherry cooked a great many highly organic whole-food meals and 'physiotheraped' aching muscles from unac-customed hard work and banished migraines with her special technique, making sure that everyone left us able to grind flour and make bread. We fitted up part of the Pye House as a kitchen, and a common room–dining room for them, with a record player, a notice board, and walls thickly coated with the posters and notices in which youth has so much faith. We must have had well over three dozen of them pass through Bocking in the course of the next 10 years, leaving in late autumn to be replaced by another four in the spring, usually two boys and two girls, and only in exceptional cases did we take them under 18.

In addition to their full board, we paid pocket money, which began at £1 a week then rose through the years, giving our students a rather better deal financially than those of Alan Chadwick in the USA, though his had informal classes by instructors who were paid out of grants from educational chari-ties. Our object was not to train young people as professional organic gardeners; it was to run our small research station and our ever-increasing organic organization. Sometimes I lectured to them, and held question and answer sessions in the common room. Many of them spent their 6 to 8 months with us making up their minds what they wanted to do. We had one very nice girl, with a degree in Icelandic, who wanted to run an organic smallholding with very little capital, and finished up teaching English in a boys' boarding school at Tunbridge Wells, and a man with a degree in Chinese who hasn't made up his mind yet. Every now and again I am greeted at Chelsea by stalwart couples I vaguely remember, who pour out their adventures and share their memories. They call me 'Lawrence', unlike the grey-haired men who call me 'Mr Hills' and can remember forgotten Chelseas.

We began to receive donations, both for our work with mul-tiple sclerosis, and £2,000, our largest yet, for research into the toxic-metal problem, especially lead and cadmium. This allowed us to pay for more work from Dr Denys Long and the Michaelis Nutritional Laboratory, including investigating a method of extracting these two metals from sewage sludge, which would have been wonderful, like so many bright ideas, if it had actually worked.

FIGHTING LIKE THE FLOWERS

Through the summer of 1972 publicity struck us again and again. *The Sunday Times* and *Reveille* both featured our 'Ladybird Hilton'. This was the neat little shed that had held an unsuccessful compost chopper, now filled with rows of small, clay drainpipes in the hope of making life easier for hibernating ladybirds. Denys Long had told me of a gatepost at Rothamsted with a wooden cap nailed on to stop the wet rotting down the end grain at the top. For 13 years ladybirds came back to hibernate under that cap, until someone backed a tractor into the post and the experiment ended.

I wondered if, by providing better hibernation quarters, I could increase the ladybird population. My first idea had been to use small plastic tubes, but I thought of the lady (and 'gentleman') 'birds' sleeping side by side in slippery plastic pipes like couples in the kind of beds found in seaside lodgings that slope in to the middle. A weekend like this is bad enough, but six months — it hardly bears thinking about! Think of looking at your watch yet again and finding it was still only January.

The smallest size of field drains, a foot long and an inch-and-a-half internal diameter, were rough inside, providing a good grip for tiny feet, and once the tubes became impregnated with the scent of ladybirds, we could send them round to members to gather the hibernation-home hunters from the surrounding gardens. The idea of nestboxes for ladybirds got my 'jump-in' letter into *The Guardian* and led to my photograph in *The Sunday Times* with a pair of soldier beetles (*Anthocomus rufus*) sitting on my spectacle frames, one each side of my nose, waving their antennae at each other, and my being televized, crammed into the little shed with Esther Rantzen, and a ladybird racing round and round my wrist watch.

The publicity, especially in the local paper, brought a stream of small boys on bicycles from miles around with ladybirds in matchboxes. Cherry will never forget the small, smooth, intent faces proudly opening their matchboxes and passing on their contribution to scientific research. It also drew B. R. Benham, M.Sc., from Manchester who was taking a Ph.D. on ladybirds. In his opinion the limiting factor on their numbers was not housing shortage but low temperatures, for the beetles started breeding only at 5°C (41°F) and could not keep pace with the aphids until 11°C (52°F). We could provide ideal conditions for them, with plenty of nettles round the compost bins offering a good breakfast of nettle aphids as soon as they woke up.

Mr Benham was a school science master with a special interest in the proportion of two-spot and seven-spot ladybirds that were black with red spots, instead of the ordinary red and black, and I asked members to send him any they found, for none of the boys brought any. He wanted to take their temperatures, to see if the black-background varieties got warmer by absorbing more sun heat, and asked us for a grant to buy himself a ladybird thermometer. The idea of a ladybird with a thermometer stuck in its mouth and a nurse taking its pulse on a front leg while asking it a Very Personal Question was so fascinating that I sent him £28, the first of the very few grants we have given. In fact, the thermometers are flat, and you sit the 'patient' on them very gently with tweezers.

All over Britain there were derelict, old-fashioned sewage farms. They were all on flat land near towns and cities that had grown up round them, land that could solve the need for council house sites or sell for very large sums with planning permission to private buyers. Labour councillors wanted the first and Conservatives chose the second. At Beaumont Leys near Leicester, the first big site, Professor Bryce-Smith had been consulted on new and more accurate methods of analysis. They were finding cadmium in quantity where earlier borough engineers had looked only for copper, zinc, nickel, and chromium.

These places differed entirely from the treatment plants such as Maple Cross, at Rickmansworth, where sludge tankers spread 6,000 to 10,000 gallons an acre of less than 100 p.p.m. lead sludge from the digesters over as much as a 40-mile-diameter circle of farmland every 3 to 4 years, with laboratory checks to keep levels of lead and cadmium low. They flooded relatively small areas of a few hundred acres with up to 300,000 gallons an acre at five-year intervals, cropping with potatoes, grain, hay, or dairy farming. As long as the land is heavily limed to keep the metals out of root-reach, there is no trouble to staff, stock, or customers until the levels of the metals rise. Most sewage farms had started in the 1870–1880 period and since then industry has continued to multiply without solving these problems.

The first case to hit the headlines was at Croydon Sewage Farm, where the allotments averaged 1,299 p.p.m. lead in the soil (dry matter, as are all these figures), and whole cabbages reached 101.6 p.p.m., only $2^1/_2$ ounces eaten would reach the daily adult safety level. The Medical Officer of Health for Croydon took blood samples from six of the allotment holders who ate their own vegetables grown on a hoard of toxic metals that had taken over 50 years to build, for many years. He was quoted by *The Daily Telegraph* (12/2/72) as saying: 'In every case the result was entirely satisfactory, being well below the average level of 30 micrograms per 100 grams of blood.' On the other hand, as Dr Denys Long pointed out, adults deposit lead in their bones so little is free to show in their blood, and these allotment holders should suffer no ill effects.

Children, however, are another matter, for lead can concentrate in their brains, producing mental retardation. The main risk is from children who put soil in their mouths to eat (a habit known as 'pica') and as little as one-645th of a pound of soil from the Croydon allotments, swallowed by a child, would be as dangerous as licking paint from the kind of toy that makes news until it is taken off the market. Though liming may lock up (or 'chelate') minerals, human digestive juices are acid, unlocking toxic metals to become deadly in small stomachs. All councils should therefore copy Croydon and build car parks, gardenless town houses, factories, schools, and sports grounds on their old sewage farms. Lead and cadmium are not absorbed through the skin, as are some pesticides, so there is no risk even to the most expensive footballer from tumbling about with bare knees on a field that was once a sewage farm.

Professor Bryce-Smith told me of yet another danger. A Professor H. V. Warren, of Vancouver, had become concerned with possible links between high metal contents of soil and high rates of certain diseases, and in 1963 he had been invited to Jersey by the local Multiple Sclerosis Society because the level of this disease was reputed to be so high. He could find no high toxic-metal levels, but a colleague in 1969 had collected four frightening samples, one of 600 p.p.m. lead. I had been trying to fix a trip to Jersey to see their famous municipal compost plant for my book, and one of our members who belonged to the Island Development Committee had invited me to speak to this body which included many members of the 'States', as Jersey calls its Parliament.

The organic movement had always been enthusiastic about municipal compost because it had none of the psychological implications of sewage, even though it could be higher in toxic metals. I had seen the last working Dano composter in Denmark on a quick trip in August. It would close down as soon as it had filled the last huge hole available, beaten by the increase of plastics and, above all, broken glass. As you come in to the Airport at Copenhagen the most striking sight is the glittering of the pieces of broken glass on the fields. The steady build-up of this lasting pollution had made their compost unsellable, apart altogether from the less visible dangers of toxic metals.

The passing of returnable glass bottles and the faster and faster increase in plastics were beating the Jersey compost plant too. The island had far fewer tits and blackbirds than Britain, but many magpies and (in 1972) these had not yet learned the trick of stealing milk, which could be delivered in waxed cardboard cartons, with no risk of birds pecking through the sides for a drink, leaving the damaged carton running to waste on doorsteps. This spared them broken milk bottles and the lead in the alluminium alloy that makes bottle tops, but gave them 70,000 cardboard milk bottles a day to compost, rising to 150,000 in the summer. Everything came to the island packed in cardboard, instead of the wooden boxes that used to be chopped for firewood, making the refuse 50 per cent paper and cardboard. This was getting out of step with the food wastes, and needing more and more sludge to help it decay. Above all, though the plastics were only 1.9 per cent of the rubbish by weight they were so light that they went a long way. Unlike glass which smashed, they tattered and hung on the fences, blew on the wind, and littered the lovely lanes.

The famous composter was wearing out, and there was nothing for it but to replace it with an incinerator, to be sited where the prevailing wind would blow the smoke out to sea and the fumes from the PVC would be well diluted.

There are no industries to speak of, except for intensive market gardening, yet I found that the lead level in their sludge was 746 p.p.m. compared with 800 p.p.m. for Swindon and 670 for Pudsey (Yorks). They took it by tanker up the narrow lanes to small tanks perched on the corners of tiny fields, for distribution by spray gun from little tankers towed behind tractors over early potatoes, carrots, and grazing for Jersey cows. As it was only 2 per cent dry matter it contained no great bulk of metals. The question was how could there be any at all without even an electroplating factory on the island?

Dr Williams of the Department of Health solved the problem of the multiple sclerosis cases very simply. This is not a notifiable disease so hundreds of wheelchair cases can come to the many nursing homes on Jersey without registering officially. Jersey imports M.S. sufferers, most of whom stay there till their death, making the M.S. death-rate higher than on the mainland though the number of new cases is average for Britain.

The final solution to the lead mystery came from one of the Development Committee who had worked out the best do-it-yourself method of making sugar from sugarbeet grown from home-saved seed during the German occupation.

For the past 400 years, he told me, the 12 Parishes of Jersey, the equivalent to British counties, have sold their road sweepings and hedge trimmings by auction as 'bonnelaise', a Jersey patois word meaning, approximately, 'good stuff from the roadside'. When they had horses and carts with slow, iron-tyred wheels grinding the stone dust from the untarred roads the grit, trimmings, and manure, stacked by the roads in a kind of large 'compost heap' were vastly more 'bonne' than today, when it could well reach the 1,000 p.p.m. lead of the road dust along the M1.

According to the Jersey Farmers' Union staff and the members who were in the office at the time, bonnelaise was used today mostly as a cheap grit to mix in tomato-potting soil and to fill in muddy patches just inside gates. Like the carefully cherished rights and rituals concerning gathering seaweed on the beaches for manuring the potato crop, bonnelaise was on the way out and sometimes heaps would stay unsold. They had to be advertised in the local paper, the *Jersey Evening Post*, because it was the law that everyone should have his fair share. After long discussion on where the heaps were in every Parish and who had bought them, my guide and I set off to collect a whole fleet of samples in polythene bags, including some from a tomato nursery's potting-soil heap. I passed these on to the sewage works manager, who told me that much of the storm-water off the roads and roofs went through the sewage works in the towns, but many isolated villages had septic tanks. Sark had no sewage works, just septic tanks, and no motor vehicles at all, but bad weather prevented us getting there to take any samples.

When the results finally arrived, they ranged from 20 to 100 p.p.m. out in the fields, and 500 to 700 p.p.m. near the gates, filling in the picture. Professor Warren had made a proper job of his samples, taking them all across the field, mixing them thoroughly and 'quartering them down' to get a representative sample. His colleague had nipped in through the gate, trowelled up a bagful then gone on to the next site. The fewer miles you do to the gallon the more lead you spread to the mile, and hired cars grinding up the hills, with a magnificent view of a clean blue sea through the rear window and the back of an over-loaded mini-bus in front, caused maximum pollution.

When I got back from Jersey I arranged to see Professor Bryce-Smith at the Chemistry Department of Reading University. He was not Britain's first professor of pollution, but of organic chemistry, which concerns substances containing carbon, and carried out all the work that made him famous in his 'spare time'. This had begun when his work on the brains of stillborn babies from London hospitals had shown him the lead that had crossed the placental barrier. He was young and spoke fast to keep up with his racing mind, and through the long afternoon we talked toxic metals and what they do to human brains and bodies.

The book I had aspired to write was a *Silent Spring* of sewage to change the way the world thinks of its wastes, as Rachel Carson altered our attitude to pesticides. It demanded far more knowledge than I possessed and the applied results of research that had never been done, to find the answers to problems whistleblowers find so easily without any responsibility for discovering solutions.

I could have based it on the practical experience and shared enthusiasm of the men who had been showing me round their sewage systems for the past 10 years, proud of their low B.O.D.s and rejoicing in the rich pastures on the farms of their satisfied customers. But suppose, instead of keeping nature safely recycling, the ever-changing sewage with its ever-increasing content of persistent, carbon-based chemicals and more and more toxic metals were to build up to disaster levels? Once the metals were in the soil they stayed as permanent poisons.

I had signed no contract with Faber and Faber for my book *Feed the Soil*, nor had I signed one with Rodale who had spent

so generously on my trip to America. So I decided to throw
away what I had already written, all my notes and all the work
I had done and the photographs I had taken through the years,
because I would not risk crops, stock, or land on a gamble that
Professor Bryce-Smith and the other conservationists might be
mistaken. To be organic carries a responsibility towards those
who buy the books and articles we write, and the food we grow
and sell.

---- 18 ----

Building a Future for the H.D.R.A.

WHEN the council surveyor made his official inspection of the finished Pye House he told me that the frontage alone of the Trial Ground was worth £8,000. Now, in the summer of 1972, when he came to approve the Bigg Building, he valued the whole site at £48,000. Joscelynes, the estate agents who had sold me No. 20, considered that the frontage, with planning permission for five bungalows, would fetch £22,000 at an auction, and secured two offers from builders trying to buy land ahead for £20,000 and £14,000. So I put the idea to the committee.

This would solve the problem that worried us both. If I were killed cycling into Braintree or my health gave out so I could no longer run the H.D.R.A., which grew larger and larger as I grew older, Cherry could not carry on the Association and the whole thing would collapse. I had gone into the question of insuring my life, but at 62 the premiums would be too high to be worth it, and even though the £5,000 would be useful in the emergency, there would be no one to write the next Newsletter, keep going the work that filled it, and answer the letters packed with problems that arrived in every post.

Therefore it was important to have plenty of time to train a successor, who in turn would have to train his successor, and we could not afford a retired senior army officer who know all about 'man-management' but had only 10 years' wear left in him. We needed someone dedicated to the organic movement and to our principles, and prepared to take on something as demanding as the H.D.R.A. which sounded hard work and was even harder than it looked. As I told the committee at the time, 'there was hope that a suitable couple could be found once there was the money to pay them with, £1,800 a year, and a three-bedroom house with a highly productive

249

garden rent-free is attractive, even in these days of high salaries, to someone who is keen enough on the job to be worth the money.'

Cherry and I had seen several of the large 'mobile home' type caravans delivered on low-loader lorries, that were never towed on the road, for their wheels were merely designed to get round the regulations. If we could get planning permission for one, we would site it south of the Pye House to get us away from the noise and fumes of the lorry traffic in Convent Lane, and pay for it out of our savings. It would cost about £4,000 including a concrete base, installing electricity and water, and a pump to lift the sewage and bathwater up the hill and along the driveway to Convent Lane.

Then it would be possible to turn over No. 20 to a young couple, perhaps with children, as a Deputy Director and wife, ready to take over from us after some years experience. No. 20 had already been left to the H.D.R.A. in my will, and this would escape the death duties which would be a large sum as its value grew with inflation.

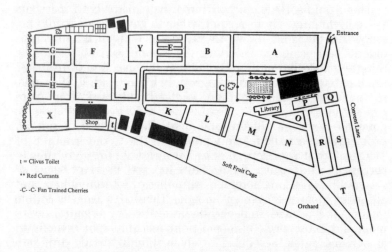

The last map 1984, showing as far as the hazelnut hedge, shows the bungalow, the Bigg building, the cedar room, the Clivus toilet, marked 't', and the ex-London prefab that finally held the office, the shop and the packing department.

Building a Future for the H.D.R.A.

Fortunately, the planning authorities refused us permission for the caravan idea, and I never had the task of cramming the Trial Ground on to almost an acre less room. Selling the frontage meant losing the widest part of the isosceles triangle, meaning less labour on cultivation but impossibly crowded open days. Still, we carried ahead with the negotiations, which Robert Pollard was determined to get through. By the time our committee met again, on October 11th, 1973, we had outline planning permission for a detached bungalow for ourselves and for two pairs of semi-detached bungalows on the rest of the frontage that would bring in £20,000, of which £13,000 would pay for our new home and the rest would be a reserve for salaries.

Again fortunately, the Right Hon. the Earl Kitchener (nephew of the nephew of the 'Your King and Country Need You' general), one of our very earliest members, became our President when Robert Pollard retired to Vice-President. He launched an appeal which brought in the £13,000 that paid for our bungalow. We grew fast enough, and trade and donations increased in step with expenditure, so we never sold the frontage, which would have made our final sale in 1985 impossible. This was for £115,000, and paid the lion's share of the cost of Ryton. Hard work by a dedicated staff and the generosity of members alone could never have grown into the largest organic gardening centre and research station in the world without inflation and planning restrictions. These turned my original $1^1/_4$ acres of leased first-class building land relatively near London into 22 acres of old riding school, on green-belt land in the Midlands, almost exactly in the middle of England with easy access from everywhere.

While we were still arguing with the planners, I put an advertisement for that young couple in the 'agony column' of *The Times* — the traditional place for unusual offers of shares in treasure hunts, places on expeditions, and the last resort of ex-public schoolboys aged 43 still willing to go anywhere and do anything. I had one reply only. This came from a couple who wanted to learn to garden organically, and to start a small-holding, like so many young people, just then, but this would have wasted their training and given them the risky drudgery of small-scale market gardening on too little capital. They were Alan Gear, M.Sc., A.M.I.C.E., a civil engineer, and Jackie Gear, B.Sc. Biology, then an analytical chemist of toxic-metal pollution at a sewage works.

They were young and keen, though entirely ignorant about gardening, and willing to live in a caravan for their first year for their keep and £5 a week each like the students, for a year on trial so that if they found they could not bear us they could still get back into the well-paid municipal world. Selling their mortgaged house and working out their notice took time and it was not until early January, 1974, that they joined our family of 3,300 members with our problems and our exciting possibilities.

Again and again in the decade before 1985, when the H.D.R.A. finally outgrew the narrow paths and non-existent parking space at Bocking and we moved it to the 22 acres that are now Ryton Gardens, I sang to my Cherry and soared away. Her diet had given me the missing health that had robbed me of a normal childhood, boyhood, and youth, and the dedication and increasing knowledge and ability of Alan and Jackie made it possible for me to leave my life work growing like a garden while I voyaged as far across the real world as I had in pencil on my old atlas when I was a white-faced little boy in a big bed.

They gave me my travelling years in my sixties and early seventies when I was young enough to enjoy the beauty of the wild green Earth and the kindliness of organic people everywhere. I lectured, broadcast, televized, and visited organic farms and gardens, rice terraces, research stations, universities, jungles, forests, and deserts. Above all, I *saw* Australia, Bali, Belgium, Canada, Cyprus, Denmark, France, Germany, Holland, India, Italy, Java, Madeira, Mexico, and New Zealand. I visited Sweden again and a paid third visit to that great empty, and generous country, the United States. Both Cherry and I have glaucoma, so sight is a wasting asset. ...

I began this book by defining organic gardening, which means far more than merely keeping to one's own compost heap and companion plants, as inorganic gardening does not consist only of buying the advertised chemicals and reading the directions. I will end this first half of my life story by defining the 'organic people' whom I have met and appreciated in so many countries. There were far fewer in the 1950s, when I started the H.D.R.A., than there are today and we shall need them as the greenhouse gases grow and the ozone holes deepen and spread.

The inorganic say cheerfully: 'I have no time for all this gloom and doom. It may be true in the long run, but in the long run we are all dead.' And they go on poisoning the future for our children. To a businessman, ten years is the foreseeable future, a politician sees as far as the next election, and a trades union leader to just beyond the next round of wage increases.

Those who think organically are united by their respect for the future. They think ahead to the fossil fuels and fertilizers running out, the toxic metals and industrial wastes in our rivers, seas, and soils, and the persistent pesticides and other pollutants adding up to danger in the bodies of all the life with which we share one world. We are all married to that world, which *is* one world because it shares a single atmosphere and seven polluted seas, for better for worse, for energy-richer for resource-poorer, in nuclear war or man-made catastrophe, till the death of our Sun shall us part. Ours is a good world, with the right moisture, temperature range, and atmosphere for our kind of life to enjoy. It is ours to love and to cherish through the sunlit centuries.

GREEN BOOKS

G REEN BOOKS are produced for the general reader. Our aim is to publish books that will enhance people's interest in environmental issues, especially in the changes that will be needed to bring about an ecologically sustainable future for our planet. We use recycled paper wherever possible for the printing of our books and catalogues.

Our titles cover a wide range of green issues, including the countryside, health, education, economics and the arts. We hope you have found this book enjoyable and stimulating, and would very much welcome your comments, suggestions and ideas about our books and the future development of our publishing programme – readers' participation is part of our philosophy.

Other titles of interest from Green Books:

Our Fragmented World by Ronald Harvey. In this timely critique of conventional thinking, the author looks at the present state of capitalism, communism, disarmament, religion, science and education, from a wholistic point of view. £7.50

Breaking Through: *Theory and Practice of Wholistic Living* by Walter and Dorothy Schwarz. A lucid and comprehensive update on the state of the Green Movement. £6.50

A Mirror of England: *An Anthology of the writings of H.J. Massingham* edited by Edward Abelson. A seminal author who passionately advocated the importance of country life, care for the land, craftsmanship, and the conservation of the British countryside. £6.50 (a Green Classic)

For our full catalogue, write to: Green Books, Ford House, Hartland, Bideford, Devon EX39 6EE.